When *Introduction à la Bible*—edited by the noted Sulpician biblical scholars André Robert and André Feuillet—was originally published in France, it was acclaimed as an outstanding accomplishment in biblical scholarship. Each of the contributors was a recognized authority in his particular field. In their approach to their topics, each author utilized all of ancient tradition as well as modern archeological, scientific, literary and historical findings in discussing the various theories on the framework of the Old Testament.

The present edition (the Old Testament portion of this monumental work) has been translated from the revised, second French edition by a group of distinguished American scholars. In addition to their adept translation of this incomparable text, these American scholars have completely updated the exhaustive bibliographies and adapted them for the English-speaking reader to offer the most comprehensive and accurate guide to Old Testament studies.

Though a work of such scholarly proportion as to require a prior knowledge of the Bible, INTRODUCTION TO THE OLD TESTAMENT is a profitable book for anyone interested in sacred scripture for the knowledge and insights it offers on the written word of God.

A. Robert — A. Feuillet

INTRODUCTION TO THE OLD TESTAMENT

VOLUME TWO

translated from the second French edition by

MSGR. PATRICK W. SKEHAN — FIDELIS BUCK, S.J.

LA SALLE P. CARON — JUNIPER CUMMINGS, O.F.M.CONV.

BRO. ALOYSIUS FITZ GERALD — ROBERT L. MAC FADYEN

ROLAND E. MURPHY, O.CARM. — PETER NICKELS, O.F.M. CONV.

PATRICK STEVENS — MARCIAN STRANGE, O.S.B.

IMAGE BOOKS
A Division of Doubleday & Company, Inc.
Garden City, New York

Image Books edition 1970
by special arrangement with Desclée Company, Inc.
Image Books edition published February, 1970

Originally published in French under the title INTRODUCTION
A LA BIBLE, Vol. I: *Ancien Testament* (Desclée & Co., Tournai,
Belgium), the present English edition is based on the latest French
edition. Moreover, the bibliography has been updated and adapted
for the English-speaking reader.

Nihil obstat—Donald A. Panella, M.A., S.T.L., S.S.L., Censor Depu-
tatus

Imprimatur—Terence J. Cooke, D.D., Archbishop of New York
New York, New York—June 25, 1968

TABLE OF CONTENTS
VOLUME 2

Section II.   The Other Hagiographers
by Msgr. H. LUSSEAU, Dean of the Faculty of Theology at Angers

Chapter I.   Proverbs

LIST OF ABBREVIATIONS

1) Books of the Bible:

Abd	Abdias	Heb	Epistle to the Hebrews
Acts	Acts of the Apostles		
Ag	Aggeus	Is	Isaias
Am	Amos		
Ap	Apocalypse	Jas	Epistle of James
		Jb	Job
Bar	Baruch	Jdt	Judith
		Jer	Jeremias
Col	Epistle to the Colossians	Jgs	Judges
		Jl	Joel
1 Cor	1st Epistle to the Corinthians	Jn	Gospel of St. John
		1 Jn	1st Epistle of St. John
2 Cor	2nd Epistle to the Corinthians		
		2 Jn	2nd Epistle of St. John
Ct	Canticle of Canticles		
		Jon	Jonas
Dn	Daniel	Jos	Josue
Dt	Deuteronomy	Jude	Jude
Eccl	Ecclesiastes		
Eph	Epistle to the Ephesians	3 Kgs	1st Book of Kings
		4 Kgs	2nd Book of Kings
Esd	Esdras		
Est	Esther	Lam	Lamentations
Ex	Exodus	Lk	Gospel of St. Luke
Ez	Ezechiel	Lv	Leviticus
Gal	Epistle to the Galatians	Mal	Malachias
		1 Mc	1st Book of Machabees
Gn	Genesis		
		2 Mc	2nd Book of Machabees
Hb	Habacuc		

Mi	Micheas	Rom	Epistle to the Romans
Mk	Gospel of St. Mark		
Mt	Gospel of St. Matthew	Ru	Ruth
		Sir	Ecclesiasticus
Na	Nahum	1 Sm	1st Book of Samuel
Neh	Nehemias	2 Sm	2nd Book of Samuel
Nm	Numbers	So	Sophonias
Os	Osee		
		Tb	Tobias
1 Par	1st Book of Paralipomenon	1 Thes	1st Epistle to the Thessalonians
2 Par	2nd Book of Paralipomenon	2 Thes	2nd Epistle to the Thessalonians
Phil	Epistle to the Philippians	Ti	Epistle to Titus
Phlm	Epistle to Philemon	1 Tm	1st Epistle to Timothy
Prv	Proverbs		
Ps	Psalms	2 Tm	2nd Epistle to Timothy
1 Pt	1st Epistle of St. Peter		
		Wis	Wisdom
2 Pt	2nd Epistle of St. Peter		
		Za	Zacharias

MT means Massoretic Text, LXX indicates the Greek translation of the Old Testament called the Septuagint.

2) Dictionaries, collections and reviews:

AAS *Acta Apostolicae Sedis* (Vatican City).

AASOR *Annual of American Schools of Oriental Research.*

ANEP *The Ancient Near East in Pictures relating to the Old Testament* (PRITCHARD) Princeton Univ., 1954).

ANET *Ancient Near Eastern Texts relating to the Old Testament*[2] (PRITCHARD) (Princeton Univ., 1955).

AOAT   *Altorientalische Texte und Bilder zum Alten Testament²*, 2 Vols. (H. GRESSMANN) (Berlin-Leipzig, 1927).

APOT   R. H. CHARLES, *Apocrypha and Pseudepigrapha of the Old Testament* (Oxford, 1913).

BA   *Biblical Archaeologist* (Baltimore).

BASOR   *Bulletin of the American School of Oriental Research* (New Haven).

Bi   *Biblica** (Rome).

BiTod   *The Bible Today* (Collegeville, Minn.).

BJRL   *Bulletin of John Ryland's Library* (Manchester).

BO   *Bibliotheca Orientalis* (Leyden).

BZ   *Biblische Zeitschrift** (Freibourg im Breisgau).

CBQ   *Catholic Biblical Quarterly** (Washington).

CSEL   *Corpus Scriptorum Ecclesiasticorum Latinorum* (Vienna, 1866 ff.).

DAFC   *Dictionnaire Apologétique de la Foi Catholique** (Paris, 1911-1922).

DBV   *Dictionnaire de la Bible** (F. VIGOUROUX) (Paris, 1895-1912).

Denzinger or DB   *Enchiridion symbolorum** (Freiburg im Breisgau: Herder).

DTC   *Dictionnaire de Théologie Catholique** (Paris).

EB   *Enchiridion Biblicum** (Rome, 1955).

ERE   *Encyclopaedia of Religion and Ethics* (J. HASTINGS) (Edinburgh).

EsBi   *Estudios Biblicos** (Madrid).

ETL   *Ephemerides Theologicae Lovanienses** (Louvain).

HE   *Histoire Ecclésiastique d'Eusèbe de Césarée.*

IB   *Interpreter's Bible* (New York, 1952 ff.).

IDB   *Interpreter's Dictionary of the Bible* (New York, 1962).

JBL   *Journal of Biblical Literature* (Philadelphia).

JBR   *Journal of Bible and Religion.*

JNES   *Journal of Near Eastern Studies* (Chicago).

JTS   *Journal of Theological Studies* (London-Oxford).

NRT   *Nouvelle Revue Théologique** (Louvain).

NT   *Novum Testamentum* (Leyden).

NTS   *New Testament Studies* (Cambridge).
OGIS   *Orientis Graeci Inscriptiones Selectae* (DITTEN-
          BERGER) (Leipzig, 1903-1905).
OTMS   *Old Testament and Modern Study*, ed. H. Rowley
          (Oxford, 1951).
PG   *Patrologia Graeca* (J. B. MIGNE) (Paris).
PL   *Patrologia Latina* (J. B. MIGNE) (Paris).
PO   *Patrologia Orientalis* (R. GRAFFIN) (Paris).
RB   *Revue Biblique** (Paris).
REJ   *Revue des Études Juives* (Paris).
REP   *Real-Encyclopädie der klassischen Altertumswissen-
          schaft* (PAULY-WISSOWA) (Stuttgart).
RGG   *Die Religion in Geschichte und Gegenwart*[2] (Tü-
          bingen, 1927-1932).
RHE   *Revue d'Histoire Ecclésiastique** (Louvain).
RHPR   *Revue d'Histoire et de Philosophie Religieuse*
          (Strasbourg).
RHR   *Revue de l'Histoire des Religions* (Paris).
RSPT   *Revue des Sciences Philosophiques et Théolo-
          giques** (Le Saulchoir).
RSR   *Recherches de Sciences Religieuses** (Paris).
RTP   *Revue de Théologie et de Philosophie* (Lausanne).
Scr   *Scripture** (Edinburgh).
SDB   *Supplément au Dictionnaire de la Bible** (L. PIROT,
          A. ROBERT, H. CAZELLES) (Paris, 1928 ff.).
STh   *Summa Theologica of Saint Thomas Aquinas*.
TD   *Theology Digest* (St. Marys, Kansas).
TLZ   *Theologische Literaturzeitung* (Berlin).
TS   *Theological Studies** (Woodstock, Md.).
TWNT   *Theologische Worterbuch zum Neuen Testament*
          (G. KITTEL) (Stuttgart).
TZ   *Theologische Zeitschrift* (Basel).
VC   *Verbum Caro* (Lausanne).
VD   *Verbum Domini** (Rome).
VT   *Vetus Testamentum* (Leyden).
ZAW   *Zeitschrift für die Alttestamentliche Wissenschaft*
          (Giessen-Berlin).
ZKT   *Zeitschrift für Katholische Theologie** (Innsbruck).

ZNW   *Zeitschrift für die Neutestamentliche Wissenschaft*
            (Giessen-Berlin).
ZTK   *Zeitschrift für Theologie und Kirche* (Tübingen).

For the abbreviations of the large commentaries, see pp. 25 f.

General Bibliography of the Old Testament

I. *Introductions to the Old Testament*

A. Catholic

A. MILLER—A. METZINGER, *Introductio specialis in Vetus Testamentum*[5]* (Rome, 1946).

SIMÓN-PRADO, *Praelectiones biblicae*[5]* (Rome-Turin, 1946).

J. RENIÉ, *Manuel d'Écriture Sainte*[6]* (Paris-Lyon, 1949).

A. ROBERT—A. TRICOT, *Guide to the Bible*, 2 Vols. (New York: Desclée, 1955 ff.).

P. ELLIS, *Men and Message of the Old Testament** (Collegeville: Liturgical Press, 1962).

B. Non-Catholic

S. DRIVER, *Introduction to the Literature of the Old Testament*[3] (Edinburgh, 1909).

J. HEMPEL, *Althebräische Literatur und ihr hellenistisch-jüdisches Nachleben* (Potsdam, 1930).

L. GAUTIER, *Introduction à l'Ancien Testament*[3] (Lausanne, 1939) ([1]1905).

A. WEISER, *Einleitung in das alte Testament*[2] (Stuttgart, 1949) ([1]1939).

H. ROWLEY, *Growth of the Old Testament* (New York: Harper, 1950).

A. LODS, *Histoire de la littérature hébraïque et juive* (Paris, 1950).

H. ROWLEY, *The Old Testament and Modern Study* (Oxford, 1951).

R. H. PFEIFFER, *Introduction to the Old Testament*[2] (New York: Harper, 1952).

A. BENTZEN, *Introduction to the Old Testament*[2] (Copenhagen, 1952) ([1]1948-1949).

O. EISSFELDT, *Einleitung in das alte Testament*[2] (Tübingen, 1956) ([1]1934); Eng. trans. *The Old Testament, An Introduction* (New York: Harper, 1965).

B. ANDERSON, *Understanding the Old Testament* (Englewood Cliffs: Prentice Hall, 1957).

N. GOTTWALD, *A Light to the Nations. An Introduction to the Old Testament* (New York: Harper, 1959).

A. WEISER, *Introduction to the Old Testament* (New York: Association, 1961).

II. *General commentaries*

L. PIROT—A. CLAMER, *La sainte Bible** (Paris) = BPC.

*The Jerusalem Bible**, Alexander Jones, general editor (New York and London, 1966).

A. VACCARI, *La Sacra Bibbia** (Florence) = SB.

*Das Alte Testament, Echterbibel** (Wurtzburg) = EBi.

Handkommentar zum Alten Testament (Göttingen) = HKAT.

*Die Heilige Schrift des Alten Testaments** (Bonn) = HSAT.

E. SELLIN, *Kommentar zum Alten Testament* (Leipzig) = KAT.

*A Catholic Commentary on Holy Scripture** (London) = CCHS.

International Critical Commentary, missing Exodus, Leviticus, Isaias 28 ff., Jeremias, Lamentations, Canticle of Canticles and all Deuteronomy (Edinburgh) = ICC.

Cambridge Bible for Schools and Colleges (Cambridge) = CBSC.

*La Biblia** (Monastery of Montserrat) = BM.

G. A. BUTTRICK, *et al.* (eds.), *The Interpreter's Bible* (New York: Abingdon, 1952 ff.).

N. J. McELENEY, ed., *Pamphlet Bible Series** (New York: Paulist, 1959 ff.).

G. E. WRIGHT, *et al.* eds., *The Old Testament Library* (Philadelphia: Westminster, 1961 ff.).

M. BLACK—H. ROWLEY, eds., *Peake's Commentary on the Bible* (New York: Nelson, 1963).

W. F. ALBRIGHT—D. N. FREEDMAN, eds., *The Anchor Bible* (Garden City: Doubleday, 1964 ff.).

Old Testament Reading Guide* (Collegeville: Liturgical Press, 1965 ff.).

N.B. The other general commentaries are either too old or too incomplete.

See also the bibliography given in reviews such as *Biblica* (Rome), *Catholic Biblical Quarterly* (Washington, D. C.), *Internationale Zeitschriftenanschau für Bibelwissenanschaft und Grenzgebiete* (Düsseldorf).

INTRODUCTION TO THE OLD TESTAMENT

PART IV

THE KETUBIM OR SACRED WRITINGS

The books which make up the third part of the Jewish canon are, generally speaking, the ones that were composed and accorded canonical recognition later than the rest. They belong to widely different classifications. After the *Psalms*, which must be given a special place, come books that treat the subject of wisdom; namely, *Proverbs* and *Job*. Five scrolls (*Megillôt*) form a collection of liturgical prayers for five great feasts (*Canticle of Canticles, Ruth, Lamentations, Ecclesiastes, Esther*). *Daniel* occupies a special place. The Jewish canon closes with the Books of *Esdras, Nehemias*, and *Paralipomenon*. In these last three books the mind of a single writer can be recognized. Each of the other books belonging to the Ketubim should be studied as a separate unit.

SECTION I

THE PSALMS

by P. Auvray

Bibliography

For introductions, translations, and commentaries, see pp. 25 f.

D. C. SIMPSON, ed., *The Psalmists* (London, 1926).

H. GUNKEL, *Einleitung in die Psalmen* (Göttingen, 1933).

N. H. SNAITH, *Studies in the Psalter* (1934); *The Jewish New Year Festival* (1947).

G. WIDENGREN, *The Accadian and Hebrew Psalms of Lamentation as Religious Documents* (Uppsala, 1936).

J. H. PATTON, *Canaanite Parallels in the Book of Psalms* (1944).

J. J. WEBER, *Le Psautier du Bréviaire romain** (Paris-Tournai, 1944).

E. PODECHARD, *Le Psautier**, 3 Vols. (Lyon, 1949-1954).

H. DUESBERG, *Le Psautier des malades** (Maredsous, 1952).

E. J. KISSANE, *The Book of Psalms**, 2 Vols. (Dublin, 1953).

W. O. OESTERLEY, *The Psalms* (London, 1953).

G. CASTELLINO, *I Salmi** (Turin, 1955).

J. J. STAMM, "Ein Viertelyahrhundert Psalmenforschung," *Theologische Rundschau*, 23 (1955), pp. 1-68.

M. TSEVAT, *A Study of the Language of the Biblical Psalms* (1955).

C. GORDON, *Ugaritic Manual* (1955).

S. MOWINCKEL, *The Psalms in Israel's Worship, I and II* (New York: Abingdon, 1962); "Psalm Criticism Between 1900 and 1935," *VT*, 5 (1955), pp. 13-33; "Traditionalism and Personality in the Psalms," *HUCA*, 23 (1950-1951), pp. 205-231.

A. R. JOHNSON, "The Psalms," *OTMS*, pp. 162-209.

P. DRIJVERS, *Les Psaumes. Genres littéraires et thèmes doctrinaux** (Paris, 1958).

J. GRAY, "The Kingship of God in the Prophets and Psalms," *VT*, 11 (1961), pp. 1 ff.

A. WEISER, *The Psalms, A Commentary* (Philadelphia: Westminster, 1962).

T. WORDEN, *The Psalms are Christian Prayer* (New York: Sheed and Ward, 1962).

P. A. H. DE BOER, *Studies on Psalms* (Leyden, 1963).

G. W. ANDERSON, "The Psalms," *Peake's Commentary on the Bible*, ed. M. BLACK—H. ROWLEY (New York: Nelson, 1963), pp. 409-443.

H. RINGGREN, *The Faith of the Psalmists* (Philadelphia: Fortress, 1964).

C. WESTERMANN, *The Praise of God in the Psalms* (Richmond: Knox, 1965).

P. DRIJVERS, *The Psalms, Their Structure and Meaning** (New York: Herder and Herder, 1965).

M. DAHOOD, *The Psalms, 1-50** (Garden City: Doubleday, 1966).

THE BOOK OF PSALMS

§ 1. Title and Place in the Bible

The Book of Psalms comes at the beginning of the *Ketubim* (Writings), which is the third section of the Hebrew Bible. In the Greek Bible it is also found at the beginning of the third section, that consisting of the didactic books. But the Latin Bible, as far back as we can go (Council of Hippo, A.D. 393), places the Book of Psalms after Job.

In Hebrew Bibles the book is called *tehillim* or *sefer tehillim*. This is an irregular[1] plural form of the feminine noun *tehillah* (root: *halal*, praise), which has a specialized meaning; it refers to a certain kind of psalm, namely *praises* or *hymns*. The word which corresponds exactly with our word *psalm* would be *mizmor* (root: *zamar*, to sing with accompaniment); it refers to a poem to be sung to the accompaniment of stringed instruments. This word is found in the titles of 57 psalms.

As a rule the LXX gives this book the title *Psalmoi* or *Biblos Psalmon*, a title which is borne out by the New Testament also (Lk 20, 13; 24, 44; Acts 1, 20). The LXX codex Alexandrinus gives it the title *Psalterion* (a word which generally means a musical instrument).

The Latin Bible also uses two titles, *Liber Psalmorum* and *Psalterium* (or *Liber Psalterii*), from which we have the French titles *livre des psaumes* and *psautier* as well as the English *Book of Psalms* and *Psalter*. *Psalter* is the title preferred in liturgical usage.

---

[1] EHRLICH thinks that this plural form *im* instead of the normal *tehillot* was characteristic of titles given to books or collections. See Esd 2, 10, *qinim* instead of *qinot*. But this is uncertain.

§ 2. Content

If we consider the Book of Psalms as it has come down to us, with its individual psalm titles and its musical and liturgical markings, it seems to be a more or less official collection of songs used in the Jerusalem liturgy during the period of the second Temple.

The collection contains 150 psalms, there being no reason to include a 151st psalm which is found as an extra in the LXX. This 151st psalm is not in the Hebrew nor in the Latin Vulgate, and it does not belong to the canonical text.

Although the number of psalms (150) is agreed to, the sources of the Book of Psalms do not all give the same divisions. Twice the LXX, followed by the Latin Vulgate, divides a single Hebrew psalm in two. Twice again two Hebrew psalms correspond to one in the LXX. In numbering the psalms this difference can be represented as follows:

Hebrew		LXX and Latin Vulgate
1–8	–	1–8
9	–	9, 1-21
10	–	9, 22-39
11 to 113	–	10 to 112
114	–	113, 1-8
115	–	113, 9-26
116, 1-9	–	114
116, 10-19	–	115
117 to 146	–	116 to 145
147, 1-11	–	146
147, 12-20	–	147
148 to 150	–	148 to 150

Most of the time it is difficult to decide which of these traditional ways of dividing is correct. An exception is the LXX
psalm 9, which is psalms 9 and 10 in Hebrew. It seems that
the LXX tradition is the better one here, since the whole
composition forms an alphabetical psalm. The problem of
these divisions will be met in particular instances in commentaries.

We cannot say exactly when this collection of psalms was
put together. The collection existed as part of the canon and
was already translated into Greek when the grandson of Ben
Sira attached a prologue to his translation of the Book of
Ecclesiasticus (about B.C. 117). In three places this prologue
mentions the three parts of the Hebrew Bible, and the third
part certainly begins with the Book of Psalms. The writer of
this prologue further implies that the psalms were already a
part of the Bible in his grandfather's day, thus at the beginning of the second century B.C. The Book of Ecclesiasticus
(47, 8-10) as well as the citation of a psalm as "scripture"
in 1 Machabees 7, 17 afford some support to this early second
century B.C. date for the collection of the psalms. This date
may be set a little farther back. In 1 Par 16 we find a song
that is made up with parts of psalms 105, 96 and 106. And
1 Par 16, 36 gives the doxology which concludes the fourth
section of the Book of Psalms. Although there are some un-
certainties here, and complete precision is impossible, we
may be right in saying that this collection of psalms already
existed in the third century B.C.

§ 3. Subdivisions

Like the Law (Torah), the Psalter is divided into five books,
and each one ends with a doxology:
  Part I: psalms 1-41
  Part II: psalms 42-72 (note psalm 72, 20 "The prayers
    [LXX: the hymns] of David, son of Jesse, are ended")
  Part III: psalms 73-89
  Part IV: psalms 90-106

Part V: psalms 107-150 (psalm 150 is a kind of doxology)

A close study of the psalms shows up many repetitions or doublets. Psalm 14 appears again as psalm 53. Psalm 70 is a reworking of psalm 40, 14-18. Psalm 108 is a reconstruction of psalm 57, 8-12 and psalm 50, 8-14. There is a very uneven use of the divine names in the psalms. The first part of the Psalter is predominantly "Yahwist" (the name Yahweh is used 272 times, Elohim 15). The second part is "Elohist" (Elohim is used 164 times, Yahweh 30). The third part divides the names rather evenly (44 to 43). The fourth and fifth books are clearly Yahwist (103 and 236 respectively against none and 7). Whatever may have been the motive for substituting the name Elohim for Yahweh, the fact that such a characteristic is present, along with the doublets, clearly proves that there were partial collections of psalms in existence earlier than the actual Psalter which we have, collections made in different places and at different times. The study of editorial notes such as the one in psalm 72, 20 and of the individual psalm titles will lead to the same conclusion.

§ 4. Titles

Many of the psalms have titles, although in giving titles the Massoretic tradition does not agree perfectly with that of the LXX. In general the LXX has more titles. While 34 psalms have no titles in Hebrew, only 19 lack them in Greek. In the Hebrew 73 psalms are attributed to David, in the LXX 84. Whatever may be the solution to this minor textual problem, the titles have their importance and deserve close study.

I. THE VARIOUS KINDS OF PSALMS

Some are called psalms (*mizmor*, 57 times), others are called songs (*shir*, 30 times), others prayers (*tefillah*, 5 times) or hymns (*tehillah*, once, Ps 145). Related to this last title (tehillah) is the acclamation *Halleluyah* which some psalms have at the beginning (10 in all) and some at the end (13)[2]; these are classified as hymns. Some of the names of the psalms are obscure: *miktam* (6 times), which was understood by the LXX as "inscription poem" and by others as "poem of gold"; *maskil* (13 times) was generally taken to mean "didactic piece"; *shiggayon* (once, Ps 7; cf. Hb 3, 1) might mean "prayer of repentance." These classifications are not complete, and they are not very exact. Therefore, they are not decisive in classifying the psalms according to their different literary forms.

II. THE INITIAL LAMED

This *lamed*, which is called the *lamed auctoris*, is ambiguous. Its actual meaning is so uncertain that some recent writers have denied the very existence of a real *lamed auctoris*. Let us look at the data.

Fifty-five psalms have the title *lamenasseah* (in Greek: *eis to telos*), which is generally translated "of (or) for the songmaster."

Seventy-three psalms have the formula "for David" (in Greek: *to David*, 84 times).

Twelve psalms have "for the sons of Asaph."

Twelve psalms have "for the sons of Core."

One psalm has "for Moses." (Ps 90)

Two psalms (72 and 127) have "for Solomon."

One psalm (88) has "for Heman the Ezrahite." This psalm also has "for the sons of Core."

One psalm (89) has "for Ethan the Ezrahite."

One psalm (39) has "for Yedutun." It also has "for David." Psalm 62 has "over Yedutun, for David." Psalm 77 has "over Yedutun, for Asaph."

Many of these persons are known—David, Moses, Solomon. The mention of the levites Asaph, Heman, etc. is a witness to the organization of liturgical song and worship as we know

---

[2] In the LXX the *alleluia* always comes at the beginning, with the exception of Ps 150 which has two *alleluias*, one at the beginning and one at the end.

it from the priestly tradition. After the Exile liturgical song seems to have been the monopoly of the sons of Asaph (Esd 2, 41; 3, 10; Neh 7, 44; 11, 17. 22). But during the period of the monarchy, starting from the time of that organization of liturgy referred to as the work of David (1 Par 6, 16-32), the priestly author of Par mentions three corporations of singers. Heading these groups were Asaph, Heman, and Ethan (who is identified with Yedutun, 1 Par 15, 16-24; 25, 1-6; 2 Par 5, 12; 29, 13-14; 35, 15). The older and larger group, which was called the sons of Core (ancestor of Heman, 1 Par 6, 7-12. 18-23), acted in various capacities such as porters (1 Par 9, 17-19; 11, 19) and bakers (1 Par 9, 31). They were linked to the levite Core of the time of Moses. Core's revolt was punished severely (Nm 16, 1-35), but he still had some descendants (Nm 26, 11).

The term *menasseah* is generally taken as a common noun (more accurately a piel participle of the verb *nasah*, to guide; see 1 Par 15, 21). Fifty-three of the fifty-five psalms which begin with this word are at the same time attributed to a specific person: 39 to David, 9 to the sons of Core, 5 to the sons of Asaph (see a similar case in the psalm of Habacuc, Hb 3, 19). The meaning of the expression is disputed.

These remarks as well as those made earlier regarding the Asaphite and Coraite professional singers, and reference to the Ras Shamra tablets with their titles (*lebaal, lekeret*) which indicate the poem or cycle of poems to which they belonged, along with the testimony of the Book of Par (2 Par 29, 30)—all these items have led scholars to speak of partial collections older than our actual Psalter or even older than the five books which it contains. There must have been Asaphite and Coraite collections of psalms as well as a collection prepared for the songmaster. In all these instances, the phrase "for Asaph," "for Core," etc., placed at the beginning of a psalm, shows that the psalm in question belonged to one or the other of these collections. The phrase, however, does not necessarily say anything about the author of the psalm. The same can be said about the title "for David." This title shows that "Davidic" collections were in existence, a fact already suggested by the editorial note of Ps 72, 20 and by the testimony of 2 Par 29, 30.

There are instances, however, in which such titles do not suggest the existence of a special collection. One psalm (90) has the title "for Moses," and two psalms (72 and 127) have the title "for Solomon." There is no question here of relating these psalms to a collection, but rather of attributing them to an author. The same should be said about those "Davidic" psalms in which the title "for David" is followed by a description of circumstances which are regarded as providing the occasion for the composition of the psalm. It doesn't matter much whether this understanding of titles led to the idea that the whole Psalter was the work of David, or whether the conviction that the whole Psalter was David's suggested this interpretation of the titles. The essential point here is that these two factors coincide. We conclude that the *lamed* was certainly understood by later tradition as a *lamed auctoris*.

III. MUSICAL DATA

Certain obscure expressions in the Book of Psalms are generally included under this heading of musical data. The expressions refer to the following:

—instruments for musical accompaniment: *bineginot*, with stringed instruments (Ps 4; 6; 54; 55; 61; 67; 76); *el nehilot*, for flutes(?) (Ps 5); *al haggitit*, on the Gath harp (Ps 8; 81; 84; according to others: on the melody of the Gattite).

—the musical mode: at the octave (Ps 6; 12; according to others: on the eight-stringed harp); for the voice of sopranos(?) (Ps 46; see 9, 1 and 48, 15 and the commentaries).

—the melodies to be used: "to the melody of *Do not destroy*" (Ps 57; 58; 59; 75; see Is 65, 8); "to the melody of *The dove of the distant terebinths*" (Ps 56); possibly also: "to the melody of *The death of the son*" (Ps 9); "to the melody of *The Gattite*" (Ps 8; 81; 84); and many others—see Ps 45; 69; 60; 80.

The meaning of these phrases is often unclear. Even less clear is the sense of the formulae *lelammed* ("for teaching,"

Ps 60; see 2 Sam 1, 18) and *le annot* ("for answering," Ps 88).

We should mention here the puzzling word *selah*, which is used 71 times in 39 psalms, 37 of these 39 psalms being in the first two books. *Selah* could mean "raise of voice" or "pause" or "interlude" (Greek: *diapsalma*).

The obscurity of all these expressions is proof of their great age. Most of them were already unintelligible in the period of the LXX translation. One may speak of preexilic notations, the meaning of which was lost during the long period when the Temple lay in ruins. But this is only hypothesis.

IV. LITURGICAL CLARIFICATIONS

The main one is found in the title "song of the steps" (Ps 120–134) which must be an allusion to the *ascent* of the pilgrims towards the Temple of Jerusalem. Others are the "song of the dedication of the Temple" (Ps 30), the "song for the Sabbath" (Ps 92), and the expressions "for commemorating" or "in memory of" (Ps 38; 70; see Lv 2, 2, etc.).

The LXX has many more notations of this kind indicating that a psalm is for the first or second or fourth or sixth day after the Sabbath (Ps 24 [23]; 48 [47]; 94 [93]; 93 [92]; or also "for the last day of the feast of tents" (Ps 29 [28]). These LXX notations are confirmed and sometimes expanded by the Mishna.

The fact that the LXX has this greater abundance of titles does not mean that they are more recent. The form of these titles rather shows that they were translated from the Hebrew. The Greek translation was using a Hebrew edition which was different from the one we have, but just as old. And like the one we have, that edition had Palestine for its place of origin.

V. HISTORICAL INDICATIONS

These historical indications fill out the details for the psalms attributed to David. They allude to his flight from Saul (Ps 7; 18; 34; 52; 56; 57; 59; 63; 142), to his repentance after his sin (Ps 51), to his wars (Ps 60), to his flight from Absalom (Ps 3).

All these indications of historical detail are found in the LXX as well as in the Hebrew Psalter. The LXX has in fact about a dozen more such indications than the Hebrew. They refer the psalms in question to David or other authors. Examples are: "Of David, before his anointing" (Ps 27 [26]); "For David, poem of Jeremias and Ezechiel, about the captivity, when they were going to leave" (Ps 65 [64]); "For David, of the sons of Jonadab and the first exiles" (Ps 71 [70]); "When the Temple was rebuilt after the Exile, poem of David" (Ps 96 [95]); "Over the Assyrians" (Ps 80 [79]); "For David, against Goliath" (Ps 144 [143]), and many others.

Conclusion

What can be said about the question of the inspiration and authority of these psalm titles? Although patristic tradition often favored the idea of taking these titles as canonical and inspired, the practice of the Fathers is not unanimous on this point. Besides, this tradition was built for the most part on the insufficient criterion of literary authenticity; that is, these titles would be taken as canonical in the degree that they were thought to go back to the very authors of the psalms. The almost unanimous practice of the Fathers was to discuss the authenticity and then the veracity of these titles.

Many recent theologians have come to doubt the inspiration of these titles. Dom Calmet[3] already in his day mentioned his contemporaries Noel Alexandre and L. Ferrand as doubting their inspiration. In our day, the great majority of exegetes who have faced the question have arrived at the same conclusion.[4] The answers of the Biblical Commission of

---

[3] *Dissertation sur les titres des Psaumes*.

[4] Most of these theologians are content simply to mention the fact that this is their position, without bothering much about the reasons for it. Basically, the idea guiding them is that these titles

May 1, 1910 (answers II and III), by the very fact that they do not oblige the Catholic exegete to consider the titles of the psalms as having unquestionable authority, seem to adopt the same position.

However, the titles of the psalms should not be under-valued. They provide positive data which bear witness to a tradition. Only good arguments to the contrary can oppose them in particular cases.

---

are editorial insertions, late, and external to the sacred text. The relation of psalm title to psalm is similar to the relation of the prologue to the Book of Ecclesiasticus.

CHAPTER II

THE TEXT

The question of textual criticism is a very touchy one in the Book of Psalms, more so than for any other book of the Bible.

I. THE HEBREW TEXT

Frequent flaws are found in the Hebrew text. From a literary standpoint, the Hebrew text has often been reworked or glossed to adapt it to changing circumstances. Besides, a text used as much as the Psalms must be copied often. This leads to errors on the part of those copyists who are not well trained in a difficult language. The comparison of doublets such as Ps 18 and 1 Sm 22 or of Ps 14 and Ps 53 points up some of the textual difficulties and leads us to suspect similar ones even in those places where there is no comparison to be made which would give concrete proof of the difficulty. If we compare the Hebrew text with the Greek version, we may conclude that in places the Hebrew text was corrupted beyond remedy even before the Greek translator got to it. Still, in practice great prudence is called for in making textual emendations.

II. THE VERSIONS MADE FROM THE HEBREW

One of the poorest translations in the entire LXX is its version of the Book of Psalms. The reason is the difficulty of the Hebrew text and its poor condition on the one hand, and on the other the mediocre talents of the translators. There are many instances of countersense in the LXX, and some of nonsense. The verbs are translated mechanically, Greek aorist translating Hebrew perfect and Greek future translating Hebrew imperfect. The supposed vocalizations are often

erroneous. All things considered, the Psalm text of the LXX
is practically useless as a translation.

Even so, the LXX is valuable as a witness to a Hebrew text
that is not always identical with our Massoretic text. And
from this standpoint the very ineptitude of the translator is
sometimes welcome, since it gives us more information than
a more careful translation ever would.

Other primary versions worth mentioning are the following: 1) The Syriac (peshitto) version, which was made from
a Hebrew text which can be easily identified with our Massoretic text, although the Syriac version was also heavily influenced by the LXX; 2) the three Greek versions or revisions
of Aquila, Symmachus, and Theodotion, the partial preservation of which we owe to the hexapla of Origen—these versions
are not too important; 3) the remarkable version of St.
Jerome which is called *iuxta Hebraeos*[1]; it was made from a
Hebrew text that was identical with our Massoretic text and
was an excellent translation for its time.

III. The secondary versions

Among the secondary versions (made from the Greek), we
mention only the following: the *vetus latina*,[2] which after a
quick revision on St. Jerome's part gives us the *Roman
Psalter*,[3] and after a more thorough revision and correction

[1] Dom Henri de Sainte-Marie, *Sancti Hieronymi psalterium juxta
Hebraeos. Édition critique** (Collectanea biblica latina, Vol. XI)
(Rome: Abbey of Saint Jerome, 1954).
[2] Of the *Vetus Latina Hispanica* (edited by T. A. Marazuela:
I *Prolegomena*, Madrid, 1953), Vol. 21 has already been published,
*Psalterium Wisigothorum-Mozarabicum** (Madrid, 1957).
[3] A rather recent edition is the one by Dom Robert Weber, *Le
psautier romain et les autres anciens psautiers latins. Édition critique**
(Collectanea biblica latina, Vol. X, Rome, Abbey of Saint Jerome,
1953). The identification of the *Roman Psalter* with the first psalm
revision made by Jerome has recently been contested by Dom D. de
Bruyne in *Le Problème du Psautier Romain** (*Revue Bénédictine*,
42, 1930, pp. 101 ff.). This learned Benedictine holds that the text
of the Roman Psalter existed before St. Jerome and was not touched
by him. But Father Vaccari has made serious objections to this posi-

gives us the *Gallican Psalter*.[4] It was this latter version that became the text of our Sixto-Clementine Vulgate.

---

tion (*Scritti di Erudizione e di Filologia** [Rome, 1952], I, 211). And Dom Weber, in his edition of the Roman Psalter (p. ix) does not commit himself completely in favor of de Bruyne's position.

[4] *Biblia sacra juxta vulgatam versionem ad codicum fidem . . . X. Liber psalmorum ex recensione sancti Hieronymi**, (Rome: Tipografia polyglotta vaticana, 1954).

CHAPTER III

LITERARY FORMS OF THE PSALMS

People have always noticed differences both of spirit and of form among the various psalms. The very psalm titles such as hymn, song, thanksgiving, etc. are an invitation to recognize these differences.

About 30 years ago,[1] with the increase of knowledge about the psalms and the improvement in methods of studying them, the problem of classifying the psalms was posed in a new way.

This kind of study must be placed on as broad a base as possible. This is done when we put alongside the 150 psalms of our Psalter a number of similar poetic pieces which are scattered through the other books of the Bible; for example, the song of Moses (Ex 15), the song of Anna (1 Sm 2), the song of Ezechias (Is 38, 10-20), the hymns inserted into the passage in Isaias 24—27, the song of Habacuc (Hb 3), the hymn of the three young men (Dn 3, 52-88),[2] the psalms inserted into the Book of Ecclesiasticus (46, 1-17), many of the Lamentations of Jeremias, etc. To all this we may add certain pieces of non-biblical literature such as the Psalms of Solomon and the thanksgiving psalms of Qumran.

Besides all this, the religious poetry of neighboring peoples can be studied with profit. Such comparative study is a difficult one and calls for much caution. It can shed welcome light on certain Israelite institutions. For a long time it has been pointed out that some of the Assyro-Babylonian religious texts are worthy of close study in connection with cer-

---

[1] This was true especially after the appearance of Gunkel's Introduction to the Psalms (1933).

[2] In many manuscripts of the LXX several of these canticles are united under the title of "Odes" and placed after the Psalms.

tain passages of the Bible. Similarities as well as differences that can be noticed will help us in our understanding of the psalms. The still recent discovery of Sumerian literature allows us to go even farther back. Even though the study of this literature is still in its rough stages, it is full of promise. When we turn to Egypt we find that, in spite of some impressive contacts (the hymn of Akhenaton and Ps 104), Egyptian literature seems on the whole to have few comparisons to offer. These few should not be neglected. Finally, in the area of Phoenicia the Ras Shamra texts which were discovered and published about 30 years ago give us an insight into the religious ideas and their manifestation in the literature of a country very near to Chanaan before the Israelites arrived.[3] There is no question of finding among these neighboring peoples the source of the Bible's lyric poetry nor of pointing out comparisons that would suffice to explain the origin of that poetry. However, such an investigation of the larger literary context will give us a better grasp of certain characteristics of biblical poetry and will help us to appreciate its remarkable originality.

§ 1.   Variety of the Psalm Form

After the general area of the psalm form has been determined, the exegete is soon impressed by the limitless variety within this form. It is very difficult to put order into so rich a variety. It isn't as if we could sort out and classify these different psalms on the basis of clear signs as to their origin or form or subject. In the literary world of the psalms, a world alive with all sorts of inspiration and showing widely different characteristics, divisions must be created in somewhat the way paths are traced in an unexplored forest. This means that the results may be disappointing to exact minds looking for order and logic. The forms that we will try to

[3] All these texts are brought together in the anthologies referred to on pp. 25 f.

define are not always clearly marked off. Many psalms remain
more or less outside any classification. Several forms seem to
overlap one another and mix. The attempt at classification is
none the less a first step in the direction that leads to a more
perfect understanding and explanation of the psalms.

It is immediately clear that there is a distinction to be
made between individual and collective psalms. Whatever
may be the precise form and content of a prayer, it can come
from an isolated individual or from a group. It can be expressed by an I or a We. This point is important and is not
merely a question of the form in which the prayer is cast.
Collective prayer usually develops in a situation of worship.
The collective psalms may be liturgical prayers that originated
in Israel's sanctuaries and were used in them in connection
with feasts and Israel's life of worship. On the other hand
an expression of individual piety can be isolated and exceptional, and it may only instruct us about the personal piety
of its author. As we will see later, however, the matter is not
quite that simple. The I can itself be collective; for example, in the case of a king or priest speaking in the name of a
whole group, and especially in the case of the "individual
lamentations"—it is practically certain that these lamentations
originated in a cultic and therefore collective situation. The
exegete must be sensitive to shades of meaning here, his
main duty being that of giving his attention to objective
data. When he attempts to place the psalms back into their
living context, the first question he must ask is whether their
orientation is individual or collective.

§ 2. The Hymns

The hymn form is found throughout the history of religious
poetry in Israel, from the song of Miriam (Ex 15, 21) and
the song of Debora (Jgs 5) to the New Testament's *Bene-
dictus* and *Magnificat*, two hymns that draw all their inspiration from the earlier Israelite poetry. The hymn form is found
in many parts of our Psalter; for example, Ps 8; 19; 29; 33; 67;

100; 103; 104; 105; 111; 113; 114; 136; 145; 146; 147; 148; 149; 150.[4] There are also elements of hymns in psalms that are more or less composite. And there are special forms like the royal hymns or the hymns to Sion. These will be considered later.

The hymn is characterized clearly by its tone of praise. It glorifies God above all for His own sake rather than for the sake of some personal benefit to the one who is praying it. The person who prays a hymn does not ask favors for himself or for those dear to him. He does not reflect on himself but keeps his attention centered in God. Since the hymn is completely involved with Yahweh and His glory, it is a very pure expression of religion.

Among all the psalm forms, the hymn has the most consistent structure. Although this structure does not exclude the use of imagination in expressing one's devotion, the variations that result from this use of imagination seem to fit into a rigid system that can be recognized easily.

The hymn has an *introduction*. It is a brief invitation to praise Yahweh. The introductory invitation is usually a plural imperative joined with an expression referring to those who are uniting in the act of praise (*Praise the Lord, you children; Praise the Lord, all you nations*). The invitation can also be expressed in the first person and in the future tense (*I will praise you, O Lord; we will praise you, O God*).

After the hymn's introduction comes a *development*. This part generally begins with "because" (Hebrew: *ki*) or some similar word. Sometimes it begins with active participles or relative clauses. The "development" names and describes the attributes of God, retells His powerful actions in favor of Israel and other men. Sometimes it lengthens out into fuller narratives (Ps 104, 6-9) or repeats the story of historical events (Ps 105; 106). In doing all this the hymn uses a wide range of forms; for example, exclamations or questions, comparisons drawn between Yahweh and the nothingness of false

---

[4] These lists of references are not complete. They aim only to point out characteristic examples.

gods, wishes and blessings, refrain-like repetitions of ideas or
formulae that have already appeared in the introduction.

Ordinarily it is Yahweh who is the direct object of this
praise, whatever may be the name by which He is called or
the epithets that are applied to Him. But some of the psalm
hymns are addressed to Sion (Ps 48; 84). It also happens that
the praise which is given to God is blended with the glorifi-
cation of His sanctuary or of the holy city.

The hymns usually end with a short *conclusion*. This can
be a more developed or more personal restatement of the
introductory formula. It can be a short blessing, a promise,
or a prayer. Sometimes it is a simple "Praise Yahweh" or
"forever," which could be said by the whole crowd in answer
to the longer expressions used by the choir.

We can gain some idea of the variation of tone among the
psalm hymns if we look at certain "cosmic" hymns such as
Ps 8; 19; 29; 104. Psalm 29 is a kind of litany to the God of
the storm. After a short invitation to rejoice in God's glory
(1-2), the author gives a detailed description of the manifestations of "Yahweh's voice." This voice makes His glory
brilliantly visible and it terrifies the proudest creatures
(3-10). Finally, a short conclusion (11) mentions Israel,
the people for whom God has a blessing.

Psalm 19 is a hymn to the beauty of the skies, and especially to the beauty of the sun because it tells the glory of
God in a special way (2-7). The psalm ends with a long
meditation on the Law. Like the sun, the Law gives light and
warmth to men (8-15). This conclusion may be a later
addition.

The greatest cosmic psalm is Ps 104. Many comparisons
have been made between this psalm and the famous hymn of
Amenophis IV to the glory of the solar disc. There are, in
fact, striking points of comparison between the two texts,
and a similar motif for the two pieces is admitted by all. But
there is probably no literary dependence to be uncovered
here, not even of an indirect kind. Within the Bible itself
two passages, Gn 1 and Jb 38—40, invite comparison with
Ps 104. All three pieces have the same point of departure;

namely, the contemplation of nature by a keenly observant man. With a sense of wonder the man in each case discovers harmonious order in the world. But each one's manner of expressing this wonder is different. Gn 1 is the product of a mind aiming vaguely at scientific expression. Its presentation is didactic, in rhythmic prose. Jb 38—40 is a grandiose page of "theodicy" read out in epic style. It is an enthusiastic picture of God's greatness seen in the wonders of creation. Ps 104 seems to stand midway between the two. It has neither the cold exactness of the first account of creation nor the fantasy of the passage in Job. Ps 104 is a good example of genuine religious lyric poetry. The author speaks admiringly to God as he describes the visible world with fine feeling for what is picturesque and colorful and for movement. It is true that at the end (32-35) he mentions the wicked, and in doing so he points out the disorder that has found its way into the world; but this is only a passing reference. The author of Ps 104 is a religious optimist. He understands and loves nature, including fierce animals and catastrophic events. Everything is for him a way of rising towards God.

In contrast with the "cosmic" hymns are the "human" hymns, which show interest in man rather than in things. They move from man to God without the help of other creatures. Ps 8 mentions the majesty of the Lord above the skies (2) and the work of God in the sky, the moon and the stars (4) only as an introduction to the contemplation of man who was created "a little less than a god" and set up as master of creation (6-9).

Ps 113, the first of the *hallel*, also mentions the glory of God "above the skies." But the author of this psalm is particularly interested in the praise of God on the lips of man and in God's generous actions in favor of men. Here the impression is given that God's glory lies mainly in His mercy. God is greater for having raised Job from his dung hill than for having created sky and earth. This kind of hymn, which is usually quite solemn, lets the human sounds of pleading and thanksgiving come through.

In this connection the most striking psalm is Ps 103. It

has been compared with Ps 104, and a similarity of structure
and tone seems to be intentionally emphasized by the fact
that they have the same introduction and conclusion formulae. But there is a big difference. The author of Ps 104, a
nature poet, goes from the exterior to the interior, from the
world to God. The author of Psalm 103 has only a moderate
interest in nature, but a very keen insight into the moral
world of man. And he shows deep religious feeling in his
praise to the Lord in connection with that world. He sees the
greatness of God in man's lowliness and in all the manifestations of divine mercy. Although as a poem it is not as fine as
Ps 104, it has a greater psychological and religious depth.

Most of the hymns give the impression of being impersonal,
and they appear to be expressions of Israel's collective piety.
Many allusions to the sanctuary and to God's presence there
can be found in these hymns. They contain indications of
liturgical actions such as prostrating, lifting the hands, shout-
ing. In them we find traces of dialogue, invitations and responses, references to processions and to sacrifices. All of
this, when taken in connection with scattered descriptions
in the historical and prophetic books, gives us a picture of
the liturgical context in which these hymns originated and
in which they were used. Unfortunately we have no ancient
ritual that would give us more detailed information. We
know only that the psalms of the *hallel* (Ps 113—118)[5] were
recited in later centuries at the three great feasts, particularly
during the paschal meal (see Mt 26, 30; Mk 14, 26).

§ 3. Supplications

The term "lamentation" is often used for this psalm form.
But it seems that the name "supplication," which is broad

---

[5] This is the *hallel* par excellence, also called the *hallel* of Egypt.
The tradition of the Talmud gives the name *hallel* also to Ps 136
(great *hallel*) and to Psalms 145—150.

enough to include the dirge character of the lament as well as other elements in this kind of poetry, is the better term.

Collective supplications (Ps 44; 79; 80; 83; etc.) are not as common as individual supplications (Ps 3; 5; 13; 22; 25; etc.). The two kinds of supplication are distinguished only by the particular grammar proper to each. At base their forms are the same. They both grow out of the reaction of the religious person in the presence of enemies or evils that assail him. When persecuted or hurt, the devout Israelite turns to God to tell Him his troubles and to ask for help.

The structure of the supplication is much like that of the hymn. But it is not as rigid as the hymn, especially in the case of the individual supplications.

The *introduction* in supplication psalms is very brief. It is an appeal to God. Sometimes it is cut down to a simple vocative; at other times it is a little more developed. It recalls God's unfailing goodness towards those who cry to Him.

The *development* in supplication psalms, in contrast to that of the hymns, is always concrete and personal. The psalmist describes his situation and admits that he is helpless. Thus the one who prays the supplication psalm puts himself forward and speaks in the first person. He describes his troubles, points out and judges his enemies, and makes his cry of distress with all the art of impassioned rhetoric. Sometimes he ends his piece by insisting again on the fact that he is weak and that none but Yahweh can save him. This avowal serves as a kind of step by which he moves to the supplication proper.

The psalmist's purpose here is to get Yahweh to intervene. Most of the time he solicits this intervention directly ("Rise up, Yahweh, save us!" Ps 44, 24, 27). But often he tells God reasons why he should intervene. These motives are Yahweh's power (and here the supplication will sound much like a hymn) and His goodness as shown in past interventions; and also the innocence and weakness and confidence of the one who is praying. The reason put forward to God can also be the opinion of onlooking strangers and Yahweh's concern for His name's honor and glory.

The *conclusion* to the supplication psalm usually expresses confidence and is marked by a conviction that God will listen and answer. Sometimes the supplication ends with words of thanksgiving.

The psalms that are dearest to the devoted faithful belong to this classification. The *De Profundis* (Ps 130) belongs here. Private devotion has made it a prayer for the souls in purgatory. Originally it was the supplication made by a man who was sick and discouraged. He made his appeal to Yahweh (1-2) by pointing out the motives he had for despairing (3-4) and by making his act of faith (5-8). The last strophe (7-8) could be the result of a later transformation of the psalm which aimed at applying it to all Israel even though originally it had been the prayer of an individual.

The *Miserere* (Ps 51) is similar in spirit to the *De Profundis* and is still more moving. The psalmist lays great stress on the sin he has committed (5-8) and on the pardon which he has asked for and expects to receive (3-4; 9-14). He says emphatically, "Create a clean heart in me. Give me once more a strong spirit" (12). These words give a more complete and precise expression to the rather flat idea of a fault being "covered" or "erased" (11). The psalmist is sure of God's pardon. He promises to express his grateful recognition in hymns (17) and to spell it out still more by offering a personal sacrifice (19). Here again, as in the case of Ps 130, the conclusion (20-21) enlarges the content of the psalm.

Ps 22, although it is not used as much as these other two in modern devotion, is famous because of the use made of it by Jesus and the evangelists. It too is a complaint. But it is the complaint of a just man who is aware of his innocence. He makes his cry of hope to God in the midst of the cruelest sufferings. The tone of his appeal and certain concrete details in his expression have led some to relate this psalm to the last of the Servant Songs in Isaias (Is 52—53). The first part (2-12) is a mixture of complaint and confidence. The second part (13-22) is a pure lamentation which describes the miserable condition of the persecuted just man. This part ends with a heart-rending appeal (20-22). In a long conclusion the psalmist makes promises. When he is delivered, he will publicly acknowledge his debt to the Lord. He will be very generous with his benefits. He will work for the conversion of the world to God. His outlook is full of hope. Moving beyond his own personal experience, he opens up still larger religious perspectives. At this point the tone of the psalm becomes that of a hymn. The psalm becomes Messianic and even eschatological. The conclusion gives to Ps 22 a prophetic and universalist meaning which is rare in the Psalter. It is easy to see why it was used so much by the New Testament writers.

The usual context or life situation of these supplication psalms was evidently the occurrence of national or individual catastrophes and the dirge ceremonies that followed them. The historical books of the Bible do not place psalms similar to those in our collection on the lips of historical persons, although the elegy spoken by David at the death of Saul and Jonathan (2 Sm 1, 17-27) is not altogether unlike them. Still, these books refer to actions of mourning (Dt 9, 18; Jos 7, 6), and they also stress the fact that mourners "wept in the presence of Yahweh" (Jgs 20, 23. 26). Sometimes the short prayers of the mourners are mentioned (Jgs 21, 3; 4 Kgs 8, 33). We also know that on certain occasions a fast was decreed and all the people were invited to make their lament in the presence of Yahweh in a cry for pity (Jl 2, 15-17). In the period after the Exile, the prophet Zacharias mentions many annual fast days such as those for the fourth, fifth, seventh, and tenth months (Za 8, 19). At least two of these solemn fast days date back to the time of the Exile (Za 7; 5). At about the same period, the feast of Expiation (*kippurim*), which was kept on the 10th of the month tishri and the days immediately following, took on an importance that was to continue in Judaism. It is very likely that the ritual for these fasts provided for lamentations in the presence of Yahweh as well as for sacrifices and purification rites. Many of our supplication psalms are more clearly intelligible in this situation.

§ 4. Thanksgiving Psalms

Like supplication psalms, these thanksgiving psalms belong
mostly to the area of individual devotion (Ps 18; 32; 34; 40;
etc.). There are only five or six instances of collective thanksgiving psalms (Ps 66; 67; 124; 129).

Thanksgiving psalms have something in common with the
hymn and with the supplication psalm. The attitude of the
faithful person who gives thanks to God is expressed easily
in words of praise. This makes his prayer like a hymn. When
an appeal addressed to God in a supplication psalm has been
answered, the one who has prayed will move on to acts of
thanksgiving. And so the connection between the two psalm
forms is evident.

The *introduction* to thanksgiving psalms is something like
the introduction to hymns. We find the following: "I will
sing . . ."; "I will praise . . ."; "Shout to God . . ." This
introduction is sometimes addressed to God, who is to be
thanked. Sometimes it is addressed to the community, which
is invited to join the psalmist as witness to God's favors.

The *development* in thanksgiving psalms is usually a narrative. The psalmist begins this development by recalling the
dangers he has experienced and the attacks or persecutions
that have been aimed at him. Sometimes he admits his faults
and confesses his weakness. At other times he claims he is
innocent and makes a protest against unjust persecution.

Then he makes his request in terms similar to those used
in supplication psalms.

At this point the thanksgiving psalm tells about the saving
intervention of God. This saving intervention is the element
of originality in the thanksgiving psalm. By proclaiming the
power of Yahweh the psalmist shows himself sure of the victory to be enjoyed by the person who places his trust in Yahweh. For this reason the thanksgiving psalm usually ends with
a hymn motif.

The *conclusion* of a thanksgiving psalm, when there is one, generally looks to the future. Man's confidence in God is renewed and strengthened. He promises to give glory to Yahweh forever. He invites the community to make a perpetual act of thanks to God. Sometimes the conclusion is a simple blessing formula.

Ps 30 is a thanksgiving psalm that has mixed elements. It glorifies God (verses 1 and 5), it narrates the psalmist's experience of danger and his rescue (3-4; 7-8), and it makes general observations about God's mercy (verses 6 and 10). Its title indicates that it was once used for the feast of the dedication of the Temple. It was applied to Israel or to the Temple of Yahweh, Israel having been at first happy and the Temple full of splendor but afterwards put to the test and persecuted and finally rescued by the intervention of God.

The first part of Ps 34 (1-11) is also a thanksgiving psalm, and it looks like a completion of the supplication Ps 25. After a hymn-like *introduction* (2-3), which is taken up again by the crowd in verse 4, there is a short description of the psalmist's rescue (5). Then the psalm becomes a kind of meditation on God's goodness (6-11). The second part of this alphabetical Ps 34 is a long *development* of a wisdom theme. This makes it sound like a teacher's instruction to his disciple. This psalm must be taken as a unit. Its wisdom development shows the turn which traditional devotion took during the period that was dominated by the scribes.

The thanksgiving psalm appears to be as old as the thanksgiving sacrifice and as old as the feasts that commemorated the great events of Israel's history. Commemorative ceremonies, great yearly feasts, dedications, anniversaries of victories—these were the situations in which many of these thanksgiving psalms originated and in which they are to be given their liturgical setting. This kind of psalm accompanied the sacrifice. It was sung in processions, perhaps alternately with hymns. However, we cannot be very precise here. The discoveries at Qumran have given us about 20 thanksgiving psalms which are full of biblical reminiscences. It is clear that they are imitations of our canonical psalms. But these Qum-

ran psalms have a rather new spirit[6] about them and are
filled with allusions to the history of the Qumran sect. They
tell us nothing about how they were used.

§ 5. Royal Psalms

Although the phrase "royal psalm" is ambiguous, it refers us
to still another kind of psalm. The term actually covers two
rather different kinds of psalms; namely, those which are
built on the idea of the kingship of Yahweh and those which
honor the Israelite king.

The psalms about the kingship of Yahweh are represented
by Ps 47 and by the series of Ps 93—100. These are basically
hymns with an eschatological turn (Ps 47; 97; 98; 99). And
they draw a great deal of their inspiration from the second
part of Isaias. During the period of the return from Exile,
Israel developed its idea of God as Ruler along with its universalist hope. Israel's devotion was moved to sing of God
as the true King of Israel and Master of the whole earth. It
seems unnecessary to hold with Mowinckel[7] that there was a
New Year's day feast of the enthronement of Yahweh. The
Bible does not give any hint of such a feast.

Other psalms have as their theme the individual *Israelite
king* (Ps 2; 20; 21; 45; 89; 110; 132). These psalms do not
present us with a new literary form. They are hymns, thanksgiving songs, supplications, etc. But the important place occupied in these psalms by the king gives them a special character which should be noted. The king held a privileged
position in the religion of Israel. His function was not simply
to serve as a guide in nonreligious matters for a people called
by God to a supernatural destiny. He was himself the instrument of God's plan. He shared in the promises and in the

---

[6] The materials to be studied in isolating this new spirit more
exactly are the hymns collected in Is 24—27 and the *hôdayôt* of
Qumran.
[7] *Psalmenstudien* II (Kristiana, 1932).

supernatural character of the history that was unfolding in and through his life.[8] He was God's representative in guiding the people, and he was their spokesman in God's presence. It is natural that some of the psalms should give the king this special attention.

Among these royal psalms we will look particularly at two, Ps 110 and 2, which resemble and complete one another. Both appear to refer to a similar ceremony; namely, the anointing or enthronement of a king. Ps 110, which has a very difficult text, shows possible points of contact with Egyptian, Assyro-Babylonian, and Ugaritic texts. Its references to the priestly character of the king and its mention of Melchisedech underline its archaic quality as well as its religious content. The fact that the recitation of this psalm was continued even after the dynasty was a thing of the past, and the fact that it was quoted many times by the New Testament writers, are signs that the Messianic meaning of this psalm was recognized very early. Ps 2 is simpler than Ps 110 and more recent. It is presented as a proclamation by a king on the occasion of his enthronement in the midst of difficult circumstances. Here too, the Messianic bearing of this psalm is emphasized by the use made of it in the New Testament and throughout Christian tradition. Ps 2 looks to the Messias in his temporal reign (Acts 4, 25. 26), or in his Church (Ap 12, 5; 19, 15), or in his end-time appearance.

§ 6. Messianic Psalms

The Israelite king was the representative of a dynasty. And the dynasty was the object of divine favors, the possessor of divine promises (2 Sm 7). When some psalms insist on the glory of the house of David and its representatives, when they sing about the greatness of this house in terms that go beyond even the exaggerations of oriental court style, when

---

[8] See J. DE FRAINE, "L'aspect religieux de la royauté israélite," *Analecta biblica,* 3 (Rome, 1954).

they stress the moral virtues and the priestly prerogatives of
the son of David, they are thinking not only of the reigning
king. These ideas look also to the future king who will "increase the empire for the sake of endless peace" (Is 9, 6).
Jesus and the authors of the New Testament were not deceived. They often quote the psalms as Messianic prophecies
that were fulfilled in the person of Jesus (Mt 21, 42 and Ps
118, 22; Mt 22, 44 and Ps 110, 1; Jn 13, 18 and Ps 41, 10;
Acts 2, 25-28 and Ps 16, 8-11; Acts 2, 34 and Ps 110, 1; Acts
4, 25 and Ps 2, 1; see also Jesus' more general declaration
in Luke 24, 44). Ancient Christian tradition has taught the
same doctrine almost unanimously, with the possible exception of Theodore of Mopsuestia. The existence of a certain
number of Messianic psalms is a revealed doctrine, as the
Catholic Church has recognized.[9] This does not mean that
all the psalms mentioned by the Fathers of the Church as
Messianic—or even by the New Testament—are necessarily
Messianic in the literal sense. This is a touchy problem for
exegetes, and it can be resolved only after a careful examination of particular cases. But Messianism is a phenomenon of
such importance in the history of Israel that the absence of
psalms representing this religious attitude would be incom-
prehensible.

Next to these Messianic royal psalms we can place certain
songs about the glory of Sion and Jerusalem. Even if the Messias is not named in them and described as he is in the royal
psalms, their perspective none the less places us in a future
which is clearly of the end-time. Like some of the psalms
about the kingship of Yahweh, many of the songs of Sion
should be studied in connection with the last chapters of the
Book of Isaias (Ps 46; 38; 76; 87). They are testimonies to
Israel's expectation.

[9] This is affirmed by the 8th response of the Biblical Commission
on May 10, 1910 (*EB*, 351: "Agnoscendi sunt").

§ 7. Didactic and Wisdom Psalms

This kind of psalm, which is quite different from the rest, was designed with a view to instruction rather than liturgical use. These wisdom psalms show certain special characteristics both in form and content. For one thing, they are filled with reminiscences of earlier texts. Because of this we may speak of the anthological method in which the writer is more a collector than an author. Such writers made use of other ordinary procedures of composition followed in the scribal schools; for instance, they use the alphabet as a kind of frame for the psalm (Ps 9—10; 25; 34; 37; 111; 112; 119; 145). The subjects of these psalms are usually the Law, wisdom, the moral life. All these are regular themes in the Old Testament wisdom books. Sometimes we find in these psalms a tendency to make historical digressions and moral reflections. Now and then they raise problems, such as that of retribution. But the writers of these wisdom psalms seldom dare to propose a doctrine tha. was unknown to their predecessors. For instance, we find that allusions to the expectation of immortality are rare in the psalms. And when such allusions are made, they are deliberately vague (Ps 16; 37; 49; 73).

§ 8. Other Classifications

Can we speak of prophetic psalms, oracle psalms, psalms of blessing or cursing, victory psalms, as special classifications? These themes appear often in the Book of Psalms. But they do not come with enough consistency or exactness for us to see in them any independent literary forms. They are rather the different shapes assumed by hymns or supplications to fit different occasions. We should not pass over these differences when we attempt to explain particular psalms, but neither should we make too much of them.

Much the same thing is to be said of those psalms that are called *mixed*. There are cases where the psalm seems to change its form and to pass from supplication to hymn or thanksgiving, or vice-versa. There are cases of brusque change in rhythm midway in a psalm that seems to cut it in two (Ps 19; 24). From this fact some have concluded that new and complex psalm forms were used in certain cultic ceremonies. Some speak of "liturgies," that is, composite pieces in which a question posed by the faithful called forth from the priests an "oracular" response, the whole ending with a blessing (Ps 14; 24). But when we look closely at the texts, the problem does not appear to be so simple. Sometimes the explanation of the *mixed* form may lie in a purely accidental union of two different psalms. We must also allow for the liberty of the psalmist, who did not feel himself bound by our stricter ideas of literary form. It remains possible that cultic ceremonies did result in some consistent psalm pattern. But the examples brought forward so far as evidence are too uncertain to establish this theory. The idea that these composite psalms are patterned on a special literary form remains a fragile supposition, and it should not be pushed too far.

Finally, two psalms must be mentioned which stand outside any classification. This very originality gives them a special place. Psalm 137 (*Super flumina Babylonis*) is a strong and pathetic evocation of history which gives us a glimpse into the Jewish soul at the time of the Exile. The psalm's conclusion seems cruel. But this understandable harshness must not make us forget the central idea; namely, the attachment of the Jewish exile to Jerusalem. Psalm 45 takes up the theme of a royal marriage and reminds us of the Song of Songs. This psalm does, in fact, present some of the same problems as the Song of Songs, and it has received as many different interpretations. Tradition has seen in both a parable or an allegory celebrating the nuptials of the Messias King with the Chosen People and with the Church.

CHAPTER IV

ORIGIN AND HISTORY
OF THE PSALMS

Our knowledge of religion in ancient Israel, the many allusions in the psalms to the sanctuary and to liturgical acts, the probabilities that emerge from a comparison with neighboring peoples, as well as general observations about the history of religions—all this has led recent authors to insist on the liturgical and therefore the collective origin of many of the psalms.

However, it is a very difficult and risky matter to attempt to describe the precise circumstances in which these psalms originated. Indications in the psalm titles are rare and not altogether sure. With few exceptions (Ps 24 is one) the data of internal criticism, such as allusions to sacrifices and liturgical actions, references to processions and dialogue recitations, are usually vague. These items call for close attention, but they simply do not tell us very much. We have already pointed out that there is no solid reason for imagining the existence of liturgical feasts when tradition tells us nothing about them. Even when we extract from the psalms themselves and from the historical books of the Bible the maximum of information that they have to offer, we must admit our ignorance about the earliest source and the original context of most of these ancient pieces.

So it would be an exaggeration to attribute a liturgical origin to all the psalms. Even if we suppose that the individual who appears in some of them is fictitious and that the one who prays is in reality a king, priest, or levite, who speaks in the name of the people, it is still certain that many of the psalms are the pure products of individual devotion.[1]

---

[1] See A. Robert, "L'exégèse des Psaumes selon les méthodes de la Formgeschichteschule," *Miscellanea Biblica B. Ubach** (Montser-

The tradition which is represented by the psalm titles placed these psalms on the lips of certain known personages of the Old Testament. The tradition, therefore, understood these psalms as being the expression of individual devotion. And even though the psalm titles are not above suspicion, it remains highly probable that in the period of the prophets, even as early as Samuel and David, individual devotion was expressed in pieces of this kind and that they were later introduced into the liturgy.

We must above all stress the fact that the psalms, whatever their precise origin, remained for a long time living realities capable of adaptation to new circumstances and to new religious conceptions. It happens often that, when an "individual" psalm passes into the liturgy, it changes or loses some of its most concrete expressions. There must also have been cases where psalms that originated in a provincial sanctuary were later adapted to the liturgy of Jerusalem. Psalms that were purely royal in their origin took on later a clearly Messianic meaning. Historical perspectives were transformed into eschatological visions. The reflections of scribes filled out or corrected more ancient ideas.

The psalms which we recognize as canonical and inspired are the psalms in their final form as they have come down to us. It would be a bad kind of archeologism to disregard or exclude every "addition" or "explanatory gloss." Still, if we are to have a better understanding of the psalm's whole meaning, it is important to reconstruct the history of the text as well as we can. Pointing out a gloss or disengaging from the text a later development often provides the answer to a difficulty and makes for a better understanding of the psalmist's mind. All this helps the modern reader to handle the ancient text better.

Then too, there is some value in following the successive interpretations of the psalms as well as we can, even when these interpretations move a long way from the literal sense.

rat, 1953), pp. 211-226; A. FEUILLET, Les psaumes eschatologiques du Règne de Yahweh*, NRT (1951), pp. 244-260; 352-363.

These "successive readings"[2] of the psalms are sometimes clarified by the LXX, by New Testament citations, and also by quotations made by the Fathers of the Church. They allow us to retrace the progress of revelation and the development of ideas across the centuries. The modern reader has something to learn from them.

§ 1. Antiquity of the Psalms

After what we have said, it will be seen how problematical is this matter of the age of the psalms.[3] It is extremely difficult to reconstruct the life situation of pieces of liturgical literature which are by definition anonymous and impersonal. Even when we think we have found a precise and concrete origin for individual psalms, they have usually been too much polished by usage for anyone to recognize in them any indications that would point to the circumstances of their origin. Only the psalm titles, about which we will say more later on, might be able to satisfy our curiosity. In spite of this scarcity of information, the actual evolution of the positions of biblical criticism over the past half-century has been remarkable. At the end of the 19th century, many scholars thought that the Psalter as a whole was postexilic and that it reflected the Jewish religion rather than the preexilic religion of Israel. These scholars confidently assigned a great number of psalms to the Machabean period.[4] Recently, however, I. Engnell of the Scandinavian school wrote, "I frankly admit that there is only one psalm in the whole Psalter which appears to me to be certainly postexilic; this is Ps 137. No matter where I look, I cannot find another psalm that is com-

---

[2] See A. GELIN, *Problèmes d'Ancien Testament** (Lyon, 1952), pp. 93-110; and the same author's "Les quatre lectures du ps. XXII," *Bible et vie chrétienne*, 1, pp. 31-39.

[3] See R. TOURNAY, "Recherches sur la chronologie des Psaumes," *RB* (1958), pp. 321-357.

[4] The most radical exponent of this opinion was B. Duhm (1899, second edition in 1922).

parable to it in content and style. How is this to be explained?"[5] Not all authors would go this far. But there is a
rather common tendency now to consider many of the psalms
as dating from the period of the monarchy. Some psalms may
date from the earliest part of that period. As for the alleged
Machabean psalms, there is no a priori argument against
them. But neither has anyone made a convincing argument
for them. What we have already said about the formation
of the Psalter as a collection would favor exclusion of pieces
written as late as the second century before Christ.

§ 2.   Authors of the Psalms

The tradition of Davidic origin for the Psalter no longer appears to be in open contradiction to the stand taken by the
majority of critics. However, the tradition is not being accepted in any simple form, and important adjustments will
have to be made in regard to it.

There is a broad historical tradition claiming that David
was a musician (1 Sm 16, 18-23; 18, 10; Am 6, 5), and that
he organized the liturgy (2 Sm 6, 5-16; 1 Par 15, 28; Esd 3,
10; Neh 12, 24. 36). This tradition attributes several important poems to David (2 Sm 1, 19-27; 3, 33-34; 2 Sm 22
(Ps 18); 23, 1-7).

There is also the fact that 73 psalm titles (84 in Greek)
assign psalms to David. Some of these titles grow more precise by proposing the circumstances in which the psalm was
supposedly written. Even if these psalm titles are not canonical and do not go back to the psalmist himself, and even if
they were not originally understood as referring directly to
the psalmist, it remains true that at one time they were for
the average reader expressions of an accepted tradition that
claimed David as author of the Psalter.

[5] I. ENGNELL, *Studies in Divine Kingship in the Ancient Near
East* (Uppsala, 1943), p. 176, note 2. He is quoted by A. BENTZEN
in *Introduction to the Old Testament* (Copenhagen, 1948), II,
p. 167, note 2.

New Testament citations bear witness to this same tradition, not for the whole Psalter but for a certain number of particular psalms (Mt 24, 43; Acts 1, 20; 2, 25; 34; 4, 25; Rom 4, 6; 11, 9).

Such are the ancient witnesses which have led Jewish or Christian authors to consider "the psalms" as being the psalms "of David." Here we have an explanation of the formula used by the Council of Trent, *"psalterium davidicum."*

We must note here the fact that St. Hilary and St. Jerome protested against the idea of attributing all the psalms to David. And the Council of Trent would not use the expression, "the 150 psalms of David." These items, along with indications in the Psalter itself, show that the attribution to David is to be understood in a general way. When it comes to particular psalms, the tradition of Davidic authorship may be questioned. And in any case it should not be exaggerated.

It is perhaps unfortunate that the only way to begin the discussion of this question about authorship is to consider the data of internal criticism. This is a difficult thing to manage, and in many instances the search will turn up no decisive argument either for or against Davidic authorship. Besides, the exegete must take into account the possibility of additions and transformations in the history of the psalms. Even a precise reference to an event, or a formula which is characteristic of a certain period, will be too slight an indication to date the whole psalm.

This is no reason for exaggerated skepticism or for renouncing all research into the history of the Psalter. While it is difficult to prove that these poems go back to a certain author or point to a certain event, it is fairly easy to assign them their true places in the development of the religious thought of Israel. A certain psalm will reflect the influence of Deuteronomy. Another shows a relationship to one of the great prophets. Many psalms present a conception of the monarchy that the careful historian will be able to situate in time and place. Some psalms appear to be full of borrowings from earlier texts. All these items can lead to fairly certain conclusions about the history of the Psalter.

If we look at modern commentaries on the psalms, we find a tendency on the part of exegetes to date the great royal psalms to an ancient period, at least to the period before the Exile (Ps 2; 45; 72; 110). The same is true of the most beautiful pieces of hymn poetry (Ps 8; 19A; 29; 84; part of 89; etc.), some of the supplication psalms (Ps 28; 61; 63), and some of the thanksgiving psalms (Ps 18). But the last word has surely not been said on this difficult problem, and the door should be left open for further studies.

In addition to the problems already mentioned, it should be said here that there are some psalms whose age is very much disputed, either because they belong to an intermediate and ill-defined period or because opposite ways of approaching them lead to opposite solutions (see Ps 42; 68; 78; 104). We have to resign ourselves to having a partial knowledge, and we should keep in mind that a religious text can be very useful without our knowing exactly how old it is.

CHAPTER V

DOCTRINE OF THE PSALMS

§ 1. Question of Method

Speaking of the doctrine of the Psalms is somewhat difficult. It is true that a number of "theologies of the psalms" can be found. These studies take the Psalter as a homogeneous whole. Wisdom psalms and royal psalms are brought together. The most ancient hymns and the more recent instructional pieces are placed side by side. This method is not to be condemned out of hand. If it is used carefully, it can provide a useful reconstruction of an important moment of history that is the climax of many centuries of evolution. The synthesis offered by this method is a part of the theology of Judaism in the period when the Psalter as a whole was fixed in its present form; namely, the period immediately preceding the Christian revelation.

But this method of constructing a theology of the psalms runs the risk of misleading those who have a tendency to project a relatively late picture back into the distant past. From what we have said about the great variety in the psalms, their different ages, their suppleness in being fitted to new circumstances, in a word, their *living* character, we can see that so static a presentation cannot satisfy those who have a sense of history.

Does this mean that we have to hold a purely evolutionary view of the psalms and attempt to trace in successive pictures the different stages of the religious thought expressed in them? Such a task would be very difficult. And even if it proved successful, the results might be deceptive. For one thing, there is great uncertainty about the date of the psalms and about the shifting paths of their development. A beginning would have to be made on the basis of an a priori outline of Israel's religious history. This would result in an arbitrary and questionable picture. Besides, the wish to stress the element of change, if carried too far, would obscure the fact that there is in the psalms a real continuity of doctrine. Revelation progresses step by step. But the progress is similar to that of a river valley increasing its soil by flood deposits. It is a matter of repeated enrichment. The past is not wiped out when history unfolds; the present is rather an organic development of the past.

Between these two opposite methods of constructing a synthesis of the doctrine of the psalms, that of a purely historical and "evolutionary" presentation on the one hand and on the other a collection of "pegs" of doctrine gathered and logically classified, we must find a middle way. This middle way must answer the demands of the historian as well as those of the theologian.[1] So much for methodology.[2] We move now to the question of the doctrine of the Psalms.

§ 2. Popular Devotion and Liturgical Life

The Psalter has been aptly named the "mirror of biblical devotion." We must note that, in the distant period when the Psalter was formed, it would be meaningless to make a distinction between devotion and theology or between dogma and moral. It is the whole religious soul of Israel that finds expression in the 150 psalms, and a very clear expression it is.

[1] This is a general problem of biblical theology. The following works can be consulted: P. VAN IMSCHOOT, *Theology of the Old Testament*, I (New York: Desclée, 1965); P. HEINISCH, *Theology of the Old Testament* (Collegeville: Liturgical Press, 1956); W. EICHRODT, *Theology of the Old Testament* (Philadelphia, 1961); E. JACOB, *Theology of the Old Testament* (New York, 1958).

[2] In this exposition many more references and quotations could be given. Since it is impossible to give them all, it seems more useful to keep them brief and to ask the reader to look into the more developed syntheses such as the article "Psaumes" in the *DTC*. He should also be encouraged to make his own personal effort at doctrinal synthesis.

It is true that other biblical books, like Judges, Samuel, and the Prophets, tell us about the ordinary manifestations of popular devotion in Israel. Many expressions of Israel's life of worship are known to us also from Leviticus, Numbers, and parts of Paralipomenon. Popular devotion seems most often to be that of an individual. It is spontaneous. It is charged with feeling and sometimes passion. On the other hand, expressions of cult are described in connection with priestly ceremonies where everything is planned and regulated. Cultic expressions seem particularly impersonal.

It is not that these two aspects of religious life are totally different. They sometimes flow together in episodes that are congenial to both. Such would be the episode of Anna at the sanctuary of Silo (1 Sm 1-2), and that of the transfer of the Ark of the Covenant (2 Sm 6). In this same line of thought, we may also find certain allusions to popular feasts and pilgrimages. But these items are relatively rare. The two forms, popular devotion and cultic expressions, are generally separated in the Bible.

Perhaps the psalms can serve as a bond of union for these two forms of religious expression, the personal and the cultic. On the one hand, the psalms grew out of the soul of the people and they express the deepest feelings. On the other hand, it is becoming more and more certain that they were introduced into the liturgy of Israel. They express the very soul of certain liturgical ceremonies, the external rites being simply the shell enclosing it.

We can note a certain harmony between some well-known liturgical ceremonies and the psalm forms. Processions and pilgrimages call to mind the gradual psalms, the psalms of Sion, and in general the hymns to the glory of Yahweh and His dwelling place. The thanksgiving psalms correspond to the holocaust, which was the ancient thanksgiving sacrifice. The sacrifice of expiation and the days of fast and penance were surely accompanied by lamentations. The peace sacrifice and the communion sacrifice seem to call for the collective hymns and in general for the hymns which evoke Israel's past greatness or its deepest hopes. These are only hints.

But we could push our search further and gain a more precise knowledge of the *Sitz im Leben*, the life context, of most of our psalms. And this would surely help us to understand better the ideas enshrined in them.

However, we should bear in mind that the psalms range over an area much wider than the liturgy. In the most ancient period this variety, the degree of which we cannot determine precisely, can be seen in the fact that the psalms often reflect strictly individual religious experiences and forms of prayer. In the more recent periods the psalms introduce into liturgical life expressions that were not originally meant for it. The devotion of the scribes, for example, which the wisdom books make known to us, is essentially individual devotion. But its main themes, such as love for the law and meditation on it (Ps 19) and the interpretation of history (Ps 78; 105; 106), form the subject of the many psalms which introduce these themes into the liturgy.

The same is true of that devotional movement which is represented by the *anawim*, the "poor ones of Yahweh," who had so important a place in the religious life of Israel after the Exile. Certain psalms appear which are the purest expression of this new spirituality (Ps 34; 37; 9–10). This spirituality, which came from the prophets, was to undergo an important development in Christianity.

§ 3. Main Doctrinal Themes

I. God

The hymn is the most characteristic as well as the oldest and most permanent literary form in the Psalter. The main subject of the hymn is God in His greatness and perfection. All the hymns are addressed to God. They speak only of Him. Every other object is related to Him, the world which owes its existence to Him, Israel whom He had chosen and guided, loved and punished in the course of its history, each believer whose steps follow His path. In the supplication and thanksgiving psalms, the relations between God and His own are presented in more varied style. Anthropomorphism is evident in them. In the more distant periods, God is often represented as having human feelings. But these are images, and in reality the psalmist knew that God was completely above His creatures.

God is unique. In spite of some surprising formulae which seem to affirm only the superiority of Yahweh over the other gods (Ps 136, 2-3; 97, 7-9), the Psalter as a whole is clearly monotheistic. Even when it borrows from surrounding literature and ideology, these borrowings have undergone a thorough expurgation. The nothingness of idols and the emptiness of false gods are frequent themes. The psalmists do know of the existence of spiritual beings and sometimes call them divine (*elohim* Ps 8, 6). But these are creatures and servants of the sovereign Master. As for demons, they are never mentioned explicitly in the Hebrew text. But the psalms do refer to enemies and evil powers who threaten and persecute the faithful man, and these expressions can mean evil spirits.

God is not only above every creature, He is also in constant relationship with every creature. He is the Providence that not only secures the order of the material world but also the rule of justice. He is the defender and avenger of the just. He is the refuge of the repentant sinner. In the case of the poor and the lowly, His goodness becomes mercy and beneficence and love (*hesed*).

II. SALVATION

God has promised men salvation. He will one day intervene to assure the just man's triumph over the sinner and sin. He will inaugurate His true reign over a world renewed. These promises are vague in the older texts, but they grow clearer all the time. Salvation will come on Sion, the holy mountain. It will be brought by the Davidic dynasty. One of the members of this dynasty will be the Messias, king and priest at the same time. He will make all the promises a fulfilled reality.

Although the Messias will be persecuted, he will also be the great conqueror. At the same time he will be the peaceful ruler equipped with all the virtues of the ideal king and charged with the office of governing and judging the whole world. The latest pictures of the Messianic age give us a glimpse of the Messias's universal reign. All the nations will converge on Sion and will prostrate themselves in the presence of Israel's God.

III. Man

In the presence of God man seems slight and full of misery. Man's cry of distress only highlights his dependence. But man is not left all alone. By prayer he obtains his Creator's blessing and help. God rescues him, and then receives his praise and thanksgiving.

Moral life means practicing justice, observing the law, and taking part in worship. These are not unrelated realities. They are simply different aspects of one same ideal. The most ancient as well as the latest psalms mention the Temple. In the late period of Judaism, the study and meditation of the law took on an exceptionally important place in the just man's life. This was not properly speaking a novelty, but rather a new stress placed on an already existing element in the religion of the Fathers.

IV. Retribution

The history of religion in Israel is dominated by the problem of retribution. So there is nothing surprising in the fact that this problem shows up in the Psalter. In most of the psalms we find a more or less explicit reflection of the ideas of the Israelite people. For them, it seemed that devotion to God and happiness ought to go hand in hand. Reversely, unhappiness was thought to be necessarily a punishment for evil. But attentive observers and alert moralists were not satisfied with a theoretical answer of this kind that often contradicted their experience. Sometimes they gave explanations which suppressed or reduced the shock. So we find a psalmist affirming that the failure of justice is only apparent, that the happiness of the wicked man is only a passing happiness and more or less illusory (Ps 37; 49). Sometimes he excitedly expresses his indignation. He complains to Yahweh and asks him to intervene. He lets fly curses against the victorious wicked ones. Sometimes he resigns himself to the apparent injustice of the present and waits for the Lord to provide an equitable retribution in a more distant future.

However, many reservations have to be made when we talk about a belief in the future life expressed in the psalms. For the most part the psalms hold fast to the traditional ideas on this subject. In sheol the soul enjoys a kind of half-life, without activity, almost without personality. It is the land of forgetfulness where no one experiences joy and no one gives praise to God. In sheol there can be neither a true reward nor true punishment. And so, according to this traditional idea, God's justice must be exercised here below by an immediate intervention in favor of the just man. Later is too late. This is what explains the indignation or the despair of the persecuted just man when God's intervention does not take place or is delayed. The great prophets and the author of Job did not await a resurrection or a survival of the soul after death. This is also the general attitude of the psalmists.

Even so, there are some psalms which seem to have a presentiment of a later revelation. This presentiment is seen in the psalms which have the faithful proclaiming by a bold image that God will "rescue" them or "make them come up" from sheol (Ps 30 , 10; 86, 13). Sometimes the psalmist staunchly asserts that not even death is strong enough to separate him from his God, and therefore that another destiny lies before him (Ps 16, 10; 49, 16; 73). But these texts provide only a glimmer of light, and their precise bearing on this subject is not beyond dispute. The New Testament will enrich and complete their meaning.

CONCLUSION

We have looked at the main themes which a reading of the
psalms will offer to our meditation. Each of the psalms can,
without much need of readjustment, express the feelings of
the Christian. However, there are some passages which are
somewhat difficult to use. The rude feelings sometimes expressed in the psalms are at odds with the law of the Gospel.
Such pieces are rare, and they often represent small fragments
inserted into a context of quite different spirit (Ps 59; 69).
If these problematical pieces are placed in their cultural and
doctrinal background, an explanation can be found for them
and their positive value can be seen. This will not, of course,
make them congenial to the Christian. But such an effort will
give him a better understanding of the soul of the ancient
Israelite. This Israelite was impatient and did not wish to
wait for a justice that was passing him by. He had confidence
in God. But God was not fully revealed to him. In such a
frame of mind, he revolted against the triumph of evil. When
the Christian reads passages where the psalmist's excessive
language appears unacceptable, he will gain a better appreciation of the newness of the Sermon on the Mount.

In any case these difficult psalms make up only a small
part of the Psalter. As a whole it gives us a remarkable synthesis of religious doctrine.

This insight was expressed very well by the Fathers of the
Church. Without making as close a distinction as we do between the literal and the spiritual sense, they found in the
Psalter a teaching that went beyond the historical context of
the psalms. "The divine scripture does not make use of historical narratives just to give us knowledge of the facts which
we learn from the actions and feelings of the ancients. It uses
these narratives in order to offer us a teaching that will guide
us in our life of virtue. The history must be accompanied by
this higher meaning" (St. Gregory of Nyssa, *Homilies on the
Inscription of the Psalms*, II). This is why St. Ambrose wrote,

"In the psalms we not only assist at the birth of Christ, but we also see him enduring His saving passion, dying, rising, ascending to heaven and sitting at the right hand of the Father" (*In Ps 1*, 8).

St. Augustine, especially in his *Enarrationes in Psalmos*,[3] found in the psalms the richest and most coherent synthesis of doctrine. For him the psalms announce not only the life of Christ but also the life and history of the Church. "Our method is not to stop with the letter alone, but to search through the letter for the mysteries. Your charity well knows that in all the psalms we hear the voice of a man (Christ) who alone possesses the head and the members" (*In Ps 131*, 2). For Augustine, the psalms already provide an answer to all the great problems of history. "The wicked are prosperous and the good are tested. How can God look on this scandal? Take and drink. Every sickness of the soul finds its remedy in the Scripture" (*In Ps 36*). The *Enarrationes* is a first attempt at writing the *City of God*.

[3] See M. PONTET, *L'exégèse de saint Augustin prédicateur** (Paris: Aubier, 1945), chap. VII, pp. 387-418.

SECTION II

THE OTHER HAGIOGRAPHERS

by Msgr. H. Lusseau

CHAPTER I

PROVERBS

BIBLIOGRAPHY

On Wisdom and Wisdom writings in general:

E. TOBAC, *Les cinq livres de Salomon** (Brussels, 1926).

W. O. E. OESTERLEY, *The Wisdom of Egypt and the Old Testament* (London, 1927).

A. VACCARI, *De libris didacticis* (*Institutiones biblicae*)* (Rome, 1929).

H. DUESBERG, *Les scribes inspirés**, 2 Vols. (Paris, 1938).

A. M. DUBARLE, *Les Sages d'Israël** (Paris, 1946).

J. C. RYLAARSDAM, *Revelation in Jewish Wisdom Literature* (1946).

H. RINGGREN, *Word and Wisdom* (Land, 1947).

M. NOTH–D. WINTON THOMAS, eds., *Wisdom in Israel and in the Ancient Near East* (Leiden, 1955).

R. MURPHY, *Seven Books of Wisdom** (Milwaukee: Bruce, 1960).

W. McKANE, *Prophets and Wise Men* (London: SCM, 1965).

W. BAUMGARTNER, "The Wisdom Literature," *OTMS*, pp. 210-237.

R. GORDIS, "The Social Background of Wisdom Literature," *HUCA*, 18 (1843-1944), pp. 77-118.

M. P. STAPLETON, "Ancient Wisdom and Modern Times," *CBQ*, 4 (1942), pp. 311-322; 5 (1943), pp. 47-62.

On the Book of Proverbs:

Introductions, translations, commentaries, pp. 25 f. (H. RENARD, *BPC**; H. DUESBERG and P. AUVRAY, *BJ**; C. H. TOY, *ICC* . . .).

H. WIESMANN, *Das Buch der Sprüche** (Bonn, 1923).

W. O. E. Oesterley, *The Book of Proverbs* (London, 1929).

B. Gemser, *Sprüche Salomos* (Tübingen, 1937).

J. J. Weber, *Le livre des Proverbes, le livre de la Sagesse et le Cantique des cantiques** (Paris, 1949).

E. Jones, *Proverbs and Ecclesiastes* (London: SCM, 1962).

M. Dahood, *Proverbs and Northwest Semitic Philology** (Rome, 1963).

R. B. Y. Scott, *Proverbs and Ecclesiastes* (Garden City: Doubleday, 1965).

R. N. Whybray, *Wisdom in Proverbs* (London: SCM, 1965).

A. Robert, "Les attaches littéraires bibliques de Prov. 1-9," *RB* (1934), pp. 42 ff., 172 ff., 374 ff.; (1935), pp. 344 ff., 502 ff.

P. Skehan, "Single Editor for the Whole Book of Proverbs," *CBQ*, 10 (1948), pp. 115-130.

G. R. Driver, "Problems in the Hebrew Text of Proverbs," *Biblica*, 32 (1951), pp. 173-197.

C. T. Fritsch, "The Book of Proverbs," *IB* (1955).

§ 1. Title

The title of this book in the Hebrew Bible: *Mešalim* fits the content well. The "mašal" is actually a very flexible literary form: it is applied to different poems (Nm 21, 27-30; Ps 49, 5; 78, 2), oracles (Nm 23, 7. 18, etc.), satires (Is 14, 4; Mi 2, 4), discourses in which the comparative element dominates (Ez 17, 2; 21, 5; 24, 3), popular sayings, maxims or proverbs that are frequently artistically patterned (1 Sm 10, 12; 24, 14; Ez 12, 22-23; 18, 2-3). Now, the Book of Proverbs, undoubtedly characterized by its comparisons and its artistically labored sayings, contains also different forms of poems about select and profound themes that are not without a religious and moral import (1, 8-9; 31, 10-31).

The Greek (παροιμίαι) and the Latin (*proverbia*) connote too exclusively the idea of *sayings* or *maxims* to do justice to the Hebrew word or the content of the work. They can be considered only as *a potiori* labels.

It is difficult to find an exact word in our modern languages that has the different meanings of the word *mašal*. If it were possible to resort to the root *mšl III*, to govern (Pedersen, Boström, cf. Bentzen, *Introd.*, I, 168), in relation to the Arabic: *to be more valuable or superior,* the substantives: *directive, instruction, rule* would seem to be indicated. But the verbal root *mšl III* has as nominal derivatives only *mimšâl* and *mêmšâlâh* meaning *government, rule,* whereas for the block of Semitic languages *mâšâl,* coming from the root *mšl I,* always carries the idea of *comparison, fable, proverb.* The English translation does not avoid the etymological difficulty. Perhaps the term *sayings* with its broad usage would be more suitable.

Be that as it may, *mešâlîm* are usually, considering the external literary form, defined as: generally religious or moral teachings founded on common observation, and usually expressed in images, open or veiled, which demand reflective effort to understand.

§ 2.   Historico-Literary Context of the Work

The Book of Proverbs is a work of Wisdom. In general, the term Wisdom designates a mentality preoccupied with the practical. The Books of the Bible which are classified as sapiential are but a part of the abundant sapiential literature found especially in the Orient. They must be situated in that context in order that their provenance and originality be better understood.

I.   WISDOM IN THE ANCIENT ORIENT

It is commonly known that there were Wise Men in Egypt, Babylonia, Phoenicia, and in all of the ancient Orient. The Bible makes many allusions to them (3 Kgs 4, 30-31; Jer 49, 7; Abd 8), which is confirmed by the Greeks' esteem of wis-

dom, mother of their own culture. And the literature of the
Middle East, recently enlarged by the discoveries of Ras-
Shamra (Ugarit), gives abundant witness to the existence of
a widely popularized Wisdom literature.

The Wise Men of the Orient are found mainly among the
ruling classes—more precisely among the members of the
court, the king's ministers, advisors, secretaries and archivists.
Their position, by reason of their role, demanded that they
be cultured men of some philosophical and moral refinement,
accomplished in the art of speaking well, but even more in the
art of worldly prudence: how to live and act. They were capable of reflecting on the facts of life and human conduct.
The religious aspect of life, however, was not excluded from
their observations; humanism for them was not atheistic.

Naturally they tried to communicate to others the *results*
of their experience, the *principles* they used, and the *means*
to succeed in their careers. Thus they were inclined to draw
from Wisdom writings—opinions and instructions from Egypt,
philosophical fables and allegories from Babylonia, picturesque maxims and parables from Chanaan and Phoenicia.
These writings were destined for the scribe class, whose role
it was to transmit sound traditions of advice and prudence
suitable for the royal household, magistrates and functionaries. Sometimes the driving force of their literary activity
was to facilitate their sons' access to positions of influence.
They had to "form" their successors to "assume a position."

Such was the case of the Wise Men of Egypt[1]: Ka-Gemni,
son of a Visier of King Ouni (3rd dynasty; beginning of the
3rd millennium), the son of Ptah-hetep, Visier of King Issi
(5th dynasty; about 2300), Meri-Ka-Re, son of a certain
Kheti, monarch of Herakleopolis (9th dynasty; about 2150),
Sesostris, son of Amen-em-hat I (founder of the 12th dynasty;
1993-1970). One does not know if these Wise Men are authentic or merely creations of literary fiction: the personal
tone and the concrete circumstances of the instruction for

---

[1] P. HUMBERT, *Recherches sur les sources égyptiennes de la littérature sapientiale d'Israël* (Neuchâtel, 1927).

Meri-Ka-Re warrant authenticity. Other Wise Men stories
come from Sumer and Mesopotamia.[2] Closer to the Israelite
royal age is the Wisdom writing that Amen-em-Ope[3] himself gave to his son (of uncertain date; between 18th and 26th
dynasties: probably between 1000 and 600). In Assyria,
Ahiguar, who perhaps wrote under the reign of Sennacherib
(705-681) or of Asarhaddon (681-669), may well be only a
legendary hero. Be that as it may, several collections have
come down to us under his name. The most ancient of these
is an Aramaic version discovered in the archives of the Elephantine Jews (5th century B.C.). The Bible itself presents
Tobias as one of his relatives. Lastly the material of Ras-
Shamra gives us the name of a Phoenician Wise Man (historical? or fictional?): Daniel. Ezechiel very probably mentions this Daniel three times (Ez 14, 14. 20; 28, 3).

One might ask to what extent the priests belonged to the
class of Wise Men. The fact is that priests and Wise Men
are identified in Babylonia. But Engnell certainly exaggerates
in generalizing this identification. Although it is true that
Wisdom literature has an indisputable relation to cult, as is
proven from religious poems, notably the Psalms, it would be
very difficult to establish that in Egypt the statesmen and
royal household were all of the priestly class, and that in Israel
the position of Esdras, priest and scribe, would have to be
considered as the rule. It must be admitted, however, that
Wisdom literature developed on a parallel with the progress
of religious sentiment. Wisdom and "theology" formed a
pair, but the Wisdom themes were not restricted to moral
laws and cultic formulas.

The high positions occupied by the Wise Men,[4] the international relations in which they were involved, and the competition in which they undoubtedly engaged (cf. 3 Kgs 10,

[2] J. J. Van Dijk, *La Sagesse suméro-accadienne* (Leyden, 1953).
[3] A. Mallon, "La Sagesse de l'Égyptien Amen-em-opé et les
Proverbes," *Bi* (1927), pp. 3-30.
[4] A. Robert, "Les scribes du roi et l'origine des Proverbes," *Revue
Apologétique* (1938), pp. 461-467.

1-3) made Wisdom an article for export. It became an international commodity.

II. Wisdom in Israel

Israel would borrow freely from this common commodity, as it drew from the sources of oriental codes of law, from rituals of neighboring peoples, as it absorbed, especially at the beginning of the institution, some of the ways of Syro-Chanaanite *nabism*.[5] But in the domain of Wisdom, as in the fields of legislation and prophecy, it surpassed them. Israel knew how to mint its own gold coin from many streams.

The more that we study the Israelite Wisdom literature, the more we note its transcendent originality. Let it suffice for now to give some general indications.

Solomon is presented as the originator of sapiential literature, just as Moses is of juridical literature, and David of psalms. The court of the great King, patterned after the model of foreign courts, abounded with counselors, archivists and scribes,[6] and these functionaries, as their counterparts in Egypt, Phoenicia, and Babylonia, were Wise Men (3 Kgs 4, 3). Solomon preached by example (3 Kgs 4, 30-34). He was a master of Wisdom, just as he was in some respects a born administrator.

Two traits characterize Israelite Wisdom. Even though it bases its teaching on *experience*, it also gives of its soul by animating its Wisdom with its faith in Yahweh, sovereign master of all Wisdom (3 Kgs 3, 4-15). "Even in the most ancient collections of Proverbs," writes A. Robert, "maxims that seem neutral are profoundly religious and subtly refer to the Torah." It is furthermore established that the Wise Men have also used the prophets, from whom they borrowed the vocabulary and the themes that were compatible with the

---

[5] See also the inscriptions of the tomb of Petosiris (B.C. 4th century); G. Lefebvre, "Égyptiens et Hébreux," *RB* (1922), pp. 481-488.

[6] Cf. p. 49 f.

laws of the genre. But precisely if they had such openness it is because, while accepting the points of view and methods from international Wisdom, from the beginning they remained in their hearts disciples of Moses. Their impassivity then was simply conformity to the laws of the genre.

The postexilic Wise Men of Israel likewise orientated their thought toward divine Wisdom. They described it by detailing its works in the cosmic order and in the context of the historical and religious evolution of the nation. Moreover the literary personification of this sovereign Wisdom would go to the limit of personification, that the New Testament will propose to our faith in revealing the Wisdom Incarnate.

Thus the Wise Men of Israel, in their way, according to the laws of the genre, and despite some legalistic rigidity, helped to prepare, through their religious humanism, for the coming of the Messias. They were, with the prophets, the spiritual guides who supported Judaism in its ascent toward the Gospel.

§ 3.   Composition of the Book of Proverbs

Many indications of internal criticism (attribution to different authors, the variety of subjects treated, the diversity of literary forms) enable us to distinguish eight sections in the Book of Proverbs. They are presented in the following table.[7]

A double collection of the "maxims of Solomon" forms the basis of the work (2nd and 4th sections). Five appendices were added to this, one to the first collection (3rd section), "remarks of Sages," and four to the second collection (5th to the 8th section). The introduction (1st section) is of a more recent date. The Greek version of the LXX adopted a different order: the appendices are placed between the two collections of the maxims of Solomon—except the praise of the valiant wife which serves as the conclusion of the work.

---

[7] Cf. *Institutiones Biblicae* (Rome, 1929), p. 51.

Sections	Subjects treated	Literary Forms	Authors
1, 8—9, 18	Invitation to acquire Wisdom. The author points out its fruits and praises it.	Strophes of about 10 verses each	Anonymous
10, 1—22, 16	Rules of conduct	Mešalim : two parallel members, either antithetic (10-15) or synonymous (16-22)	" Solomon "
22, 17—24, 34	Duties toward neighbors. Rules of temperance. Concerning idleness.	Four-membered synonymous parallelism.	" The Sages "
25—29	Various maxims	Two-membered. Comparisons. Antithesis.	" Solomon " and the scribes of Ezechias
30, 1-14	Divine Wisdom. The smallness of man.	Four-membered synonymous parallelism.	" Agur "
30, 15-33	Numerical mešalim	Synthetic and synonymous parallelism	Anonymous
31, 1-9	Counsels for kings	Four-membered synonymous parallelism	" Lamuel "
31, 10-31	Praise of the valiant wife	Alphabetic poem in synthetic parallelism	Anonymous

A certain number of repetitions (10, 1 and 15, 20; 10, 2b and 11, 4b; 10, 6b and 10, 11b; 10, 8b and 11, 10b; 10, 13b and 19, 29b) could suggest the idea that section 10—22, 16 is itself a collection of smaller collections, compiled by the last editor. This hypothesis is admittedly very probable, and could be applied to other sections, especially to the collection 25—29 on which the scribes of Ezechias worked. But the material is too fluid to permit a well-founded exact reconstruction of the text.

§ 4. Origin of the Sections and the Book

The two major sections (10, 1–22, 16 and 25–29) are attributed to Solomon, the second with this precision that it was
collected under the reign of Ezechias (about 700). If it is not
certain that the son of David, whose renown for Wisdom is
amply established (3 Kgs 3, 4-15; 4, 29-34; 10, 1-10), is the
author of all the maxims, it is at least very probable that a
number of them could have been composed by him and collected by the court scribes. It is only natural to suppose that
the monarch would make it a point of honor not to be surpassed in this art by members of his household. Moreover, the
collections listed under his name seem to be the oldest in the
work: the predominant literary form is the simple and primitive doublet. The maxims are generally the fruit of daily experience or current customs. The terms in which they speak
of the king (14, 28-35; 16, 10-15; 20, 2. 8. 28; 25, 1-6; 29, 4
etc.) and the allusions to the life of the court (10, 8; 11, 2;
15, 1; 16, 14. 15. 18; 19, 12; 22, 11; 25, 6-7; 29, 23) have
led some to think, perhaps too readily, that their setting is
royalty at its most flourishing moment.

Nevertheless, some Aramaisms, sometimes explicable by
the fact that certain outlying countries (Edom on the border
of Arabia) were Aramaized quite early, lead one to believe
that additions and retouchings were done at a late date. Moreover several maxims are related to the Prophets and Deuteronomy. It would not exceed scientific limits to argue that at
the time of the captivity sapiential reflection enjoyed a renais-
sance, and that if at such time all that remained of the
Solomon tradition was collected, new sayings would have been
added to the older works. Thus in all probability the Solomon collections grew with the centuries, especially the second collection, for which the Exile would provide a favorable
terrain.

The identity and age of the Wise Men remain unknown to
us. There is, on literary grounds, an obvious comparison to be

made between the 3rd section of the Book of Proverbs (especially 22, 17–24, 22) and the Wisdom of the Egyptian Amen-em-Ope, a high official of Egypt living at Panopolis. The papyrus that contains his work was published in 1923-1924 by Sir Wallis Budge, director of the British Museum's Service of Egyptian Antiquities. There are, however, problems to be solved before it will be possible to date the works of the Wise Men by means of this papyrus. On one hand, the dating of Amen-em-Ope's writing oscillates between B.C. 1000 and 600; on the other hand, the relation of the two works is still an open question. While Fr. Mallon holds that the quatrains of the Wise Men depend on Egyptian Wisdom, others assert that the two works depend on a common source, whether Egyptian or Hebrew. Dhorme considers the similarities accidental, and Fr. Humbert, with Duesberg, insists on the transcendence of the biblical quatrains regardless of the influence of foreign literature.

The names of Agur and Lamuel seem to designate Wise Men of the tribe of Massa (Gn 25, 14), unless the expression is part of the literary genre (oracle, vision, cf. Is 13, 1). We know nothing, however, of the age in which they lived. The position of their writings in the work and the numerous Aramaic expressions of the piece attributed to Lamuel would seem to indicate a postexilic period.

It is the last editor who added, by way of conclusion, the 8th section (31, 10-31), and who added the 1st section (1, 8–9, 18) as an introduction.

During the age of Sirach (about B.C. 200), the Book of Proverbs existed in its present form (cf. Sir 47, 17; Vulg 18, and Prv 1, 6). It may even have been translated into Greek (cf. Sir Prologue).

§ 5. The Doctrine of Proverbs

We will consider the general doctrine found in the work as a whole, and then the peculiar aspects of the various collections.

I. General doctrine of the work

The scribes of the Law   The reader of Proverbs can easily find himself fascinated by the sharp, incisive, enigmatic character of the statements. It is necessary to rise above this plane to arrive at the level of doctrine in which the Wisdom writers of Israel transcend their foreign colleagues.

The Israelites, in fact, already possessed a treasure acquired in the desert. They received from Moses a body of principles from which their religious, moral, and social obligations sprang. The teachings of the prophets and the organic development of the Torah anchored and made more profound the old codes. For centuries and centuries they had already gathered insights concerning God, the world, society, the family, the human person. When they undertook to express themselves in Wisdom language, they not only added to their acquired treasure the rules of good conduct drawn from a foreign culture and adapted them to their new conditions—as for example the sayings especially destined for members of the court, functionaries, statesmen—but they animated all that imported material with their profoundly monotheistic and Mosaic spirit. They were not ostentatious in their beliefs, observances, and piety. They were not devout as Ani, nor members of several brotherhoods as Amen-em-Ope. They did not encumber themselves with theological speculation as Kheti, nor multiply prayers to Yahweh as did the Prince of Herakleopolis to Thoth. But they did retain well a sense of the divine, a supernatural orientation, and an awareness of the authentic providential order. They were scribes of *the Law*.

Good conduct of life   They knew that everything good comes from God (10, 22); it is necessary then to avoid whatever He abhors and to do what pleases Him (11, 1; 12, 22; 15, 3. 8; 16, 1-9). The fear of Yahweh is the beginning of wisdom and justice (1, 7; 14, 2); it is the source of life and the assurance of happiness (12, 28; 14, 27; 16, 20; 18, 10;

29, 6. 25). One must further love and practice the Law (29, 18), hold in high regard justice and equity (21, 3).

It is Wisdom which is the foundation of the authority of kings, and inspires their actions (8, 15-16). The prince is not to be greedy (29, 4) nor intemperate (31, 3-5), but just and loyal (14, 34; 16, 12; 17, 7; 25, 5; 29, 4. 12; 31, 9) and kind to the needy (20, 28). He should know how to surround himself with good counselors (14, 35; 25, 13), to be prudent in war (20, 18; 24, 16) and distrust liars (29, 12). He should, in exchange, be able to count on his collaborators, on the integrity of the judges and the respect of his subjects (17, 15. 23; 18, 5; 20, 2; 24, 21. 23; 28, 21).

For the rest, individual, family and social virtues are the object of precise and concrete recommendations. One should practice justice and charity toward his neighbor (11, 17; 14, 9. 21; 17, 17; 21, 3), generous fidelity toward a true friend wisely chosen (3, 28; 11, 13; 13, 20; 22, 4; 25, 9; 27, 10). Almsgiving and the pardon of injuries call down the blessings of God (14, 31; 19, 17; 22, 9; 28, 27).

Spouses should be faithful (5, 15-21). The husband should provide for the family (27, 23-27). The ideal companion and mistress of the house is honored with resounding praise (31, 10-31). A husband can measure his happiness by the degree of misfortune caused by a senseless wife (14, 1), by a wicked one, a quarrelsome one, an unfaithful one (7, 6-23; 12, 4; 14, 1; 19, 13; 21, 9. 19; 25, 24; 27, 15-16). The education of the children is a life-long work (22, 6): who loves well punishes well (13, 24; 23, 13); in exchange the children will be docile (1, 18; 6, 20; 23, 22), in order to avoid many miseries (19, 26; 20, 20; 28, 24). Although it is fitting to be firm with servants (29, 21), one must not neglect them in their need (31, 15-21).

At times the generally vigorous condemnation of vices is the occasion for picturesque descriptions. It is thus that pride (6, 17; 11, 2; 13, 10; 15, 25; 16, 18; 25, 6-7; 29, 23), avarice (15, 27; 23, 4-5; 10, 12; 11, 4. 28), lust (5, 1-14; 6, 20—7, 27), envy (14, 30), gluttony (23, 29-35; 21, 17), anger (15,

18; 26, 21; 29, 22; 30, 33), sloth (6, 6-11; 10, 4-5; 24, 28-34; 26, 13-16) are censured.

Life is subject to many trials (24, 16). Certainly God is the sovereign master of existence (16, 1. 33; 19, 21). We are, nevertheless, most often the shapers of our own happiness or misery. The sayings aim generally to orientate us on the way of success by turning us away from obstacles.

Proverbs and the ancient traditions of Israel In all these respects the teachings of Proverbs, as indeed all of the Wisdom literature, harmonize well with the pedagogy of the narrators who have left us the precious accounts in which the basic maxims of religious, social, and professional life are actualized by being situated in real life. For example, the heroes of patriarchal history, notably Joseph, conform in their conduct to a practical wisdom which is essentially religious. They show themselves in every circumstance attentive and submissive to the management of Providence (Gn 12, 4; 15, 6; 22, 1-3; 24, 10-14. 21. 26-27. 31. 40. 42. 48. 50-52. 56; 31, 9. 12-18. 49. 53; 40, 8; 41, 16. 25; 43, 23; 45, 5-13; 46, 3; 48, 9. 11. 15-16. 21; 50, 19-20. 25), penetrated with a reverential fear of Yahweh (Gn 17, 3; 39, 9; 42, 18; 44, 7. 17), at ease with confident prayer (Gn 18, 16-33; 19, 17-22; 24, 12-14; 28, 16-22; 32, 10-13; 48, 15-16, 20; 49, 24c-26), well able to take care of their personal or family interest (Gn 13, 2; 21, 25; 23, 17; 25, 31; 26, 12-14. 18-22; 30, 29. 43; 31, 36-42; 33, 9; 39, 2-6; 40, 14; 41, 34-46; 46, 31-35), but respectful, with some exceptions (Gn 27, 6-40; cf. 35; 30, 42—31, 1), of the rights of others (Gn 13, 8-9; 14, 23; 23, 1-18; 30, 33; 31, 45-53; 33, 9; 43, 11-12). The examples of conjugal fidelity, still tainted with polygamy (Gn 16, 2-3; 25, 1; 29, 30), the candid views of mutual devotion of spouses, the perfect honesty of Joseph in warding off the advances of a loose woman (Gn 39, 7-12), the integrity, savoir faire, and administrative talent of Pharao's minister (39, 7-20; 47, 13-26), the prudence and shrewdness with which he treated his brothers (Gn 42—45), the generous pardon he granted them (45, 3-7; 50, 15-21), the tender affection he showed his father (46, 28-29): these are so many concrete teachings which play on very basic themes, less overtly religious, but all the more accessible to the profane. The Book of Proverbs develops and casts them in metal. What harmonious agreement, soundly pedagogical, between rule and application! It underscores the profound connection between the sapiential and historical genre in Israel.

II. PARTICULAR ASPECTS OF THE COLLECTIONS

The Solomon sections The sections attributed to Solomon, but which in fact largely overflow into subsequent centuries, are especially distinguished by the richness of observation they contain. Sometimes the concrete observations, metalic in their resonance, imply no evaluation, but are content to fix an experience, somewhat as one sets choice gems: success of the rich, the crafty (14, 35), the flatterers (19, 6), unscrupulous merchants (20, 14); the powers of the tongue (15, 2. 4); the efficacy of bribes (17, 23). These finely applied touches let one nevertheless see, here and there, in caricature (19, 24; 20, 4; 26, 13-16: sloth; 27, 15: quarrelsomeness), or with discrete approval (25, 4: refined silver; 11: apples and rings of gold), a hint of judgment in the practical order.

Critical evaluation in most cases confirms this observation. There is a well-defined line between the good and the evil, the wise and the foolish. The authors delighted in discovering and multiplying a veritable flood of contrasts in which these extremes clash, and inserted them in the framework of arresting antithetical parallels (10, 3. 6. 7; 21, 26; 29, 6-11): the praise of virtuous people (10, 31-32; 12, 5. 15. 16; 15, 18; 19, 11; 29, 11), of exemplary children (10, 11; 15, 20), of wise and reserved women (11, 16; 18, 22; 19, 14) and reproach of perverse men, whom he vigorously takes to task (12, 5. 17; 13, 5. 10; 16, 28. 29; 21, 24; 28, 24. 25; 29, 11), for unruly women, whom he mercilessly unmasks (11, 22; 19, 13; 21, 9. 19; 25, 24), for perverse children, whom he covers with shame and curses (19, 26; 20, 20; 28, 24).

The moral criterion used by the Wise Men does not seem

to rise above *personal interest* and the domain of the present life. It is with that reservation that one should note the parallelism of the two ways: the way of virtue leads to success and to life (10, 11; 13, 4; 16, 22; 12, 31), the way of evil leads to ruin and death (10, 16-17; 11, 19). Virtue and happiness, vice and misery go hand in hand. Is this thesis well founded? Undoubtedly, order generates good, disorder evil. But the Wise Men usually limit themselves to assertions of an experimental nature. Now these are often such as to lead to the opposite conclusion. The equation is often inverted. The authors of Proverbs might well have raised the problem of the suffering of the just and the prosperity of the impious. If they avoid it, it is due to the fact that beyond the data of experience to which they make appeal, they place their *faith in God* who blesses the good and confounds the wicked (10, 3. 6. 27. 29; 22, 12), who probes hearts (15, 3. 11; 16, 2; 17, 3; 20, 12; 21, 2) and lays bare intentions (21, 3. 27; 28, 9). It is He who holds in His hands the progress of the universe (19, 21), the stream of human destinies (16, 1. 9. 33; 21, 31), the conduct of all life (20, 24; 21, 1). The enigma of the suffering just and the wicked who prosper remains an exception, no matter how numerous the incidences. At most, the author of the introduction, who wrote at a much later date, suggests that God tests the just out of love (3, 12). Job will prove more demanding. But the answer that Yahweh gives him invokes practically the same confidence which the Wise Men had in Him. The hour to reveal sanctions in the next life has not yet arrived.

Supplementary sections   The supplementary sections attributed to the Wise Men (22, 17—24, 34), to Agur (30, 1-14), to Lamuel (31, 1-9) and those lacking all indication of authorship (30, 15-33; 31, 10-31) present more special themes.

The collection of the Wise Men intends to educate the ideal functionary. We can understand that the Egyptian influence is preponderant here (Amen-em-Ope) and that the practical advice concerns the main qualities of the "honest man," who is upright (22, 22-23; 23, 10-11), friend of good manners (13, 14. 22; 23, 1-2), sober (23, 20-21, 29-35), orderly (23, 26-28). This is the same kind of advice that Lamuel, candidate for the throne, received from his mother.

Agur gives the impression of a more rough nature, but the accent of his enunciations is profoundly religious; it is the faith of a peasant which is expressed, inspired by nature and blossoming in prayer (30, 1. 4; 7, 9).

The *numerical mešalim* (30, 18-33), which are not peculiar to the Book of Proverbs (cf. Ps 61 (62), 12; Jb 5, 19; Mi 5, 4; Eccl 11, 2; Sir 23, 16; 25, 7; 26, 5. 19 etc.), aim to attract attention and aid the memory.

The praise of the *valiant wife* (31, 10-31) is an alphabetic poem (cf. Ps 9A; 9B (10); 24 (25) . . . ; Lam 1—4; Na 1, 2-10; Sir 51, 15-29) of a high moral and religious plane. The lines that etch this portrait, borrowed from the customs of the surroundings, testify that the Wisdom writers remained perseveringly faithful to the observation of the world, and that their fine and penetrating psychology attained to a classical ideal of universal application. They penetrated the inner secrets of the human heart.

The introduction   The introduction to the Book of Proverbs, with its unity of composition and thought, stands in contrast to the Solomon collections. This literary and doctrinal block is almost entirely composed of the exhortations of a master who aims to arm his disciple against bad companions (1, 8-19) and corrupt women (5, 1-23; 6, 20—7, 27) and to develop in his heart the cult of Wisdom, whose usefulness (2, 1-22), practice (3, 1-35) and advantages (4, 1-27) are dwelt on at length.

It is evident that the author of these paternal exhortations is much closer to the stream of biblical tradition than to any foreign wisdom whatsoever. He lives, thinks, meditates, in an atmosphere, an ideological climate, the components of which are the doctrines contained in the more ancient sections: such as his advice concerning loyalty (4, 11), mercy (3, 27-30), docility (1, 8; 5, 13), greed (1, 19), violence (1, 11.

16; 3, 29-31), bad company (1, 10-16). He is also in the
tradition of earlier proverbs in his exhortation to knowledge,
prudence, fear of God (1, 1-7) and the passages concerning
misconduct and adultery (2, 16-19; 5, 3-23; 6, 20-35).

Moreover the Wisdom writer used especially, although in
different degrees, Deuteronomy, the writings of Jeremias and
Second-Isaias. He was not tied to the letter of his sources,
but he arranged the formulae and adapted them to his own
purpose. He introduced elements of these ancient sources,
transforming them into the structure of his composition. He
thus obeyed the genius of the race, which, moved by an ever
watchful instinct, delighted, just as in the midrashim,[8] in
provoking doctrinal developments within the organic unity
of a single current of living thought without breaking with
the past.

We have not pointed out the passage 6, 1-19, a sort of
parenthesis which interrupts the uniformity of the exhortation, and must be compared to the sections attributed to
Solomon. We have yet to consider the pericopes in which
Wisdom itself speaks (1, 20-33; 8, 1-9. 12). These celebrated
passages give us the occasion to conclude our work by treating
of Wisdom in the Book of Proverbs.

§ 6.   Wisdom in the Book of Proverbs

The technical term in Hebrew is *hokmâh*. He who possesses
it, or at least seeks to acquire it, is a *hâkâm*.

I.   THE WISDOM OF MAN

Applied to man, *hokmâh* appears as a complex quality,
thanks to which human acts are oriented to their true end. It
is situated, then, in the order of action limited to the domain of morality. Its components are, however, diverse:
hokmâh is the result of *attentive observation* (*bînah, te-*

8 See p. 195.

bûnah: cf. 1, 2. 6; 2, 5. 9; 8, 5-9; 14, 8; 19, 25; 20, 24; 28, 5;
29, 7 . . .), *judicious reflection* (*sekel:* cf. 16, 20; 21,
12 . . .), *foresight* (*tušiyyah:* cf. 3, 21; 6, 14), *cleverness,*
astute when necessary (*'ormah:* cf. 12, 16. 23; 13, 16; 14,
8. 15; 22, 3; 27, 12), *perspicacity* (*mezimmah:* cf. 1, 4; 2,
11; 3, 21; 5, 2; 8, 12), every disposition that ultimately informs, elevates and adapts to action "the knowledge of
Elohim," the *practical knowledge* whose source is the Creator
(*da'at:* cf. 1, 2. 4. 7. 29; 2, 5. 9. 10; 3, 20; 4, 1; 5, 2; 8, 10.
12; 14, 10; 17, 27; 31, 23 . . .). When it arrives at this degree, Wisdom attains perfection: it lets itself be guided by
reverential fear of God (15, 33) or filial piety (*yir'ah*), the
principle of *hokmâh* (1, 29; 2, 5) and source of all the advantages that, along with justice (*sedeq* or *sedaqâh:* cf. 1, 3;
8, 8. 15), Wisdom promises its disciples (long life: 10, 27;
security: 14, 26; abundance of wealth, honor and life: 15,
16; 22, 4; cf. 10, 3. 6. 7. 11. 20. 21. 31. 32; 11, 21. 28; 12,
3. 5. 7. 10; 13, 5; 15, 28; 20, 7; 21, 26; 29, 7 . . .).

II. WISDOM PERSONIFIED

Now Wisdom does not appear only as a quality: it disen-
gages itself from conceptual trappings and assumes the physi-
ognomy of a living being. It stands in the wide open, in busy
places, at noisy crossroads, at the city gates (1, 20-21; cf.
Jer 7, 2; 11, 6; 17, 19-20; 22, 2-6; 26, 2)—like a prophet.

By its calls it endeavors to attract attention. Like the
prophets it addresses sinners first of all, the ignorant in this
context (1, 22a: *petayim:* babblers; 1, 4; cf. 20, 19; 7, 7; 8, 5;
9, 4. 16; 14, 15. 18; 19, 25; 21, 11; 22, 3), scoffers (1, 22b:
lesim: cf. 3, 34; 9, 8; 15, 12; 19, 25; 21, 11), the inane (1,
22c: *ewilim:* cf. 15, 5; 17, 28; 22, 15). Its call, at first plain-
tive (1, 22), changes to a pressing, friendly, engaging invitation (1, 22-23). It speaks the language of prophets, which is
that of God (1, 23b; cf. Ez 36, 24-27; especially Is 44, 3) and
like prophets it reacts with menaces (1, 24-27; cf. Is 28, 7-22;
Jer 7, 24-29; 11, 8; 17, 23; Is 65, 2. 12; 66, 4). It will have
its day of vengeance when, faced with misery, the recalci-

trants will turn to their divine messenger (1, 28-31). Too late!

Prophet that it is, Wisdom also takes on the traits of a generous hostess (9, 1-6). In the house that she builds she invites her own to feast. All men are invited there. One can imagine, inspired by the imagery (building, victims, meals) borrowed from the service of the material temple, a prefiguration of a transcendent feast in a spiritual sanctuary. Wisdom here fulfills a doctrinal function. In any event, its teaching is presented to us as tasty and substantial. Dame Folly, who runs a hotel across the street (9, 13-18), can only exalt, by the contrast of her behavior, the marvelous invitation of provident Wisdom.

Also, *hokmâh* is capable of self-praise (8, 1-21) and sets forth its claims to nobility (8, 22-36). It places itself before all men; its mission is decidedly *universal* (8, 1-3; cf. Is 40, 9; 49, 6; 52, 7-9; 55, 5). The goods it promises are so surpassing that all mortals are attracted to it. It is its own dignity that confers on these goods their exceptional value. For that which man has by effort, Wisdom possesses by nature (8, 12-14): savoir faire, knowledge, perspicacity, reflection, foresight, penetration, power (cf. Is 11, 2; 35, 6). It confers moral rectitude and authority upon leaders (8, 15-16). It loves those who love it; those who search for it find it (cf. Mt 7, 7-8; Lk 11, 9-10), and have their fill of it (8, 17-21).

III. DIVINE WISDOM

How can such pretentions be justified? Wisdom is intimate with God, who gave it being in all eternity. He gave it birth, enthroned it (8, 22. 26): Yahweh was always wise. During the whole of creative activity, *hokmâh* was master of the work, bringing into effect, as if at play, the building of the universe (8, 27-31a), seeking with pleasure the company of men (8, 31b).

For this reason, listening to its instruction (*torâh*) is for them a question of life or death (8, 32-36).

Many exegetes view the labeling of Wisdom with the traits

of prophet and hostess as simple literary personifications.
Others (Lagrange, Gressmann, Procksch, Eichrodt, Robert,
Jacob) consider, not without solid reasons, that the sacred
author goes much further. One must at least concede that
the path is opened that permits authors of the New Testament to make explicit the relation of Wisdom Incarnate to
the Father. The description uses terms such that one cannot
fail to compare it with the prologue of St. John. Thus, in
light of the New Testament, the Fathers of the first centuries
and the great majority of exegetes have applied this passage
to the second person of the Trinity. In a broad sense, this
interpretation cannot be called into doubt.

By way of accommodation, the Church in its liturgy applies the entire passage describing eternal Wisdom to the
Blessed Virgin Mary, predestined in all eternity in the divine
mind to the role of Mother of the Incarnate Word: *Sedes
Sapientiae.*[9]

§ 7. Canonicity and Liturgical Use

The Book of Proverbs is protocanonical. The rabbinical discussions about it were terminated at the Council of Jamnia.
It is not certain that Theodore of Mopsuestia formally denied
its inspiration, but he certainly underestimated this work by
stressing that it could be explained by human wisdom alone.
To be noted, however, is the fact that the biblical opinions
of Theodore of Mopsuestia were discussed at the Council
of Constantinople, in a context that examined them, but
one can not maintain, as is generally the case, that they were
the object of a formal condemnation.[10] To the same type

[9] A number of the Fathers and the Scotists apply the Wisdom
passage specifically to the Second Person Incarnate; hence the aptness
of liturgical accommodation to Mary, predestined with her Son by
the same decree. (*Translator's note.*)

[10] See the councilar texts in MANSI, and the article of Fr. DUBARLE
in *RB* (1954), pp. 68-69. Cf. also below the note concerning the
Canticle, p. 120.

of objection put forward by Spinoza and Leclerc, Richard Simon answered that numerous inspired books would fall into the same category, if one must exclude, in order to assert their divine origin, the ability of the human author to compose them by himself.

The Book of Proverbs is frequently cited in the New Testament. It was nevertheless scarcely commented on by the Fathers of the Church. Besides the passages applied to the Blessed Virgin, the liturgy uses the poem of the valiant wife (Common of Holy Women and feast of St. Anne).

CHAPTER II

JOB

BIBLIOGRAPHY

Introductions, translations, commentaries, pp. 25 f. and 79 (P. LARCHER, *BJ**; A. B. DAVIDSON, *CBSC*; S. R. DRIVER–G. B. GRAY, *ICC* . . .).

P. DHORME, *Le livre de Job** (Paris, 1926).

G. HÖLSCHER, *Das Buch Hiob* (Tübingen, 1937).

E. J. KISSANE, *The Book of Job** (Dublin, 1946).

W. B. STEVENSON, *The Poem of Job* (London, 1947).

J. J. WEBER, *Job et l'Ecclésiaste** (Paris, 1947).

S. R. DRIVER–G. B. GRAY, *A Critical and Exegetical Commentary on the Book of Job*[2] (New York: Scribner, 1950).

A. WEISER, *Das Buch Hiob* (Göttingen, 1951).

T. H. ROBINSON, *Job and His Friends* (London, 1954).

F. STIER, *Das Buch Ijjob* (Munich, 1954).

S. TERRIEN, "The Book of Job," *IB* (1954).

——, *Job, Poet of Existence* (New York, 1957).

J. DANIÉLOU, *Holy Pagans of the Old Testament** (New York, 1957).

M. BOURKE, *The Book of Job, I and II** (New York: Paulist, 1962-1963).

M. POPE, *Job* (Garden City: Doubleday, 1965).

A. LEFÈVRE, "Job," *SDB*, IV (Paris, 1948), cols, 1073-1098.

E. SUTCLIFFE, "Notes on Job, Textual and Exegetical," *Biblica*, 30 (1949), pp. 66-90.

O. J. BAAB, "The Book of Job," *Interpretation*, 5 (1951) pp. 329-343.

H. W. ROBINSON, "The Cross of Job," *The Cross in the Old Testament* (London: SCM, 1955), pp. 9-54.

H. ROWLEY, "The Book of Job and Its Meaning," *BJRL*, 41 (1958), pp. 167-207.

R. A. F. McKenzie, "The Purpose of the Yahweh Speeches
in the Book of Job," *Biblica*, 40 (1959), pp. 435-445.
P. Skehan, "Strophic Patterns in the Book of Job," *CBQ*, 23
(1961), pp. 129-143.

§ 1.   The Book

I.   Position in the bible and general theme

Always listed among the *ketûbîm* in the Jewish catalogues,
the Book of Job is found in different places within that group.
It is found sometimes in the second place, sometimes in
the third place of the block it composed with the Psalms and
Proverbs. The Psalter usually headed this three-membered
group. If one notes that in the Catholic canon the location
of Job is likewise variable (between the Pentateuch and Josue
in the Syriac version, at the head of the didactic books in
the Vulgate), one is led to think that in part at least these
differences are a result of uncertainty about the origin of the
work and the era of the hero.

The general theme of the work is relatively simple. Job is
presented as a just man whom God permits Satan to test.
Three of his friends take it upon themselves to convince
him that he suffers because he is a sinner. But the unhappy
man energetically rejects the opinion of his accusers. A
fourth person intervenes and pretends to solve the enigma
by affirming the instructive power of suffering. At last Yahweh appears. He unrolls, like an immense film, the marvel of
creation, and reproaches Job for the indiscretion of his complaints. The book closes with the restoration of the proven
just man to his original happiness, blessed moreover with
new benefits.

II.   Literary structure

The work is obviously complex. Two parts are in prose: the
prologue (1—2) and the epilogue (42, 7-17). Between these

two sections a long poem intervenes (3, 1—42, 6). It is itself
a compilation. There is first an argumentative dialogue in-
stigated by a monologue of Job (3, 1-26). The dialogue
develops in three series of discourses, each containing three
exchanges: one of Eliphaz (4—5; 15; 22), the second of
Baldad (8; 18; 25 and 26, 5-14), the third of Sophar (11;
20; 27, 13-23 and 24, 18-24). Job replies to each of these
nine discourses with a defense of his cause (6—7; 9—10; 12—
14; 16—17; 19; 21; 23—24, 17 and 24, 25; 26, 1-4 and 27,
1-12; 29—31). It must be noted that the end of the dialogue
is not presented clearly in the book in its present form. The
texts must be rearranged to assure harmony of ideology and
composition.

Chapter 28 is a special problem. It is inserted as an interlude between the third intervention of Sophar and the last
answer of Job (29—31).

The dialogue is immediately followed by a series of discourses (32, 6-33; 33; 34; 35; 36, 1-21; 36, 22—37, 24: the
harangues of Elihu).

The poem ends with two discourses of Yahweh (38, 1—40,
2 and 40, 6—41, 26) each followed by a response of Job (40,
3-5 and 42, 1-6).

III. The origin of the composition

The apparent unity of the book   It cannot be denied that
a certain homogeneity emerges from the complexity of the
work in its present form. But it is a unity of the doctrinal
order: the problem of the suffering of the just confronted
with the prosperity of the impious constitutes the work's central object.

This homogeneity is also founded on considerations of the
psychological and literary order. The attitude of Job is dis-
cernably the same in the prologue-epilogue and in the poem,
granting a heightened vividness of language used by the hero
in the dialogue. This is accounted for by the laws of the
literary genre used, the necessity to stand up to the imperti-

nency of the accusers, and to bring out clearly the agony of the trial.

The consistency with which the divine names are distributed and grouped should be noted. That of Yahweh is never placed on the lips of Job (except in 1, 21: a common formula), nor on the lips of his friends; the names Elohim (five times in the poem), El, Eloâh, and Šadday (more frequent) are artfully distributed in the poetic work.

Finally, the mutual references of the prologue and epilogue (1–2 and 42, 6-17; compare 1, 5 and 42, 8; 1, 11 and 42, 7-9), of the dialogue and the theophany (implored by Job: 13, 3-12; 15, 27; 16, 19-21; 19, 25-29; 31, 35-37 and by his friends: 5, 8; 8, 5; 11, 5-6; compare 19, 27 and 42, 5), the discourses of Elihu and the dialogue (Elihu recalls the talk of the friends and Job: 31, 1-22; 33, 9-11—cf. 10, 7; 16, 17; 23, 10; 27, 5;—34, 5-6—cf. 27, 2; 29, 15; 30, 21; 35, 3—cf. 7-20), of the dialogue and sapiential references (inaccessible Wisdom is alone capable of solving the enigma) constitute so many ties that associate and bind the different elements of the writing. It is not surprising then that the unity of the Book has been defended by the majority of critics.

Traces of revisions In any event it is not a question of a unity without fault. There is evidence against the perfect homogeneity of the Book. The absence of Satan and Job's wife (42, 7-17) is to be regretted as a flaw in the harmony of the prologue and epilogue. There are more nuances in the attitudes of Job in the prologue-epilogue and in the poetic dialogue than one would suspect. Even in the dialogue there are indications of disorder in the last discussions (24, 18–27, 25) that, although reparable, disturb the harmony of the overall beautiful order.

But it is especially the calling upon Wisdom, and the present form of the discourses of Yahweh and the harangues of Elihu which cause difficulty.

The invocation of Wisdom seems to be an interpolation. The initial conjunction "for" hardly fits in the context where we read it. One might even say that the theme does not seem to be occasioned at all by the statements of Job and

his friends. To see here, with Budde, a reproach of God by
Job for not having revealed to him the plenitude of Wisdom
(28) seems to be a poorly founded conjecture. One would
well be more tempted to affirm that neither Job nor his
friends, in spite of 11, 6; 15, 8; 26, 3, thought of any other
intervention than God's.

Likewise it would be very unreasonable not to consider the
divine intervention as an essential element of the poem. One
must however agree that the discourses of Yahweh in their
present form suggest that there have been additions and revisions. It is possible that God held only one discourse (38,
1—40, 2); even so it is not certain whether the description
of the ostrich and the horse (39, 13-24) were part of the original passage. To this discourse one would have added the
powerful reference to Behemoth (the hippopotamus: 40, 13-
24) and to Leviathan (the crocodile: 40, 25—41, 26). Thus a
break would have resulted that would have necessitated the
introduction that we read in 40, 6-14 (compare 40, 6 and
38, 3) and Job's second answer (42, 1-6).

It must be admitted that the harangues of Elihu are an
addition to the original plan. Elihu was not expected at all.
He speaks and reasons in an entirely different manner from
the accredited accusers. He seems to refer to the preceding
discourses, but a later author could have used that device.
Above all he delays the intervention of Yahweh who speaks
over his head directly to Job (compare 31, 35 and 38, 1-3)
and ignores the pretentious babbler in 42, 7-17.

Conclusion To conclude, we find that there are clear
indications of unity and signs of disunity, the latter being
more pronounced. But the differences notwithstanding, the
fundamental theme is consistent. Thus we think that while
admitting a lack of literary unity, we must admit an organic
unity. The poet found himself with a popular work (*Volks-
buch*), the substance of which is contained in the material
of the present prose section. To it he probably added the
friends of Job (2, 11-13), composed the poetic dialogue and
the discourses of Yahweh, and to conclude reintroduced the
three accusers as a necessary denouement (42, 7-9).

The same author, or another one, finding the work in that condition, probably balanced it by lengthening the discourses of Yahweh, and then introduced the character of Elihu, who seems to bring a new element into the discussion (33, 19-30). Elihu could not be placed after Yahweh; he actually serves as a prelude to Him (36, 22—37, 24) in a hymn to divine Wisdom. Perhaps it seemed well to a later editor to close the discussion with a similar procedure. It was probably at the same time that the praise of Wisdom in 28 assumed its present place. At that time it seemed to fit well, if not in the literary and psychological context, at least in the ideological context.

It is thus possible to explain the organic unity by a process of growth beginning with a basic work (the prose book, dialogue, theophany), which its author, or another, enriched with new elements quite artistically joined to the original.

§ 2. The Problem

I. A COMMON THEME IN ANCIENT LITERATURE

The problem is that of the suffering of the just, along with the related one, which serves to accentuate it: the prosperity of the sinners.

It is a perennial problem, but it becomes more pressing in proportion as the demands of morality are more deeply felt. From the time of the Middle Empire, Egyptian thinkers had deplored in vehement terms the misery of the poor (*Plaint of the Poor Peasant*). In the measure that they accepted or rejected the efficacy of funeral rites, they celebrated death as an entering into happiness (*Dialogue of the Despairing:* poetic section), or as a fall into nothingness (same work: prose section), on occasion ridiculing the cult of afterlife (*Antef*). Around 1350 a poet composed an unqualified praise of death, slanted toward a criticism of skeptics.

But it does not appear that anyone in Egypt sought to resolve the anguishing problem. On the other hand, already in the year 2000 the problem challenged the wisdom of a great poet of Akkad, probably a king: Shushi-Meshri-Nergal (gather-riches-Nergal). Fallen from power, inflicted with illness, the unfortunate professes his justice, and ends, by virtue of moving prayers, by obtaining his cure from Marduk. About ten centuries later another afflicted man converses with a friend, whom he moves to pity by proclaiming his innocence.

Greek philosophical works and tragedies, contemporary with the Book of Job, raised the same question. Prometheus is certainly not innocent, but his excessive punishment embitters him and makes his despair. Oedipus Rex, for an offense against the gods for which he was not responsible, undergoes an accumulation of misfortunes, a Machiavellian destiny. Heracleus, though, is a just man, and it is the sadistic cruelty of the gods which crushes him. There is no way out of the pessimism which fatalism engenders. The philosophers, notably Plato, did succeed in giving the insoluble question its precise form, without arriving at any other solution for it than a recourse to some evil divinity.

If it remains difficult to place the Book of Job in the exact framework of these oriental writings, it is at least certain that the sacred author first of all shared the properly human preoccupation which they reveal, and undoubtedly captured some of the sense of suffering which they suffuse. It might even be possible to assert an external dependence (material similarity of thought and expression) of the canonical writing upon the Babylonian poems. Most likely this dependence reached its high point by way of the Accadian "Suffering Just Man," which the author of Job could have known through Chananeo-Phoenician tradition. But it is above all biblical speculation which gave birth to the inspired work.[1]

II. THE PROBLEM OF RETRIBUTION IN THE BOOK OF JOB

The biblical context   It will be recalled that in the Old Testament, retribution of good and evil, considered at first

---

[1] J. STEINMANN, *Le Livre de Job*, chaps. II and III, has conveniently brought together the principal extrabiblical texts relating to the problem.

as collective (Ex 20, 5-6; cf. Nm 16, 31-33; Jos 7, 1c-5; 2 Sm 3, 2; 21, 1-5; 24, 11-17, etc. . . . .), then as individual (Dt 24, 16; cf. 4 Kgs 14, 1-6; Ez 18; 33), is situated, until the last centuries of Judaism, in an earthly perspective, and in a framework of temporal sanctions. It is only since the first half of the second century that we find belief in spiritual and eternal sanctions manifested (Dn 12, 1-3; 2 Mc 7, 9. 11. 14. 23; 12, 43-46; Wis 1—5). The progress achieved in proportion as the historical situation evolved seems to have been the result of critical reflection, which, under the light of revelation, directed tormented spirits (cf. Ez 18, 2; Jer 31, 29; Mal 2, 17) little by little toward conceptions more and more in conformity with reality. The Book of Job finds its fitting place in the age when individual and earthly retribution came to grips with insoluble difficulties of the experimental order.

The propositions in the book   The friends of Job defend the commonly accepted opinion.

Eliphaz, like an Idumean Wise Man (Abd 8. 9; Jer 49, 7; Bar 1, 22-23), in a calm, magisterial, and slightly pretentious tone, expounds it at greatest length. His personal reflections (4, 8. 12; 5, 3. 27), confirmed by a revelation in a dream (4, 12-16) and by the witness of the ancients (15, 17-19), lead him to affirm that the innocent will not perish (4, 7), that sin calls down punishment (4, 8. 9), and that God finds fault with all men (4, 17-19; 15, 14-16), Job included (22, 6-10). To be sure, punishment is for correction (5, 17-18), and the latter restores prosperity (5, 19-26).

Baldad is more spontaneous and direct. He poses as an apologist for God, to whom he thinks it would be injurious to admit mysteries in the rule of providence (25, 1-6; 26, 5-14). Tradition is enough for him (8, 8-10). However, he occasionally emphasizes the current doctrine in a somewhat fatalist accent (18, 2-21). He insists upon the lot that awaits the just and the wicked (8, 11-22). He acknowledges, just as Eliphaz, that conversion brings about a return of good fortune (8, 6-7).

Sophar is decidedly aggressive, subtle, pessimistic. He appeals only to his own authority (20, 2; 24, 25), is determined to sting Job (11, 2-4), holds that there is no remedy for the sinner's punishment (20, 5-29), and goes so far as to admit unconscious sins (11, 5-12). Nevertheless, he too considers conversion the principle of restoration (11, 13-20).

Job stands out for the firm, constant defense of his cause. He opposes his personal case to the current doctrine: he is innocent and he is suffering (9, 21; 13, 23; 16, 16-17; 30, 25-37). His final answer (29–31) poses the problem in all its sharpness. But how to resolve it? The anomaly incarnate in him is explained, in his view, by a violent persecution of God who relentlessly pursues his servant (7, 11-12; 10, 2-4; 13, 24-28; 14, 16-17; 16, 7-14; 19, 6-12. 21-22; 30, 19-23). Admittedly he puts forward a quite bold conception of God, in that he attempts to link divine Wisdom with a kind of tyranny that would constitute His essential property. God is always just, whether He strikes the innocent or makes the culpable prosper. His omnipotence seems arbitrarily to create its own morality. The conclusion of this singular theodicy is that man must remain silent before God. He is inaccessible to human reason, based on a concept of morality that divine transcendence surpasses (9, 2. 3. 12. 19-20).

There are in this some excessive statements, whose intent, however, is to safeguard the sanctity of Yahweh. "Job fights to rediscover God," writes Fr. Larcher (op. cit., p. 21), "feeling that he is cut off from Him, while the others content themselves with speaking well of Him. And it is Job alone who faces the problem of God. . . ." Finally, after having given up all hope of satisfaction, he takes refuge in confidence in Him who remains, beyond suffering and death itself, his ultimate goel and his friend (19, 25-27).[2]

---

[2] A difficult passage. It would be profitable to read the study Fr. LARCHER has made of it (op. cit., 27-31). It is certain that Catholic tradition is unanimous in proclaiming the dogma of the resurrection of the body. But it is equally incontestable that tradition has not been unanimous in so interpreting the famous text of Job. The Vulgate's translation is influenced, here as in many other passages, by the theology of the age.

Contemporary exegetes are for their part far from agreement on

The statements of Elihu intend to point out the inaccuracies of Job and his friends. It likewise delights this singular speaker to place in relief those elements of a solution which the dialogue presents: God instructs men not only by dreams (33, 15-18), but also by suffering (33, 19-23). Is this not an instrument of salvation (36, 15)? If He does not seem to listen to the outcries of those under trial, the reason is that they have neglected to call upon Him as Creator and Lord (35, 9-13). Should a mediator intercede for them, His benevolence would show itself (33, 23-30)! To be sure, God saves the penitent (34, 31-32; 36, 11). Job will be delivered from his anguish (36, 16), but he must beware of falling back into sin (36, 18-21).

God's intervention does not bring the solution which might be expected of Him to whom Job and his friends had appealed. The reason is that Yahweh is not a gambler who takes up the challenge. He speaks as God and not as man. In this respect He grants several points to Job, who better grasped the mystery of divine transcendence. It is precisely this transcendence which bursts forth when the Creator and Arranger of the universe unfolds the panoramic spectacle of His enormous works (38, 1–42, 6). His power and His wisdom overcame the forces of chaos and brought stability to the cosmos. Is it not an unavoidable conclusion that such wisdom and power cannot fail to resolve the problems which the spirit of man is not capable of solving?

Further development The response to the problem posed remains therefore hidden in God. But one senses in advance that there is an answer. Only its revelation is deferred. Daniel's last vision (12, 1-3), the Second Book of Machabees (7, 9. 11. 14. 23; 12, 43-46), and the Book of Wisdom (1—5) will unveil the eternal destiny reserved for the just and sin-

---

the object of the patriarch's vehement declaration. Some allege the object is a cure (Bickell, Hudal, Bigot, Szcygiel); the assurance of well-being that Yahweh will promulgate, either here below (Vetter, Peters, Ceuppens, Beel), or after the resurrection of the body (Knabenbauer, Royer, Hontheim, Sales, Vaccari, Lagrange); the separated soul's vision of God (Dillman, Welte).

ners, and the New Testament, in developing the teachings
of the Servant Poems (Is 53, 1-12), will succeed in giving
the solution which the just man who suffers could still find
desirable on the plane of life here below: the suffering of the
just has redemptive value (Rom 5, 6-19; 1 Cor 15, 3; 2 Cor
5, 15; Col 1, 14. 20. 24, etc.).

§ 3. Date, Author, Literary Genre

I. DATE

The patriarchal coloring of the prose passage leads one to
think that the foundation of the popular legend sinks its
roots into the far distant past. Still it is right to observe that
the character of Satan is not mentioned until late in the Bible
(Za 3, 1, where he is matched, to one side of the throne of
God, with the "angel of God" who stands on the other side;
cf. also 1 Par 21, 1: Satan there has replaced the anger of
Yahweh of 2 Sm 24, 1). In any case, the principal part of
the work, of incontestable literary perfection, is certainly of
more recent composition.

The art demonstrated by the plan, the power of expression,
the elegance of style—these traits have led some to suggest
the golden age of Hebrew literature (10th–8th centuries):
from the reign of Solomon to that of Ezechias. But does this
dating, forcibly obtained by way of comparison, take into
sufficient account the fact that many works not long ago attributed to ancient writers are commonly regarded as having
acquired their definitive form in a more recent age? And
moreover the literary perfection of the work must be able to
be reconciled with the Aramaisms which, taking into account
the liberties which a poet familiar with several dialects could
have permitted himself, of themselves impose as probable the
end of the royal period (Pfeiffer).

But there is more. A number of literary ties, implied in
historical references, encourage one to go further along this
path. The figure of the "just man who suffers" which domi-

nates the Book of Job, suggests a relation to the Book of
Jeremias. Is it not quite possible that there is some relation
between the reference to the prosperity of the wicked (Jb
21, 7-34) and the strong protest against God over the
happiness of the evildoer (Jer 12, 1-3)? The same holds for
the bitter complaints of Job (3, 3-26) and the morbid curses
of Jeremias (20, 14-18).

More discretion is necessary in comparing the "suffering
servant," whose traits are described by Isaias (42, 1-7; 49,
1-9; 50, 4-10; 53, 1-12), with the patriarch misunderstood by
his friends. The problem is stated in Job in a more pointed
way, but it is in Isaias that the solution is given (Is 53, 4-6.
8. 10-12): the just man suffers to save the many.

As far as other claimed relationships are concerned (Ps 107
(106) and Jb 5, 16; 12, 24; Prv 13, 9; 24, 20 and Jb 18, 5-6),
they are not sufficiently clear to be of help in solving the
problem at hand.

No matter what relationships might be suggested by comparisons and references, it is certain that the historical background which agrees with the preoccupation of the characters
of the Book of Job is one not prior to the Exile.

We must go further and state that it is posterior to the
Exile. Without insisting too much upon the allusions to the
deportations which we read in Job (12, 17-25; 36, 7-12), it
might not be amiss to suppose that the morale of Ezechiel
(18; 33) could have appeared insufficient only after the accumulation of trials undergone by the best of the sons of
Israel, those who returned to Juda from Babylonia. Aggeus
and Zacharias sustained their courage for a while. But after
the disappearance of these prophets, the unhappy Jews felt
dearly the insufficiency of the solution of the son of Buzi.
Might it not be during the course of this crisis that the Book
of Job was written?

It would be further from the truth, it seems to us, to go
back further than the age of Esdras and Nehemias. The
Prophet Malachias, a contemporary of the pioneers of the
restoration, was certainly not ignorant of the complaints of
the people (2, 17; 3, 13-15), but he was better instructed

than the characters of the Book of Job concerning the outcome of the painful situation (3, 16-20). With more reason,
then, the reader will note, as Dhorme does, some connections
between Malachias and the discourses of Elihu.

In any case, there is no reason to situate the book in the
Hellenistic age, whatever possible relations there might be
between the biblical writing and the tragedies of Aeschylus
and Sophocles or the dialogues of Plato. We have already
said that the Book of Job belongs more to the family of
Babylonian rather than to Greek writings.

In sum, we place the redaction of the work between the
return from captivity (538) and the Hellenistic invasion
(330). The end of the fifth century would seem the most
appropriate date.

II. THE AUTHOR

The author has not told us his name. But he did at least
reveal the high character and outstanding quality of his spirit,
profoundly religious and moral, capable of sharp psychological reflections, endowed with moving sympathy for the unfortunate. He most probably experienced sadness himself.
Many traits of his writing lead one to believe that he was an
intellectual: even if the imagery he employs is Palestinian,
the Assyro-Babylonian, Phoenician and Egyptian associations
justify the conclusion that he was a writer of vast culture.
Quite a number of details of the Book of Job clearly suggest
the notion of some relation to the Egyptian world (28, 1-11:
the mines of Sinai; 40, 15–41, 26: Behemoth and Leviathan;
9, 26: boats made of reeds; 8, 11: papyrus; 40, 11-12: lotus).
Nevertheless, these relations have been contested recently by
Tournay.[3]

---

[3] RB (1956), p. 134, in reply to Fr. HUMBERT, Recherches sur
les sources égyptiennes de la littérature sapientiale d'Israël, pp. 75-
106; see also the moderate conclusion of Fr. LEFEVRE, SDB, IV, art.
Job, cols. 1074-1075.

III. THE LITERARY GENRE

The Book of Job is fundamentally a didactic writing. It is
not however impossible that the hero did exist. And it is not
only the discovery of his name under the form *'ayyab*
(El-Amarna: A-ia-ab, king of Pi-hi-lim, today Fahil) that suggests this. The allusion of Ezechiel (14, 14. 20) refers only
to a proverbial Wise Man. On the other hand, the absence of
a genealogy would not appear to be an unfavorable sign: Job
is presented to us as a stranger to the people of Israel. The
appendix of the LXX rightly places the land of Us on the
border of Idumea and Arabia. But it is easier to draw from
these geographical particulars an argument for the homeland
of the author than for the historicity of the hero. Many modern authors, Pfeiffer among them, actually hold that the
poem has deep roots in Idumean soil; without going so far,
it is not out of order to ask oneself to what extent Idumean
wisdom, which is called to mind by the origins of the characters, influenced Israelite Wisdom. The origin of oriental
traditions, which are generally the products of real facts, perhaps warns against rejection of the absolute historicity of Job
and the basic elements of the prose section; but in the book
the case at hand is generalized and raised to the level of a
type.

As a Wisdom writing, the Book of Job belongs by its literary form to various genres. The question treated gives the
dialogue a philosophic turn; the interacting characters and
the development of the action make it a sort of drama; the
sentiments expressed, the bold imagery, the evocation of
the miraculous raise it to the heights of lyric and epic.

§ 4. Job in the Progression of Revelation

If one reads the Book of Job after that of Proverbs, he discovers at once that reflexive questioning, which calls easy
solutions into doubt, follows the simple teaching founded

on observation. It is also easy to see that a self-seeking
morality gives way to an investigation of the causes which
would be capable of justifying the failures which this morality
records. The questioning takes the form of a long emotional
complaint. So it pleased the Spirit of God to lead the spirit
of man toward a solution of the mystery that causes him
most anguish. The cry of Jeremias echoes throughout Job.
The insufficiency of personal and earthly retribution breaks
forth. The author of Ecclesiastes may try to stop the quest
by affecting the attitude of a disillusioned sage; his apparent
skepticism only deepens the emptiness which he himself
suffers.

The liberating solution, which the Servant of Yahweh
songs had incidentally sketched by proclaiming the redemptive value of the sufferings of the just, will find its full expression in the eschatological revelations of Daniel (12, 1-3) and
the Book of Wisdom (2—5). The trials of the just, already
worthwhile on account of their expiatory value, will be transformed into eternal happiness, while the prosperity of the
impious will give way to eternal damnation. We who are more
blessed than Job, who live in the brightness of the New
Testament, can contemplate in Christ, who suffered for us
before entering into glory, the perfect example of the solution to the never ending—but forever solved—problem.

CHAPTER III

THE CANTICLE OF CANTICLES

BIBLIOGRAPHY

Introductions, translations, commentaries, pp. 25 f. (A. MIL-
LER, *HSAT**; A. ROBERT, *BJ**; J. FISCHER, *EBi**; D. BUZY,
*BPC** . . .).

G. RICCIOTTI, *Il cantico dei cantici** (Turin, 1928).

M. HALLER, "Das hohe Lied," *Die fünf Megilloth* (Tübingen, 1940), pp. 21-46.

H. ROWLEY, "The Interpretation of the Song of Songs," *The
Servant of the Lord and Other Essays* (London: Lutterworth, 1952), pp. 189-234.

A. BEA, *Canticum canticorum** (Rome, 1953).

A. FEUILLET, *Le Cantique des Cantiques** (Paris, 1953).

R. GORDIS, *The Song of Songs* (New York, 1954).

G. KNIGHT, *Esther, Song of Songs, and Lamentations* (London: SCM, 1955).

H. SCHMÖKEL, *Heilige Hochzeit and Hoheslied* (Wiesbaden,
1956).

A. M. DUBARLE, "Le Cantique des cantiques," *RSPT* (1954),
pp. 92 ff.

R. MURPHY, "Recent Literature on the Canticle of Canticles,"
CBQ, 16 (1954), pp. 1-11.

J. P. AUDET, "Le sens du Cantique des cantiques," *RB*
(1955), pp. 197-221.

T. J. MEEK, "The Song of Songs," *IB* (1956).

——, "Babylonian Parallels to the Song of Songs," *JBL*, 43
(1924), pp. 245-252.

M. SEGAL, "The Songs of Songs," *VT*, 12 (1962), pp. 470-
490.

B. ULANOV, "The Song of Songs: the Rhetoric of Love," *The
Bridge*, 4 (1962), pp. 89-118.

In the present Hebrew Bibles, the Canticle of Canticles is placed at the head of the *Megillôt*.[1] The name it bears expresses its eminence; it is a *superlative*, akin to the superlatives which were used to designate the most sacred part of the Temple (the Holy of Holies), the greatest king (the King of Kings), the ultimate nothingness (vanity of vanities). "All the Sacred Writings are holy," wrote Rabbi Aqiba in the 2nd century, "but the Canticle is sacrosanct." The Pesshita even carries this subtitle: "*Wisdom of Wisdoms of Solomon.*" In the synagogues the Canticle is recited on the octave of the Passover.

§ 1.   Historico-Literary Content of the Canticle

The Canticle is a love song. Before starting our study, it would not be useless to place it in its historical and literary milieu, even if it soars above the other examples of the genre.

The fact is that the milieu of the Canticle is first of all profoundly human, and as such, universal in time and space. Nevertheless its characteristics relate it more strictly to the customs and love songs of the Orient.[2] Week-long marriage feasts, jubilant and expressive, are still known there today. It was no different long ago. Nuptial songs constituted a specific and richly varied genre: these were popular songs, often risqué and derisive, and higher class poems, sometimes artistically composed.

It was an unwritten law to praise the beauty of the spouses. The existing Syrian *wassf* is a very ancient legacy. Not that hackneyed expressions were always lacking. Some descriptions smack of artificiality. They have nonetheless this peculiarity that they associate nature with the well-being of the spouses. Moreover any real ugliness perceived during these days of rejoicing served as point of comparison with the physical

---

[1] See p. 26.
[2] S. SCHOTT, *Les chants d'amour de l'Égypte ancienne*, French transl. Fr. KRIEGER (Paris, 1956).

beauty of the bride and groom. To praise of physical charms were always added good wishes, among which that for fecundity was never lacking. In this way, the songs rose to a religious plane, becoming veritable nuptial blessings, matching the incantations to ward off the effects of sorcery, the "evil eye." It happened that in this context obscenities or at least realistic expressions, tempered by euphemisms, were not at all excluded. A number of Egyptian pieces (cf. Pap. Harris, about B.C. 1200) nevertheless extol love, the joy of loving, lovesickness, and love potions without shocking expressions. They often expressed, notably in the case of marital misfortunes, tender and affectionate sentiments, mixed on occasion, if jealously intervened, with accents of indignant anger.

The love songs of the Chester Beatty I papyrus deserve special consideration. "They do not lack agreement down to detail with the material form of the Canticle," writes E. Suys.[3] "One especially merits attention because of an obvious similarity of plan, although the basic ideas differ. It is a question of a complex and somewhat artificial composition in seven couplets . . . The author is "the grand amuser," in other words, the woman in charge of entertainment. At first glance it is astonishing that the author is a woman. But it must be recalled that on the bas-relief of El-Amarna representing dramatic, or if one prefers, orchestral performances, it is a woman who is directing" (p. 209-210).

Israel, placed as it was at the crossroads of the great oriental nations, could not ignore the literary genre of wedding chants and love songs. The week-long wedding feasts which unfolded at Harran (Gn 29, 27. 28) must have found a place in the family ritual of the descendants of the patriarchs (Jgs 14, 10-18). Jeremias (16, 9; 25, 10) prophesied that these joyful melodies would soon cease in the face of invasion. Psalm 44 (45) has preserved the record of a marriage feast in which the groom seems to be a real prince and not just king for a week. The description of the royal couple is

[3] *Bi* (1932), pp. 209-227.

the work of a delicate writer. This piece puts us on the path
to the object of our present study.

§ 2. General View of the Canticle

At first reading the Canticle appears to be a poem of married
love, presented in alternating chants whose plan resists rigor-
ous and precise determination. Thus analysis differs according
to the opinion one holds concerning the unity of the work
and its literary genre. Fortunately, it is not necessary to take
a stand in order to acquire a general understanding of the
work.

Whether one divides it into five sections (C. a Lapide),
five poems (Robert), six scenes (Kaulen, Pelt, Muntz),
seven songs (Bossuet, Calmet, Lorath), or even more
(Budde finds twenty-three of them), it is apparent it concerns two separated lovers who are avidly searching for one
another. They proclaim their mutual love, they are reunited
and separated again, waiting to succeed, after a trial over
which the lover triumphs, in possessing one another definitively.

The absence, at least apparent, of a logical thread through
the poems, the diversity of *places* where the events take place
and of *situations* in which the characters are placed, the repetitions of themes, images and words—all these factors do not
succeed in destroying the unity which results from the
development of the plot, and from the likeness of spirit and
form of the various songs. The striking color and richness of
imagery, spread through the whole work, is convincing evidence that the work should not be denied a basic homogeneity.

§ 3. Diverse Interpretations of the Canticle

A deeper study of the Canticle can only be done within the
framework of an interpretation. The best must be selected

from among many. We will first present a historical summary of the systems proposed. As a preparation, a few notions from the science of interpretation will be helpful.

Every *inspired* book has a *literal* sense, proper or figurative, which emerges from the terms of the text, interpreted according to the ordinary rules of human language, taking into consideration time, place, and literary genre. The *figurative literal sense* can assume various modalities: it can be parabolic or allegorical; allegory itself can be subdivided, being capable of attaching itself to a historical foundation, or merely providing its own foundation. A *typical* sense can be added to the literal sense, proper or figurative. It pertains to Revelation to make it known to us, since the typical sense is itself inspired: God may, in effect, will that persons, situations, or events signify higher realities as a prefiguration of future events. The Canticle has given rise to interpretations corresponding to these various classes of senses.

I. Ancient interpretations

It has been doubted whether the Jews admitted any other interpretation than the allegorical. How else could they have overcome the difficulties which arose, at the end of the first century of our era, concerning the canonicity of an apparently profane book, if this book had been, in their tradition, an anthology of radically sensual songs? The author of the Apocalypse of Esdras is a witness in favor of this figurative interpretation when he calls the people of Israel garden, lily, dove (4 Esd 5, 24. 26; cf. Ct 2, 2. 10; 4, 12). That is also the interpretation of the Targum[4] and the Talmud, which consider God the Beloved, and the nation of Israel the spouse of Yahweh. The substance of this explanation has remained intact among the best Israelites down through the centuries. A few exegetical blunders, more or less fantastic, did not succeed in obscuring the essential idea the Jews had of the

---

[4] E. Vulliaud, *Le Cantique d'après la tradition juive* (Paris, 1925).

Canticle: *the work sings of the mystical marriage of the Lord and the Chosen People.*

In the beginning the Christians' way of thinking was no different. They merely adapted the allegorical interpretation to the conditions of the New Testament. The name of Christ was substituted for that of Yahweh and the Christian people for the people of Israel. The Canticle celebrates the mystical marriage of Christ and the Church. A normal evolution took place in exegesis; it took on more particular applications according as the spouse became all mankind, the faithful soul, or, in the Middle Ages, the Virgin Mary (St. Bernard). There was no departure from the line laid down by Jewish exegesis. At most, one could conclude that the evolution, without breaking with the allegorical interpretation, leads toward the superimposition of meanings of the kind tinged with typology, and toward applications in an evidently *accommodated sense.*

Nevertheless, there was a discordant voice: Theodore of Mopsuestia (350-428) interpreted the Canticle as a souvenir of Solomon's marriage to an Egyptian princess—a prelude to the "Banquet" of Plato. The interpretation of Theodore, which granted the work only a proper literal sense, was dealt with unfavorably at the Fifth Ecumenical Council.[5] It was proposed again in the 16th century, and the Jewish exegete who revived it, Sebastian Castellion (1547), had no followers. It is evident though that there was a movement toward making the literal sense more *concrete.* In 1621, Panigarola was a spokesman for the movement when he proposed to see in the Canticle an idyllic drama between a shepherd and

---

[5] Fr. DUBARLE makes a point of calling the condemnation of Theodore's opinion into question (*RB*, 1954, pp. 68-69). Cf. VOSTÉ, *RB* (1929), pp. 390-395; R. DEVREESSE, *RB* (1930), pp. 362-377; *Studi et Testi*, Bibl. Apost. Vat., 141 (1948), pp. 34-35. L. PIROT (*L'œuvre exégétique de Théodore de Mopsueste*, Rome, 1913, pp. 134-137) does not mention any condemnation. But the judgment of the Fathers was decidedly contrary: the "*commenta*" of Theodore are "*infanda Christianorum auribus.*"

a shepherdess. For Catholics anxious to conciliate, the door
was open to a more complex interpretation.

It was this path, already indicated by Honorius of Autun
(*PL* 172, 347-496), that P. Sherlog (1633-1640), F. Q. de
Salazar (1642), Bossuet (1693) and Dom Calmet (1726)
followed. According to them, the Canticle recalls the love
of Solomon and one of his wives (the daughter of Pharao or
Abisag the Sulamite). But the marriage of the prince was
ordained by God to signify the mystical union of Yahweh
with Israel and of Christ with the Church. The typical interpretation was born.

II. FROM THE 18th CENTURY TO MODERN TIMES

From the 18th century on, then, there were three currents.
The old allegorical tradition always had adherents. But the
boring genre (A. Robert) which marks them all, leaves room
for philosophical and political variations: the marriage of
Solomon to Wisdom (Rosemüller: cf. Prv 7, 4; 9, 5; Wis 8,
2-9; 9, 1-10; and Ct 5, 1); the attempt to unite Israel and
Juda (L. Hug, 1813, followed by I. G. Herbst); conflict followed by pacification of Yahwism and human civilization
(A. Torelli, 1892). Fr. Joüon (1909) strove to put an end
to these products of the decadent age by introducing into
the ancient theme precise historical references: according to
him the Canticle recalls the various phases of the Alliance
from the Exodus to the coming of the Messias.

Alongside the allegorical interpretations developed that of
Theodore of Mopsuestia. In 1771 Jacobi revived Panigarola's
opinion in a new form: the shepherdess was stolen from her
fiancé and placed in Solomon's harem. But she refuses the
king's advances and gifts, and he is forced to free her. Renan
was the champion of this interpretation in France, while the
observations collected by Wetzstein, German consul at
Damascus, concerning wedding feasts in Auranitis, gave
K. Budde the idea for a folklore explanation: the Canticle is
a collection of love songs destined to celebrate the new
spouses, king and queen for a week (Week of the king).

The typological current likewise holds its own. Its promoters were Casazza (1846) and P. Shegg (1865). Then after the interpretation of Budde became popular and predominant, Zapletal (1907), J. Hontheim (1908) and A. Miller (1927) modified the figurative element, which ceases to be a marriage of Solomon, in order to draw nearer to the current opinion, which was considered sufficiently founded upon details of the Canticle. But they firmly retained the reference to the reality represented in figure: mystical union, which pure allegorism had found just beneath the letter. According to A. Miller, the literal sense of the Canticle is to be applied to an ideal marriage typically prefiguring the union of God and man.[6]

III. PRESENT POSITIONS

It is apparent, therefore, that the substance of the primitive interpretation has held its ground. Neither the revival of Jacobi's interpretation, which for the rest was unmasked by Pouget and Guitton (1934),[7] as at least an accommodated interpretation, nor, even more so, the efforts of a poorly conceived comparative method undertaken by Meet (1922) and Wittekindt (1925), seem to have been successful in eliminating the inspired allegorical sense, at least typical. Moreover Fr. Buzy (1950) thinks that the literary genre of the Canticle is a descendent of pure poetry, allowing for parabolic reflections, while A. Robert and A. Feuillet, having rejected all parabolic interpretation, hold that the poem signifies immediately the union of Yahweh and Israel. R. J. Tournay agrees with this exegesis. On the other hand, A. M. Dubarle (1954) and J. P. Audet (1955) have turned to an exactly

---

[6] Cf. op. cit., p. 89.

[7] According to POUGET-GUITTON, in the proper literal sense, the only one intended by the sacred author, the work declares the doctrine of marriage (indissolubility, conjugal fidelity, monogamy), under the form of a dramatic presentation; but the proper literal sense contains the germ of the spiritual sense (union of God and Israel). In the course of time this germ developed and blossomed into the allegorical sense. (Cf. op. cit., pp. 126-127.)

opposite opinion: the Canticle celebrates human love just as
God willed it; it took its normal place in the wedding cele-
brations of Israel until the rabbis, at a more recent date,
interpreted it allegorically.

What conclusion is to be drawn? Admittedly, those interpretations which welcome an appeal to the material, the
worldly, the profane, remain acceptable if they do not reject
all religious significance. They are all the more acceptable if
they admit the existence of a typical sense. It is not contrary
to inspiration to admit that in this case, as in others, likewise
disputed (Gn 3, 15; Is 7, 14; Ps 44 [45]), historical events
can be raised to the dignity of symbols which point to
supernatural realities. And if some rearrangement or reinterpretation was necessary right from the beginning to obtain the
desired result, we do not think such a purification impossible.
Who knows whether the Jewish doctors were not the first to
effect this transposition, thus qualifying human love songs,
purified of all profane meaning and elevated under divine
influence, to take their place in the canon of sacred
writings?

Still we find it preferable to settle for the figurative literal
sense, that is, the allegorical. Thus we take into account the
extension that this sense can acquire when under the proper
circumstances the mind rises from the union of Yahweh
and Israel to that of Christ and the Church, Christ and the
individual soul, and the Holy Spirit and the Virgin Mary.

§ 4. A Brief Analysis of the Canticle

We can now analyze the plan of the work. With A. Robert
we distinguish five poems, preceded by a prologue and followed by two appendixes.

In the prologue (1, 2-4) the bride is searching for her
bridegroom.

The first poem (1, 5—2, 7) describes the anxiety of the
separated one (1, 5-7); the chorus urges her not to lose hope
(8). The bridegroom appears; he allows himself to give in

to the charms of the beloved (9-11). A dialogue informs us
of their sentiments of mutual admiration (1, 12—2, 5). Their
union, however, is not yet assured (6-7).

The second poem (2, 8—3, 5) depicts the mutual search
which the two spouses renew. The bride describes the beloved running toward her (2, 8-16); she rushes to search for
him and meets him in the city (2, 17—3, 4). Is possession
achieved? Not yet (3, 5).

The third poem (3, 6—5, 1) opens with a description of a
triumphal procession presided over by Solomon (3, 6-11).
The bridegroom demonstrates more and more that he is in
love (4, 1—5, 7). He establishes a meeting place (6) and
invites his beloved there in passionate terms (8-15). The
bride accepts. One gathers that she will soon yield (4, 16—
5, 1).

The fourth poem (5, 2—6, 3) presents a still withdrawn
bride (5, 2-3). She finally opens the door, but too late! The
bridegroom has left (4-6ab). The exasperated bride searches
for him again (6c-8) and describes him to the chorus which
is struck by so forceful an attachment (9-16). There is another meeting. Mutual possession is now very near (6, 1-3).

The fifth poem (6, 4—8, 4) leads to the denouement. The
groom again describes the beauty of his beloved (6, 4-12).
He replies to the chorus, which invites him to turn around
(7, 1a), with ever more vehement declaration of love (1b-
10a). Then the bride expresses her passion (10b—8, 3). But
she has not achieved her dream (4).

The denouement is reached (8, 5-7). It is the bridegroom
who awakens her (5). He demands eternal love (6-7).

Two appendixes, which were added later, seem to be reflections suggested by the Canticle (8, 8-14).

§ 5.   The Bible as Milieu of the Canticle

The allegorical sense of the Canticle seems to us to be required by its vital relation to a long biblical tradition of
which it is the product. What is spread over its pages under

a form that reaches the heights of poetry are those same themes that are spread through the Bible, and whose common object is the mystical conjugal union of Yahweh and Israel.

One has only to read the sacred book. Yahweh has married Israel (Os 2, 2; Ez 16, 8), but the nation did not remain faithful (Os 2, 7; Jer 2, 20-25; 3, 2. 6. 8b-10; 13, 27; Ez 16, 15-34; 23, 2-8. 11-21), God repudiates her as an adultress (Os 2, 4-6; Jer 3, 8a). The rejection was not definitive: Israel does not cease to be a bride dear to her bridegroom. In order to correct her, He gives the nation over to the infamy and adventures of a vagrant life (Os 2, 8. 9. 11-13; Ez 16, 35-41; 23, 9-10. 22-26. 28-35. 45-48). So great is His desire to bring the unfaithful back to Himself (Jer 3, 7b. 12-18; 4, 1-4; Ez 3, 26-27)! He knows that the sinful people themselves want to return (Os 2, 9; Jer 3, 4. 5a. 22; 4, 31). Pardon must however be delayed (Jer 3, 1. 5b. 22), because God will not be satisfied with empty promises (Jer 2, 29-37). The people must be constrained besides to confess their insufficiency (Jer 31, 19; Is 63, 15—64, 11). Yahweh must intervene with the fullness of His power and mercy (Os 11, 8-9). He will Himself bring about the reconciliation, and will restore to His spouse all her rights (Os 2, 16-25; Ez 36—37; Jer 31, 20-40; Is 51, 52, 54, 60, 61, 62). Then the idyl of the desert will live again (Os 2, 16-17. 21-22): the bride and groom will possess each other forever.

Is this not the theme of the Canticle? The only difference is that in this book the bride has to yearn for a long while before realizing the final outcome, which God will transform, by an act of His omnipotence, into a definitive conversion.

That is the process described for us. Each of the sections, as A. Robert notes, could be summarized in two words: *tension* and *repose*. "The tension is expressed in the admiring contemplation, the openly expressed desire, the appeals and their response, the anxious search"—all elements whose order can vary. "By repose, one should understand 'mutual possession' (Buzy): the goal of each section."

To thematic connections must be added the climate

created by the style. It is a very biblical climate, one in which sumptuous images spring up spontaneously: perfume, oil, nard, myrrh, aloe, clusters of grapes, vineyard, narcissus, cinnamon, Lebanon, flocks, shepherd, king, tower of David. . . . If the Yahwist influence does not appear explicitly, is it not there in filigree, in the complex of thought and expression? Is this not the way, without revealing itself expressly, that it informs the development and the doctrine of the classic works of Wisdom?

It is understandable, therefore, how well the originality of the Canticle stands out when compared with the writings which have been invoked in order to give it a naturalist interpretation. It is only natural that love poems show a similarity of expression. Besides, we can well imagine that oriental imagery would illustrate isolated works of this genre in the same glistening colors in Palestine, Assyro-Babylonia, Egypt and Arabia. Just as Wisdom literature spread throughout the Orient and encountered Israelite thinkers on its way, so it should not be surprising that this or that type of love-literature—we are thinking especially of the Egyptian—may have provided the author of the Canticle some technical suggestions (dialogue, romantic intrigue, couplets recited by a chorus, etc.). To go further would prove that one has not understood the genius of the Canticle. It is not a common imitation, nor a skillfully handled borrowing or recasting: it is a true creation. Its transcendence is evident.

§ 6. Literary Genre of the Canticle

Despite appearances, the Canticle is not an anthology of poems, in which each is complete in itself, and all together leave the work a mere accidental unity. There is at least an *organic unity*, which our analysis revealed.

Does this unity justify the conclusion that the writing belongs to the dramatic genre? Some, following Panigarola and Jacobi, have thought so. J. Guitton shares this view. As a matter of fact the Canticle does contain a plot, crises, a denouement. It draws characters, particularly the bride and groom on whom it concentrates its attention. In our estimation, we would be dealing with no more than a lyric drama, a cantata in dialogue, composed of long recitations and interludes more sentimental than dynamic.

Besides, it is not a question of history. Even if the Canticle directs one's thought toward an idealized synthesis of the relations of Yahweh and Israel, it does not permit one to extract from it a detailed evolution of this union. It would not be amiss, however, to see there a future projection of God's fidelity to His promise, and consequently to allow the work a prophetic character. Would it be unreasonable to compare the Canticle with Daniel and the Apocalypse, two works which in like manner applied the past to the future? The eschatological flavor of a number of passages of the Canticle (2, 11-13; 3, 6-11; 8, 1-2) incline one to accept this view.

§ 7. Date and Author of the Work

Attribution of the Canticle to Solomon is obviously a literary fiction. As in the case of Proverbs, Ecclesiastes, and Wisdom, it proves no more than that the son of David was considered the originator of the sapiential genre. Besides, the language of the Canticle is full of expressions belonging to the Hebrew of a later age: Aramaisms are numerous. On the other hand many indications point if not to the Greek period (Hellenistic influence is contingent), at least to the Persian period, which is evidenced in several expressions ('egôz, nut: 6, 11; pardes, garden: 5, 1; nerd, nard: 1, 12; karkom, saffron: 4, 14, etc. . . .).

Moreover, is not the postexilic age sufficiently indicated by the basic theme of the work, which supposes a certain reflection upon prophetic data from which it borrows its general development? The age of trials that gave birth to the Book of Job was an apt time to emphasize the irreversibility of

the design of God and the depth of His attachment to Israel.
The "optimistic bent" of the Canticle too reflects very well
the religious fervor which resulted in the reforms of the Jewish community under Nehemias and Esdras. The tone of the
work also accords with the era of political peace of the first
half of the 4th century. Dussaud, Tobac, Ricciotti, and Buzy
likewise consider this epoch the literary period of the
Canticle.

§ 8. Canonicity and Liturgical Use

The silence observed by the Canticle in regard to God, to
the *legal covenant*, to *prophetic preaching*, and to the *great
events* of Israel's history led some rabbis to doubt its inspiration. But the synod of Jamnia considered it necessary to decide, not its introduction, but its maintenance in the Hebrew
canon. Rabbi Aqiba strongly defended this decision in the
second century.

With the exception of Theodore of Mopsuestia, whose interpretation tended to minimize the inspiration of the writing, the Canticle was always regarded as canonical, even
though it is not cited in the New Testament.

The Protestant tradition is equally favorable to its canonicity, even though many contemporary Protestants consider it
a purely profane work.

The missal and breviary frequently cite passages of the
Canticle which they apply, in an accommodated sense, to the
Blessed Virgin and to holy women. Especially to be noted is
the use made of it in the Office and Mass of Mary Magdalen.
That is certainly a precious argument in favor of the allegori-
cal, or at least typical, sense of this work.

Every Christian soul can draw salutary lessons from it.
There is the drama of sin, of repentance, of the conversion
(never ending here below) which shines through the symbols
of the marriage life of Israel and Yahweh. Sin breaks the
bond of love; repentance is necessary to resume intimate

relations with God. Justification is a gratuitous gift, and the return to favor is perfect joy.[8]

[8] The exegesis of the Canticle which we propose seems to receive valuable confirmation in the New Testament. In Ap 12, 1 the woman clothed with the sun and with the moon under her feet is considered by most commentators, including Fr. DUBARLE (Cf. *Mélanges bibliques rédigés en l'honneur de A. Robert*, Paris, 1957, pp. 512-518), as a recollection of Ct 6, 10. The liturgy itself associates the two texts and applies them to the Blessed Virgin. Now Ap 12, 3 clearly brings to mind the ideal Sion of the prophets, spouse of Yahweh, and mother of the people of God in the age of grace (cf. especially Is 60, 19-20; 66, 7-8). Cf. *RB* (1959), pp. 67-72. Ap 3, 20 would seem to refer to Ct 5, 2, and constitute another New Testament confirmation of the allegorical interpretation of the mysterious love poem.

CHAPTER IV

RUTH

BIBLIOGRAPHY

Introductions, translations, commentaries, pp. 25 f. (A. VIN-
CENT, *BJ**; R. TAMISIER, *BPC**; A. SCHULZ, *HSAT** . . .).
P. JOÜON, *Ruth** (Rome, 1924).
C. LATTEY, *The Book of Ruth** (London, 1935).
W. RUDOLPH, *Das Buch Ruth* (Leipzig, 1940).
H. H. ROWLEY, "The Marriage of Ruth," *The Servant of
the Lord and Other Essays* (London, 1952), pp. 163-186.
J. M. MYERS, *The Linguistic and Literary Form of the Book
of Ruth* (Leiden, 1955).
G. KNIGHT, *Ruth and Jonah*[2] (London: SCM, 1956).
A. CLAMER, "Ruth," *DTC*, XIV, 1 (Paris, 1939), cols. 373-
382.
M. HALLER, "Ruth," *Die Fünf Megilloth* (Tübingen, 1940).
L. P. SMITH, "The Book of Ruth," *IB* (1953).
THORNHILL, "The Greek Text of the Book of Ruth," *VT*, 3
(1953), pp. 236-249.
G. GLANZMAN, "The Origin and Date of the Book of Ruth,"
CBQ, 21 (1959), pp. 201-207.

In the LXX and the Vulgate the Book of Ruth stands between the Book of Judges and the first Book of Samuel. The
modern Hebrew Bible places it in the canon of the *Ketûbîm*,
among the *Megillôt*, between the Canticle and Lamentations.
It is difficult to determine which of these traditions represents the order of the primitive Hebrew canon.

Origen and St. Jerome claimed that originally Ruth was
joined to Judges as a kind of third appendix. Melito of Sardis
and St. Athanasius likewise placed it in their canons after

Judges. The order of the modern Hebrew Bible, which is of recent date, especially concerning the *Ketûbîm* (cf. Bentzen, *Introd.* I, 32), is not a decisive witness against these assertions.

Nevertheless it would be difficult to admit that the Book of Ruth was transferred from the more esteemed canon of the prophets to the less esteemed canon of the holy writings. It would be better to grant its insertion among the "former prophets" as retrospectively justified by the opening words of the work (1, 1: "Once in the time of the Judges") and the purpose of the story (the ancestry of David). Moreover, the Babylonian Talmud (Baba Bathra, 14b), which holds that Ruth was written by Samuel (and that Job was a contemporary of Moses), did not dare to list Ruth outside the canon of the *Ketûbîm*, where it places it at the head of the group, ahead of Psalms. Is this not a proof that the authentic place of the Book of Ruth was among the Writings?

§ 1.   Content of the Work

In the age of the Judges, Elimelech of Bethlehem was forced by a famine to emigrate to Moab with his wife Noemi and his two sons Mahalon and Chelion. He dies there, and the two sons marry Moabites, Ruth and Orpha. Then they too die.

After the famine had ended, the three widows leave Moab for Juda. But Orpha accedes to the entreaties of her mother-in-law, and returns to her fatherland. Ruth, however, stays at Noemi's side and goes to Bethlehem with her. It is the time of the barley harvest.

Since the two women had only meager means, Ruth gleans where the harvesters have passed. In doing this she meets Booz, a rich owner and relative of Elimelech. He is very considerate of her.

Heeding the suggestions of her mother-in-law, Ruth musters courage to ask Booz to exercise his right of "goel" in her favor. One night she goes up to her benefactor while he sleeps on his floor, and covers herself with a corner of his cloak.

Booz understands Ruth's gesture, and promises to accede to her wishes, if a closer relative of Elimelech is willing to forfeit his right to him. After this other relative forfeits his right at the city gate in the presence of the ancients, Booz solemnly takes possession of Elimelech's land and takes Ruth as his wife with the obligation of providing legal offspring for the deceased. Of this union is born Obed, father of Jesse and grandfather of David.

§ 2.   The Characteristics of the Writing

For anyone who reads it after Josue and Judges, the Book of Ruth evokes an emotional idyl that rests the spirit from the intensity of combat and the brutal scenes he has just witnessed. The simple and candid atmosphere of the patriarchal age comes again into its own. The account of Samuel's birth too belongs in such a climate.

The noble simplicity of family life, all fidelity and mutual devotion, is described with sober magnificence. Elimelech accepts expatriation in order to provide a living for his family (1, 1); Noemi is more preoccupied about the future of her daughters-in-law than about her own affairs (1, 8-13); Ruth places her attachment to her mother-in-law above all other considerations (1, 14-18); Booz is kind and charitable toward his relative (2, 8-17).

But the principal center of interest of the work goes beyond this framework, or better, brings to it a new dimension. The Book of Ruth allows us to grasp in the concrete the procedure called "goel," the law of solidarity of the clan. It is not a matter here of freeing a relative who has fallen into slavery (Lv 25, 47-49), nor of revenging the blood of a member of the group (Nm 35, 19; Jgs 8, 18-21), but of redeeming the land of Elimelech (Lv 25, 25-28) and marrying Ruth (Dt 25, 5-10). This last obligation was known under the name of "levirate law." It pertained to the next of kin—nor-

mally a brother of the deceased—to exercise the rights and
duties of goel. The words "near relative" and goel were used
interchangeably (cf. 3, 12: "if I am goel . . ."). Thus we see
that when Ruth, at the urging of her mother-in-law, pleads
with Booz to assume the classic obligation, the latter accepts
only after the nearer relative forfeits his right (3, 12-13; 4,
1-12).

We conclude likewise from the Book of Ruth that marriages between Israelites and foreigners were not so strongly
prohibited by law. Neither Mahalon nor Chelion is repre-
hended in the least for marrying a Moabite, and it would require a lack of feeling to protest the action of Booz who, by
introducing Ruth into the people of Yahweh, was to assure
the birth of David and become a link in the ancestral line of
the Messias (Mt 1, 5).

§ 3. Date of the Work

Faced with a writing that seems so classical and natural, we
are tempted to accept the opinion suggested by the LXX and
the Vulgate and to date the Book of Ruth, with the Talmud-
ists, in the age of Samuel. Have not some ancient and modern commentators (Keil, Cassel, H. Weiss, Schenz, Cornely-
Hagen) subscribed to this opinion?

Lamy, Kaulen-Hoberg, Seisenberger, Goettsberger did not
consider it certain. Anyone who has examined the text in
depth cannot reasonably hold that opinion.

A few superficial observations suffice to place the redaction
after the end of the age of the Judges (1, 1) and by no means
before the reign of David (4, 18). The archeological parenthesis between 4, 6 and 4, 8, which does not seem an editorial addition, makes it apparent that the symbolic removal
of the sandal had not been in use for a long time when the
author wrote. But it would be hazardous to allege on the
basis of this short verse that the Deuteronomic era was already long passed (Lods), because the event recorded in Dt
25, 9 does not have the same meaning as that in Ru 4, 8

(Vincent): it could be considered an addition to the custom which it supposes. If the goel does not remove his shoe, the offended widow removes it by force and spits in his face. Accordingly Dt 25, 9 presupposes the ceremony recorded in Ru 4, 7 (Rudolph).

Nevertheless, other indications suggest a date later than Deuteronomy. Thus in Ruth (1, 9-13; 3, 1) the remarriage by levirate law seems to have as principal aim the happiness of the widow, while in Dt 25, 5-10 the aim was first and foremost to keep the name of the deceased husband from falling into oblivion (cf. Ru 4, 9-10).

Even though the Aramaisms are not so numerous that their presence alone would suffice to consign the work to a recent age, certain neologisms (1, 13: *nâsâh nâšîm*, to take a wife, instead of the classic *lâqah'iššâh*, Gn 4, 18; 6, 2; 11, 29; 12, 19; 24, 4. 7, etc. . . . ; *âgan*, in niphal, to forbid (marriage), a Talmudic formula of Aramaic origin; 4, 7: *qiyyam*, to validate; cf. Est 9, 31-32; Ez 13, 6, in place of *qômêm*; 1, 13: *sibber*, in the sense of to hope for, to expect, instead of to reduce to pieces, to break, Ex 32, 19 (E); 34, 1 (J); *hâlahên*, what is the reason for . . . ; cf. Dn 2, 6. 9; 4, 24, in place of *lâmâh* or *lammâh*, Is 1, 11) leave no possibility of considering a preexilic date.

Finally, the place that Ruth seems to have occupied in the primitive Jewish canon is convincing evidence that its redaction was postexilic. Its exterior aspect and its object, however, led it to be placed among the "former prophets."

§ 4. The Author's Purpose

We grant that the hypothesis of a recent date favors the opinion that finds in the author's plan a somewhat aggressive intention underlying the calm surface of the account.

Without doubt not all historical preoccupation should be excluded. Even if one admits that the book's conclusion (4, 18-22; cf. 1 Par 2, 10-15) is an obvious addition (because Obed does not appear to be the offspring of Mahalon or of

Elimelech, despite 4, 10. 17), and that the conclusion of the story (4, 17) could have been revised (because the text does not present the expected formula or name), nevertheless the author certainly wanted to make known a tradition about the origins of David.

It is equally incontestable that an intention of illustrating family virtues was not alien to the author's perspective. The description stands out too well not to have been intentional. We encounter here a "morality story."

This stage of thought, at which Gunkel and Gressmann stop, should be further developed. Beneath the story, so simple in appearance, lies a polemic concern: *non sine felle columbinus*. Has it been sufficiently observed that Ruth "the Moabite" is insistently presented as a foreigner to the Chosen People? Notwithstanding that, she enters into an Israelite family; she accepts Yahweh as her God; she conducts herself with the utmost loyalty towards her relatives; she merits the praise of her neighbors and divine favor. She will be David's great-grandmother!

Certainly Ruth is a special case. It is by the way of goel and the levirate law that the foreigner becomes an Israelite citizen. But precisely, is there not in this an indication in favor of some mixed marriages, an insistence on the validity of the practice, at least when it is in accord with family virtues? All the more so since the writer seems to take pleasure in recalling a whole group of customs: redemption tied to the levirate law, the shoe ritual, adoption . . . It would seem that that is enough to suggest that the story is the author's protest against a certain contemporary rigorism. One is imperceptibly led to consider the Book of Ruth as an appeal for moderation in the application of the measures taken by Esdras and Nehemias against mixed marriages (Esd 9–10; Neh 13, 1-3. 23-27), at least in special circumstances. It is an appeal to a fuller appreciation of a past whose customs produced beautiful examples of virtue. The work must have pleased a good number of contemporaries. It is a fact that the prescriptions of Esdras and Nehemias encountered fierce opposition. Did they not arrive at the extremes that we read about in Deu-

teronomy (23, 4-7; cf. Neh 13, 1-3) concerning Ammonites
and Moabites, and in Leviticus (18, 16; 20, 21) by prohibit-
ing any union of brother-in-law and sister-in-law, without regard for the levirate law? And was it not somewhat difficult
to reconcile the divorces demanded by Esdras (10, 1-11) and
the strict interpretation of Malachias (2, 14-16) who
preached fidelity to the first spouse?

By means of this reaction—and this is the essential point—
one sees likewise the tendency to uproot the hatred that Judaism encouraged between Jews and pagans. Like the Book of
Jonas, that of Ruth has universalist tendencies. The God of
Israel does not disdain the homage of a foreigner. He places
one in the ancestry of the Messias.

We can thus appreciate the importance of the Book of
Ruth in the historical context of postexilic Israel, and even
perhaps use this context to give the work a more precise date.
In this regard, one can hardly go amiss if he settles for the
years which followed the weighty decisions concerning mixed
marriages.

§ 5. Historicity

The characters that dominate the narrative, the underlying
intention of the work, the circumstances and late date of the
redaction—these are so many arguments which put one on
guard concerning the historicity of the content of the work.

There could be no doubt that the Book of Ruth, like that
of Esther, is a work of art whose simplicity does not exclude
a certain literary arrangement. Certain contrasts are obviously
contrived: Orpha, who takes the easy way out (1, 14a), makes
the steadfastness of Ruth stand out (1, 14b-17); the near
relative who forfeits his right because of self-interest (4, 4-6)
brings the generosity of Booz to the fore (4, 9-10). The
laments directed to Noemi (1, 19) are counterbalanced by
the congratulations given her (4, 12-17). These are features
which, without presenting an obstacle to historical truth, are
evidence of a plan of presentation.

The symbolism of the names is somewhat more disturbing: Noemi, my pleasantness; Mahalon, languor; Chelion, consumption; Orpha, she who turns her back; Booz (Boaz= Baalaz: Baal is strong): cf. Salambo=sâlêm Baal. Does this not give the writing a certain symbolic value?

On the other hand, the presentation of the past contains certain valid references. Furthermore, it was only by appealing to history that the opposition to the legal prescriptions of the age of Esdras and Nehemias could find an audience. And it cannot be excluded that when David sought a refuge for his relatives in Moab (1 Sm 22, 3-4), he did it because of his ancestry.

All things considered, it is wise not to reject the hypothesis of a primitive tradition which the fame of David enhanced. The apparently symbolic names are perhaps the product of popular fancy. The emphasis given to the custom of goel would be the storyteller's own contribution. He has passed on to us a pleasing account, nearer to what we call a short story than to a midrash of the ponderous type we find in Paralipomenon.

CHAPTER V

LAMENTATIONS

BIBLIOGRAPHY

Introductions, translations, commentaries, pp. 25 f. (L. DENNEFELD, BPC*; A. GELIN, BJ*; T. PAFFRATH, HSAT* . . .).

G. RICCIOTTI, Le Lamentazione di Geremia* (Turin, 1924).

A. CLAMER, "Lamentations," DTC, VIII, 2 (Paris, 1935), cols. 2526-2537.

W. RUDOLPH, Die Klagelieder (Leipzig, 1939).

M. HALLER, "Die Klagelieder," Die fünf Megilloth (Tübingen, 1940).

A. GELIN, "Lamentations," SDB, V (Paris, 1950), cols. 237-251.

G. KNIGHT, Esther, Song of Songs and Lamentations (London: SCM, 1955).

N. K. GOTTWALD, Studies in the Book of Lamentations (London: SCM, rev. ed. 1962).

B. ALBREKTSON, Studies in the Text and Theology of the Book of Lamentations (Lund, 1963).

This work is classified among the *Ketubim* in the Hebrew Bible, where it is called *'eykâh* (how; cf. 1, 1; 2, 1; 4, 1) or *qînôth* (lament). In the LXX, under the title Θρῆνοι, and in the Vulgate, under that of *Lamentationes*, it is placed immediately after the Prophet Jeremias. It belongs to the group of the *megillot*. It was read each year on the 9th of Ab, the day of fast commemorating the burning of Jerusalem in 586.

§ 1. Contents

The collection is composed of five poems, the common subject of which is the destruction of Jerusalem and the Temple
by Nabuchodonosor.

In the first poem the author recalls the fall of Jerusalem,
the enslaved queen sorrowing, weeping, abandoned, humili-
ated, deprived of leaders and consolers (1, 1-11). The holy
city, emotionally personified, implores the compassion of men
and the pardon of God (1, 12-22).

The second poem describes divine punishment's most terrible aspects. Yahweh has acted as an enemy: He has leveled
the sanctuary and the altar. The Israelites who survived the
sword succumb to famine (2, 1-12). Sion is being reminded
why God treats her thus and how she is to take refuge in
Him. The poet takes Yahweh as witness to the misery of His
people (2, 13-22).

Although the calamities had in their variety and intensity
reached the point of tragedy (3, 1-21), the poet nevertheless
expresses in the third poem his confidence that God, although
He has severely chastised His people, has not annihilated
them. Their sins must have been many (3, 22-42). Would
that the aid of God come to sweep away the enemy (3,
43-66)!

In the fourth poem the poet describes the miserable state
of even the nobles and princes (4, 1-12). It is the sins of the
priests and false prophets that are the cause of all the misfortune (4, 13-20). Let Edom rejoice; its turn will come (4,
21-23)!

The fifth poem, entitled the *Prayer of Jeremias the Prophet*
in the Vulgate, is an ardent supplication which the author,
in the name of his brethren, directs to the Lord who has punished the nation. The plea is expressed in heartrending terms
(5, 1-6): the sons are paying for their fathers, the worst of
afflictions have been visited upon them, sadness holds sway

over all flesh (5, 7-18). May God at last have mercy (5, 19-22)!

§ 2. Literary Genre

We are dealing with dirges, funeral wails. The Israelites, like all oriental peoples, were acquainted with funeral rites which involved either hired mourners (Jer 9, 17; cf. Am 5, 16-17), or relatives and friends of the deceased (2 Sm 1, 17; 3, 33), accompanied by musical instruments, especially the flute (Mt 9, 23). The chants proclaimed the profound change death had brought about. The opening exclamation, *'ey, 'eykâh*, underlined this metamorphosis—what a difference! It is true that in this way a person showed his personal sorrow, but he also thought that he was fulfilling a religious obligation toward the departed (cf. Ex 20, 12). The name of Yahweh, however, was not mentioned in these couplets. He was not the God of the dead, but of the living (Ps 113B [115]; Mt 22, 32).

The personification of groups induced poets to expand the genre of the dirge to apply it to individuals embodying the state or to nations considered as persons. Most frequently these dirges by extension take on the aspect of satiric compositions addressed to enemy princes or states (Na 3, 18-19; Is 14, 4-21; Ez 26, 15-18; 27, 3-36; 41, 10-18; 42, 17-18). But some are also motivated by the misfortunes which brought Israel to the brink of the grave: imminence of the exile (Jer 9, 7-22; cf. 10, 17. 18-19. 20); public calamity (Jer 14, 2-6); destruction (Am, 5, 2); etc.

Some of these dirges are presented in the framework of a public gathering where the laments over the calamities are pronounced by the people or their representative and accompanied by ardent supplications (Ps 73 [74]; 78 [79]; 79 [80]; 88 [89]; Jer 14, 2-6; Is 63, 7—64, 11: note 63, 19b—64, 1, a distraught appeal to the coming of God the Saviour). Others are more openly individual (Ps 3; 4; 5; 7; 21 [22]).

The Lamentations of Jeremias are related to these various

forms; they are as a kind of synthesis of all of them. The 1st, 2nd, and 4th poems are, on the whole, public laments marked by vehement invocations of Yahweh, urgent appeals, and earnest confessions. The 5th lament is clearly a community prayer. As for the 3rd, it assumes a more individual character, like the confessions of Jeremias (Jer 11, 18—12, 6; 15, 10-21; 17, 12-18, 18-23; 20, 7-18) and the laments of Job (16, 8-17; 17, 6-9; 30, 1-23 . . .), without ceasing to be evocative of the national catastrophe, and as such an echo of the common sadness of Israel. Could it be that this third lamentation, which in theme and imagery is close to the Book of Job, depends on it? In that case it would be more recent. It is also true that the dependence could be inverted. The question merits further study.

§ 3.   Literary Evaluation

The metric and strophic pattern of Lamentations gives evidence of a conscious literary effort whose artificiality could have degenerated had the fundamental theme not been so tragic.

Each poem has as many strophes as there are letters in the Hebrew alphabet (22). All of them except the fifth are acrostic, that is, the initial letter of each verse follows the order of the normal alphabet (*pe* and *'ain* are inverted except in the first poem). The third is peculiar in that each of the three verses which compose its strophes begins with the same letter.

Added to these alphabetic arrangements are symmetrical repetitions of one or more words, a method of stressing the more important thoughts and making the structure of the strophe more evident.

The first four poems observe the rhythm of the *qînâ*. Dropping the voice on a shorter second member gives the impression of sorrow, which the author so obviously meant to express. In the fifth, the frequent repetition of the same ending produces a sort of rhyme, even when the ending does not always coincide with the end of a member.

The literary value of these poems has been universally acknowledged. After so many centuries, the intense emotion that emerges from them moves us still, just as we marvel at their wealth of imagery. The last one in particular remains one of the most heartrending cries that ever sprung from an anguished heart. Palestrina must have thought the same; he made it the theme of one of his best compositions.

§ 4.   Date and Author

Certain historical references verify the event indicated in the work, the destruction of Jerusalem and the Temple. It suffices to recall 1, 1-4 (the deserted city, suspended cult); 1, 19 (famine during the siege); 2, 7 (invasion of the Temple and palace); 2, 9 (gates beaten down, king and leaders in exile); 2, 15 (insults of passers-by); 4, 17 (defection of the ally Egypt); 4, 19 (the captured fugitives; cf. Jer 39, 4-5). There is every indication that the terror and anguish still hold sway. It is usually admitted that Lamentations were composed sometime after 586, certainly before the liberation (538). It should be observed that the 2nd and 4th poems seem to be the oldest. Rudolph goes even further and dates the 3rd and 5th poems at the beginning of the invasion which preceded the fall of Jerusalem, and the 1st on the morrow of the siege of 597. In any case it is true that the spirit of these poetic pieces is shot through with the literary thought of Jeremias (3), Ezechiel (2 and 4), and anticipates in places (especially 1, 3, 5) the tone of Second-Isaias.

The influence of Jeremias is predominant throughout the work (cf. 1, 15; 2, 13: virgin, daughter of Sion, and Jer 8, 21. 22; 14, 17—; Lam 1, 16; 2, 11. 18; 3, 48. 49: fountain of tears, and Jer 9, 1. 18; 13, 17; 14, 17—; Lam 1, 14: chained neck, and Jer 27, 2—; Lam 1, 14; 4, 13-15: sins of the priests and false prophets, and Jer 2, 8; 5, 32; 14, 13; 23, 10. 40, etc. . .). It was only natural that in the search for an author the choice would settle upon this prophet, whom a text of Paralipomenon (2 Par 35, 25) calls the author of lamentations. After all, was he not the witness who was most closely and sadly related to the events? It is evidently for that reason that the Jewish tradition, represented by the LXX, the Targum and the Talmud, attributes the work to the prophet of Anathoth. Origen (*In Ps*, 1), St. Hilary (*Prol. in Psalt.*, II, 15), St. Epiphanius (*Haer.*, VIII, 6), St. Jerome (*prol. Gal.*) seem to attest that in the beginning the work followed Jeremias in the Hebrew. The transferal could have been caused by liturgical use.

Still these arguments are not decisive. Internal criticism presents a number of difficulties which weaken the force of the alleged connections between the two books. Could Jeremias have subjected himself to such a complicated and artificial genre of poetry? How could he have celebrated the memory of Sedechias (4, 20; cf. Jer 22, 13-28; 37, 17-21), or have recalled the hope of aid from Egypt (4, 17; cf. Jer 37, 7-8), or have been a witness against the existence of prophetic revelation after the national catastrophe (2, 9; cf. Jer 42, 4-22), or still extol collective retribution (5, 7; cf. Jer 31, 29)? Furthermore, the reminiscences of Ezechiel and the Book of Consolation turn one's thought to a less unilateral hypothesis. And while it is true the title in the LXX is found likewise in Latin manuscripts and the Sixto-Clementine edition, it remains true that it is lacking in the Massoretic text and the Peshitta. This would seem to give greater importance to the correctness of the position the Book of Lamentations occupies in the Hebrew Bible, among the *Ketubim*.

Not only is it doubtful that Jeremias is the author of the work, but when the complexity of literary dependencies is examined, it would be reasonable to give some credit to the opinion of Eissfeldt and Haller (1940), who envision the plausibility of several authors. Even Rudolph (1939), who favors unity of origin, was constrained, by the date he placed on the first poem (597), to attribute it to a special author.

§ 5. Liturgical Use

The Catholic Church has introduced the Lamentations into the office of Holy Week. The Church sees in them, just as the Jews of the exilic and postexilic era did (cf. Za 7, 3; 8, 19), an expression of repentant sorrow, the fruit of faith in the irreversible salvific will of God, and a stimulant to confidence in His merciful pardon.

CHAPTER VI

ECCLESIASTES (QÔHELETH)

BIBLIOGRAPHY

Introductions, translations, commentaries, pp. 25 f. (D. Buzy, BPC*; R. Pautrel, BJ*; A. Allgeier, HSAT*; G. A. Barton, ICC . . .).

E. Podechard, L'Ecclésiaste* (Paris, 1912).

H. W. Hertzberg, Der Prediger (Leipzig, 1932).

E. M. de Manresa, Ecclesiastes* (Barcelona, 1935).

M. Haller, "Der Prediger," Die fünf Megilloth (Tübingen, 1940).

R. Gordis, The Wisdom of Ecclesiastes (New York, 1945).

J. J. Weber, Job et l'Ecclésiaste* (Paris, 1947).

A. Bea, Liber Ecclesiastae qui ab Hebraeis dicitur Quohelet* (Rome, 1950).

H. L. Ginsberg, Studies in Koheleth (New York, 1950); "The Structure and Contents of the Book of Koheleth," Suppl. VT, 5 (1955), pp. 138-149.

M. Danhood, "Canaanite-Phoenician Influence in Qoheleth," Biblica, 33 (1952), pp. 191-221; "Qoheleth and Recent Discoveries," Biblica, 39 (1958), pp. 302-318; "Qoheleth and Northwest Semitic Philology," Biblica, 43 (1962), pp. 349-365.

G. R. Driver, "Problems and Solutions," VT, 4 (1954), pp. 225-245.

R. Gordis, Koheleth (New York, 1955).

R. Murphy, "The 'Pensées' of Coheleth," CBQ, 17 (1955), pp. 304-314.

O. S. Rankin, "The Book of Ecclesiastes," IB (1956).

E. Jones, Proverbs and Ecclesiastes (London: SCM, 1962).

R. B. Y. Scott, Proverbs and Ecclesiastes (Garden City, N. Y.: Doubleday, 1965).

The term "Ecclesiastes," a transcription of the Greek Ἐκκλησιαστής, corresponds to the Hebrew *qôheleth*, which comes from the root *qhl* whose sense in the qal form is to assemble. *Qôheleth* then as participle would signify either the assembler or the preacher of an assembly. The same meaning is arrived at if the word is derived from the substantive *qâhâl* which itself means assembly. In any case it is not necessary to identify the person thus designated with Wisdom, as might be suggested by the reference to Prv 8 and the feminine ending of *qôheleth*. On the one hand, in the passages in the work where we meet this term (1, 2. 12; 12, 8. 9 and 7, 27; read here: *'âmar haqqôhelet*), the modifier is in the masculine. On the other, it is known that nouns which signify a function or connote a quality or title take the feminine ending (cf. Esd 2, 55: *sôferet*; 57: *pôkeret*).

Taking these considerations into account, *qôheleth* would be the outstanding preacher, the master of Wisdom, the head of a group of sages.[1] To consider the assembly itself in reaction against the preacher (Pautrel), is an interesting suggestion, but one difficult to prove.

§ 1.   General View of the Work

The author of Ecclesiastes proposes to draw up the balance sheet of the good and evil that constitute the lot of human life, and to investigate whether this life is worth living (1, 3). The reader gathers immediately (1, 2-21) the pejorative character which marks the enquiry.

The investigation is erratic. It is not presented under the form of a dialogue, but rather a monologue or soliloquy. After having investigated various opinions, the author discusses them, and passes on to other forms of thought which present him the occasion to correct or rectify the previous opinions. The developments are often partial, fragmentary, controlled by narrow points of view.

[1] PODECHARD, *op. cit.*, p. 134; JOÜON, in *Bi* (1921), p. 53 ff.

Still it is possible to distinguish two series of reflections, the one built into the other. The first is by far the more important, and develops the book's main theme. It stands out for the critical and sharp turn the inquiry takes, and this relates it to Job. The second is much briefer and consists of small groups of opinions which counterbalance the preceding developments. And this relates it to Proverbs.

Tobac has shown how well this general conception, when applied to the detail of the work, reveals immediately its composite character. We here follow his analysis.

After the prologue (1, 1-11), which puts us in the ideological climate of the whole work, three sections describe the disillusionment that Wisdom and pleasures leave (1, 12—2, 26); human efforts ruled by events, tyrannized by those in command, destined for death (3); the contradictions found in the social order (4, 1—5, 8). In this context a double series of maxims appears: the first group (4, 9-12) suggests, in reply to 4, 7-8 (an appeal for the solitary life), the advantages of the common life; the second group (4, 17—5, 6), in a poorly chosen context, contains counsels relative to cult.

There follows a fourth section on the deceptions of riches (5, 9—6, 12). A third series of sayings (7, 1-12) opposes the stabilizing practice of moderating Wisdom to excesses in conduct (wantonness, mockery, anger). We read much the same in the fifth section: disillusionment caused by the contradiction in the lot of the just and the wicked (7, 13—9, 10). Two more series of advisory sayings aim to lessen the paradox; the one appeals to the universality of sin (7, 18-22), the other to submission to authority and the eventual judgment (8, 1-8).

The sixth and last section recalls the fickleness of fate, no matter what conduct, work, talent, or wisdom one employs to determine it (9, 11—11, 6). Just as previously, two more series of maxims intervene: the one praises Wisdom (9, 17—10, 4), the other, virtue and work (10, 10—11, 6). The allegory of old age (12, 1-8) is nothing more than a literary prolongation (we would call it a "sequence") whose gloomy character cannot but accentuate and urge the precept on which it hangs: Be mindful of your Creator . . . (12, 1).

The epilogue contains a brief praise of Qôhelet and the words of the sages (12, 9-12). It resumes in closing the impressions which emerge from the book: fear God, obey Him, prepare for the judgment (12, 14).

§ 2. Doctrinal Content

A deeper examination reveals that the literary complexity of the work is not without relation to its doctrinal complexity. Ecclesiastes has many facets. It is peppered with ideological contrasts, but still replenished by a pure religious spring.

There can be no doubt that, against the melancholy background of this long "confession," the dissonant elements are the first to stand out and clash. The author appears *disillusioned*. He sees only a reason for sadness in the perpetual movement of the universe (1, 4-10) and in the miserable state of mankind (1, 14. 18; 2, 1. 11. 16-23). So much so that death seems preferable to life (2, 17; 4, 2; 6, 3). Nevertheless, here and there, the reaction is to accuse this disillusioned man of epicurism. No matter how lamentable life is in his eyes, it still leaves open the possibility of enjoying *earthly pleasures*, especially those of the table (2, 24-25; 3, 12-13. 22; 5, 17-19; 8, 15; 9, 7-10; 11, 7. 8). Is this not the best that man can hope for, in effect, his final goal (2, 24; 3, 22; 5, 17c)? Naturally, such an attitude is conceivable only at the price of a certain rejection of the afterlife. And that is the point: Ecclesiastes seems to reject even that admittedly minimum of Revelation concerning the next life, which has filtered down. He is, in effect, so skeptical that he is not content to call into question the rightness of providential dispositions (3, 16; 6, 1-3; 8, 10. 14; 9, 5). The ever present incertitude which envelops the conditions of the future life seem to leave him with not only the unsolved problem of otherworldly retribution, but also even that of the immortality of the soul (3, 18-21).

But this pessimist, this epicurian, this skeptic, as he has been called, presents himself as a convinced Yahwist. For Ecclesiastes affirms his *faith in God*. He praises divine Wisdom (7, 12. 20; 9, 13-18) and convincingly professes the reality of Providence (3, 11. 14-15; 8, 17; 11, 5). It is God who gives and takes away life (5, 17; 8, 15; 9, 9; 12, 7), riches (5, 18; 6, 2), joy (2, 24; 3, 13; 5, 18-19); it is He who distributes good and bad fortune (7, 14). In addition, Qôheleth does not ignore the distinction between good and evil (3, 16; 4, 1; 5, 7; 7, 16; 8, 10. 14; 9, 2), and if he confesses ignorance about the nature of eternal retribution, at least he has no doubt about a future judgment (3, 17; 11, 9; 12, 13-14). Thus the notion of a moral act does not entirely escape him (2, 26; 7, 27; 8, 5. 13). So many positive convictions hold his skepticism in check.

Could not one say the same about his epicurism? Though Qôheleth understandably does not rise to the height of Christian asceticism, he does hold that earthly pleasures are gifts of God (2, 24; 3, 13; 5, 18; 9, 7). He condemns their abuse (7, 26-27; 9, 3); he goes so far as to proclaim their vanity (2, 1-2; 11, 8-10). These convictions stand in contrast to hedonism.

While we cannot justify the paradoxical lesson of optimism that some ancients claimed to discover in the work, even the author's pessimism does not exclude opinions that reveal to us at least a friend of existence (11, 7), who has confidence in the foreknowledge of God (6, 10), his sovereign judge (12, 14) and the goal of man (12, 7). In a word, he is a realist.

The coexistence of such dissonant themes, together with the unusual structure of the book, poses a problem, that of its composition.

§ 3. Composition of the Work

The hypothesis of a primitive work which successive authors edited is unavoidable. So thought Siegfried and Podechard.

The present form of several sections partly substantiates this view. Attention centers especially on the epilogue (12, 9-14). There the title Qôheleth is twice given to the author (12, 9. 10), while he attributes it to himself only once (1, 12). The author of the epilogue, then, must be distinct from Qôheleth. As a fervent disciple of the master, he probably also edited those passages in which the Sage is spoken of in the third person (1, 2; 7, 27; 12, 8).

The maxims inserted in the course of the work which are in metric form (4, 9-12; 4, 17—5, 6; 7, 1-12. 18. 22; 8, 1-4; nearly all of 10; 12, 2-6) betray a different hand. Do they not seem to mitigate the statements of Qôheleth?

This determination to correct is more evident in 12, 13-14; the author of the epilogue has recourse to a settling of accounts, while this perspective is more limited in the rest of the work. And would it be an exaggeration to say that other verses fit better in the same class as 12, 13-14 than in the general outlook of the work (cf. 2, 26ab; 3, 17; 7, 26b; 8, 2b. 5-8. 11. 13; 11, 7b; 12, 1a)?

Thus we are led to distinguish from Qôheleth, to whom belongs the substratum of the work, an epiloguist, a Sage (hâkâm), a pious author (hâsîd), and perhaps even more editors. Orthodoxy is not thereby offended, since Catholic circles admit that inspiration can use a number of writers to produce the work in its present form. But on the scientific plane this analysis remains problematic, except in the case of the epilogue. And Kuenen is probably right in saying that it is more difficult to deny the unity of the work than it is to demonstrate it.

§ 4.   One Author

In effect, the coexistence of contrasting opinions can be explained in the case of a single author. Without refusing to admit, in such a fluctuating matter, the hypotheses which recur, more or less successfully, to stylistic criteria (presentation of diverse opinions, hints of a tortured soul, incomplete or interrupted editing), might not one simply see in the work the result of a critical reflection, which, while not arriving at a complete understanding, much less a solution, of the problems of the contingency of things created and of the retribution of good and evil, betrays the confused state of observations of unequal value? In reality, Qôheleth is a tortured Yahwist who meditates on the picture of disoriented human nature, and strives to describe its frustrations. Instead of situating the problem of the human condition above the accidental contingencies which give it such a divided appearance, he prefers to place it in the concrete context of experience in which, as a matter of fact, mankind is involved. This does not prohibit him from sensing, or even affirming, the solutions that faith in Yahweh offers for the unrest and uncertainty of the human spirit. Not that he presents faith as an easy solution. One even gets the impression that he arrives at it only with effort. There is, however, no contradiction between those alternatives of doubt and conviction. Did not Paul too experience like agonies, and commend to the grace of God the task of realizing that unity to which the disconcerting duality that we are aspires? And will one not find in St. Augustine, Pascal, and many other troubled souls, the same answers that Ecclesiastes gave?

§ 5. Date of the Work

Such a state of soul, however, demands placing the work in a quite recent age. Now it is clear that the reference to Solomon (1, 1. 12) is no obstacle to a late date; the work's Aramaisms, and its appreciation of royal administration (1, 17; 4, 13; 5, 7; 10, 5-7. 20) are incompatible with Solomonic origin. Qôheleth is not the son of David. The author makes use of a literary fiction of his day. He introduces Solomon, the originator of Wisdom Literature, and, in the circumstances, he undoubtedly demonstrates understanding, because Solomon would not perhaps, in some respects, have refused to subscribe to this or that opinion of the work. That is the most one can say.

On the other hand, without going so far as to claim that the writing depends directly upon some Greek master or a Hellenist system of philosophy, it is certain that it fits well in the world of thought which characterized the Hellenistic epoch. The breaking of ideological ground at which the Sages worked could hardly have attained before this period the state of perfection which an analysis of Ecclesiastes supposes. In certain respects Qôheleth seems to be a contemporary of Job. Both write about similar problems: the enigma of life, suffering, evil, the uncertainty of the fate of man. Neither of them gives them a completely satisfying solution. They leave the ultimate explanation to be sought in God, in a still imprecise future life. Nevertheless, Ecclesiastes marks progress over Job. The latter considers earthly happiness an adequate satisfaction; Qôheleth goes so far as to join sorrow to the happiness one can experience here below. Job is astonished that the just is not overflowing with good things; Ecclesiastes maintains that even if he has his fill, he is still not happy. Earthly insatisfaction creates, more deeply in the Book of Qôheleth than in the Book of Job, the emptiness which Revelation will fill. Ecclesiastes is more recent than Job.

Besides, it is incontestible that the climate of the Ptolemaic domination (B.C. 300-170) provided an excellent occasion to present to the Jews questions about the insufficiency of earthly happiness. The world was then moving toward the ease, the comfort, and even the luxury of Greek civilization. Without being a moralist preacher, nor a philosopher who has worked out a thesis, nor a prophet who communicates a message, Qôheleth presents himself as one who recounts familiarly the results of his experience, in order to raise his compatriots to a more precise concept of earthly happiness: "If you want to be happy, enjoy the passing goods of existence, without forgetting that one day God will demand an account of your use of them." If the Jews had accepted Greek culture with these wise reservations, the crisis they were about to face could have been avoided. Wisdom will propose to adapt Judaism to the Greeks; Ecclesiastes seems to have wanted to measure out to the Jews the satisfaction they could draw from Hellenism.

§ 6. Ecclesiastes in the Progress of Revelation

The reflections of Qôheleth are centered on the nothingness of earthly pleasures. They constitute one of the last steps in the path that will end in the discovery of sanctions beyond the grave. From then on the terrain is sufficiently prepared for the Spirit of God to sow with profit the seeds of the last doctrinal harvest of the Old Testament. The conception of collective retribution was already left far in the past. Insistence on the person, responsible for his acts, permitted the notion of individual retribution to emerge (Jer 31, 29-30; Ez 18; 33). But this still remained in the framework of earthly existence, and consequently exposed to the contradictions of life (Job). It was necessary to rise to the as yet unexplored heights of eternal sanctions. Such an effort supposed that, docile to both divine pedagogy and intellectual reflection, the sages would cease to consider temporal happiness as an unalloyed good, as a sovereign ultimate goal. It is to bring about this detachment that the author of Ecclesiastes dedicates himself with a rude frankness bordering on excess. While still looking with favor on earthly goods, he so forcefully affirms their vanity that imperceptibly he orients the mind of his disciples toward a certain "beyond the grave" preceded by the judgment of God (12, 13). The Book of Wisdom (2–5), in borrowing and developing the oracle of Daniel (12, 1-3), the faith of the seven martyred brothers and their mother (2 Mc 7, 9. 11. 14. 23. 29), as well as the conviction of Judas Machabeus and his historian (2 Mc 12, 43. 46), will open horizons on the destiny of mankind which Christ will illumine (Mt 5, 3-11; 25, 31-46; Lk 16, 19-31 . . .).

§ 7. Canonicity

The Book of Ecclesiastes is protocanonical. It had a place in the Jewish canon in the 1st century of our era (4 Esd 14, 18-47; Josephus, *C. Ap.*, 1, 8); there are no indications that it was not included earlier. The doubts which were raised about its inspiration between 90 and 190 (despite the decision of the synod of Jamnia) were not successful in shaking Jewish belief. It is interesting to note that fragments of the book were found at Qumran. Theodore of Mopsuestia was the only Christian who minimized the inspired character of the work. The Second Council of Constantinople disapproved of his opinion in 553.[2]

[2] Cf. note 5, p. 120.

CHAPTER VII

ESTHER

BIBLIOGRAPHY

Introductions, translations, commentaries, pp. 25 f.
(A. BARUCQ, BJ*; L. SOUBIGOU, BPC*; J. SCHILDENBERGER, HSAT*; L. B. PATON, ICC . . .).

L. BIGOT, Esther*, DTC, V, 1 (Paris, 1924), cols. 850-871.

M. HALLER, "Esther," Die fünf Megillôth (Tübingen, 1940).

T. GASTER, Purim and Hannukkah in Eastern and Western Traditions (New York, 1950).

B. ANDERSON, "The Book of Esther," IB (1954); "The Place of the Book of Esther in the Christian Bible," JR, 30 (1950), pp. 32-43.

G. KNIGHT, Esther, Song of Songs and Lamentations (London: SCM, 1955).

The Book of Esther reads very differently in the Hebrew text and the LXX. The latter contains important passages which are not to be found in the Massoretic text. These fragments, which pose more than one problem, are besides arranged differently in the common Greek text than in the Lucian version, which seems to be a complete re-editing of the whole. Since these additions are listed among the deuterocanonical writings, we do not treat them here. The study of these Greek fragments will be treated in the next part.[1]

[1] Cf. pp. 263 ff.

§ 1.   Content of the Hebrew Work

A young Jewess named Esther, having been chosen queen by
Assuerus after the repudiation of Vasthi, succeeds in saving
her countrymen who were destined by a decree of the king to
extermination. She is guided in her undertakings by her uncle
Mardochai, who is exposed to the hatred of the first minister,
Aman, whom the Jew, loyal to the king, has offended. Esther
obtains Aman's condemnation, and Mardochai becomes first
minister. The extermination decree is changed to an authorization for the Jews to defend their lives. Which is exactly
what they did, massacring, on the day when they themselves
were to have been slaughtered (13th Adar), 75,000 Persians,
without counting those who died the following day. The feast
of Purim recalls the event.

At first view the account leaves an unpleasant impression,
that of exaltation of the hate which existed between the Jews
and the pagans. In fact it is Aman who sets off the drama
(3, 6), but is it not Mardochai who provokes the extreme
reaction against the Jews by his arrogant behavior toward the
minister (3, 2-5)? And does the defense of their life authorize the Jews to abandon themselves to the excess of a massacre
which resembles bitter revenge (9, 1-10)? And what is to be
said of Esther who requests a second day of slaughter (9,
11-15)! In addition, the name of God is not mentioned in
the work. We could consider as an indication of disdain for
this strange story the fact that neither Christ nor the authors
of the New Testament cite it, especially since they were acquainted wtih the more religious Greek version.

Still, a more attentive reading of the book allows us to
make a less severe judgment. God is not named, but He nonetheless directs the action. As in Racine's "Athalie," He is the
principal actor. The characters, moreover, display by their
actions their belief in Providence. Does not Mardochai appeal discretely to Providence when he suggests to Esther the
meaning of her elevation to royalty (4, 13-14)? It would be

reasonable to regard likewise as appeals for heavenly aid the penitential acts of Mardochai (4, 1), the invitation to fast addressed by the queen to all the Jews of Susan, and the example she and her servants give (4, 16). Mardochai and Esther, instructed about the mighty deeds of God in Israel, and convinced of the ascendency which Yahweh wanted to exercise in the midst of the pagans (Gn 45, 5-8; Dn 1, 9. 17), could not believe that in the end justice would succumb to iniquity. The faith of Abraham, so deeply anchored in the souls of his descendants, expected from the Almighty the revenge of good over evil. And it is the inevitability of such revenge that explains somewhat the massacre, undertaken, let it be remembered, in a tactic of legitimate defense (8, 10), since the decree of extermination of the Jews, untouchable like the sovereign decisions of the Achaemenids, could not be annulled.

The Greek fragments develop the import of the Hebrew work; they do not give it a new meaning.

§ 2.   Historical Evaluation

The literary genre of the work will permit us to determine its historical value.

One would willingly enough incline to accept it as objective history, if he were content to take note of the exactness of certain details: distinction between the castle and the city (3, 15, suggested in 8, 14 and 9, 6. 11), between the royal residence and the harems (2, 13. 14); the impulsive and sensual character of the king (1, 11-12; 2, 1. 12; 3, 10; 6, 1-10; 7, 8-10; 8, 7-12; 9, 11-14) attested by history; the intolerance of Aman, who was not a Persian (3, 1); the administrative customs of the Achaemenids (1, 13-21); the irrevocability of the royal decrees (1, 19; 8, 8; cf. 11). But a fictional account can present traits of reality just as well as a work of history.

It is the contrary that cannot be verified. Now in the Book of Esther there are numerous unlikely facts. The impulsive-

ness of the king seems exaggerated: he surrounds himself
with counselors before promulgating the deposition of Vasthi
(1, 13-21), and authorizes without prior deliberation the
massacre of his subjects (8, 11-12). The decree to extermi-
nate the Jews contrasts with the benign tolerance of the
princes toward the Israelites (cf. Esdras-Nehemias). And how
imagine, on the plane of efficiency, the delay of eleven
months (3, 12-15) or of nine months (8, 5. 13) granted the
victims, so much so that the Jews would profit from them,
but not the Persians! In addition, if Amestris was, at the
time of the biblical account, the wife of Xerxes and the
queen of Persia (cf. Herodotus, VII, 61; IX, 108-113), what
likelihood is there of the investitures of Vasthi and Esther?
One would also like to have an explanation of the king's prolonged ignorance of the origins of the heroine, whereas
Mardochai, who is so solicitous for his niece, compromises the
secret by his indiscretion (3, 4) and his comings and goings
(2, 11). Besides, how old would Mardochai be in the reign
of Assuerus (486-465) if he was deported to Babylonia by
Nabuchodonosor in 597?

These indications against the historicity of the Book of
Esther suggest an interpretation of the work in the framework of a literary genre more in accord with its appearance.
The idea of intrigue, at first limited to the rivalry of two
characters, Aman and Mardochai, then extended to the hostility of two peoples, Persian and Jew, reveal a concern in
composition that smacks of the fictional. The characters follow well the author's plan: Aman and Mardochai, firmly set
in an attitude of implacable opposition, cunning and crafty,
wagering the highest stakes; Vasthi and Esther, the one a
victim, the other exalted, the first foretelling in her humiliation the brilliant victory of her rival; Assuerus, a fanciful and
puppet king who is manipulated from both sides with in-
decent facility. The handling of the action, wisely spiced with
incidents which either slow or hasten the pace, interspersed
with pleasant descriptions—this only heightens the impression
that the author, who is obviously familiar with the methods
of dialogue and protocol formulae, is, literarily speaking,
more a dramatist than a historian.

ESTHER   159

Thus we are led to define better the nature of the work by comparing it to other writings which are related to it by quite evident characteristics.

There is a striking resemblance between the canonical book and the account left to us by Herodotus of the false Smerdis, whose imposture is denounced by Otanis with the aid of his daughter, a concubine of the king, and is punished by the massacre of the tribe of the Magians. The third Book of Machabees presents in a Jewish background an account that seems to copy Esther: Ptolemy Philopator, expelled from the Temple by the Jewish authorities, decrees that the Jews be thrown to elephants. His joyous banquets make him forget the order. He then recalls it, but it is the elephant drivers whom the elephants trample. Whereupon the prince reverses the order. He praises the loyalty of the Jews and permits them to feast at his expense and to massacre the apostate brethren. It is remarkable that the accounts of Herodotus and the third Book of Machabees both end, as does Esther, with the institution of a commemorative feast.

Even in the Bible, situations similar to the story of Esther are not lacking. It will suffice to recall the instance of Joseph, calumniated and imprisoned for his fidelity to virtue, then freed and made minister of the kingdom in which the sons of Jacob are to settle; of Judith, who saves the besieged people of Bethulia; of Daniel, Esdras and Nehemias, exemplary Jews, who for the good of their compatriots gain the favor of foreign princes.

In sum, the Book of Esther is another witness in favor of providence, which insures the triumph of the Jews over the gentiles, a triumph which in their own way the Wisdom writers, especially that of Wisdom, have put in bold relief (cf. Wis 10—12).

So many indications permit the placing of Esther in the category of midrash of the haggadic type,[2] without denying its authentic historical ring, a quality in which it excels.[3]

---

[2] On *midrash* and *haggadah*, see pp. 173-175 (French ed.).
[3] Cf. A. ROBERT, *Guide to the Bible*, I (New York: Desclée, 1960), p. 308.

§ 3.   Esther and the Feast of Purim

The Book of Esther ends in a passage that seems to attach
the events described with the institution of the feast of
Purim (9, 20-32; cf. 3, 7). What is to be made of this allusion?

It is certain that the Jews had a feast called Purim (lots)
(Josephus, *Ant.*, XI, 6, 13). Its Babylonian name justifies
considering it of Persian or Babylonian origin; beyond that,
its origin is difficult to trace.[4] A close similarity has been noticed between Mardochai and Marduk, Esther and Ishtar. At
the beginning of the year lots (purim) were cast and the
victory of Marduk was celebrated. A number of Babylonian
poems also celebrated the exaltation of Ishtar. Here is an
instance of Jews and Babylonians joining their traditions
against a common enemy. Keeping in mind the literary
genre of the work, one does not have, however, the right to
conclude solely upon Est 9, 20-32 and 3, 7 that the Jews in
Persia instituted their feast in memory of their deliverance.

---

[4] The feast of *parwardîgân* comes to mind, *pordigan*, *phourdigân*
in modern Persian; cf. the reading of Lucian: φρουραια. It is a feast
of the dead, which occupied the last five days of the year (interca-
lary). Thus is explained the absence of the name of Yahweh in the
Hebrew text of Esther. But would the Jews have accepted a feast in
honor of the dead? Meissner appealed to the *Sacées*, a popular feast
akin to the Bacchanalia and Saturnalia: during these feasts social
conditions were overturned with pleasure. Thus Aman and Vasthi
would be dethroned by Mardochai and Esther, the first couple representing the gods of winter, and the second the gods of spring. But
the *Sacées*, according to Strabo, were celebrated in the month of
July, and it is improbable that the Jews were inspired by a mytho-
logical feast. Other historians have thought of the new year: Persian
(*neurouz*) or Babylonian (*zagmuk*). In the first hypothesis, the
Purim would designate the gifts; in the second the lots. It seems that
the origin of the Jewish feast is to be sought in the almost universal
mentality which these various feasts reflect, but cannot be identified
with any one of them. Cf. A. BEA, "De origine vocis pûr," *Bi* (1940),
pp. 198 f.

The second Book of Machabees (15, 36) mentions a feast commemorating the liberation of the Jews from Persia, known in this period under the name "Day of Mardochai." The passage which we read in Est 9, 20-32 seems to be a complicated addition (an overburdened text) destined to give meaning to the feast, whose quite vulgar and in any case clearly pagan attraction was displeasing, by relating it to the story of Esther which was read on the occasion. It was doubtless following this addition that the mention of "Purim" was added in 3, 7.

The matter can be thus summarized:

1) The Jews had a feast of pagan character, of Babylonian origin, analogous to the feasts which were celebrated nearly everywhere at the beginning of spring (Adar: end of February—beginning of March).

2) This feast was put in relation to the triumphal liberation of the Jews from Persia and was also called the day of Mardochai (2 Mc 15, 36).

3) Since it was the custom to read the Book of Esther on this day, it seemed good to justify the feast, which had lost none of its popular origin, under the name which had designated it from the beginning. The Book of Esther then received the appropriate additions.

4) Flavius Josephus is witness to the existence in the sacred calendar of Judaism of the feast of Purim which commemorates the deliverance of the Jews by Esther.

§ 4. Date and Author

The Hebrew text of the Book of Esther cannot be dated later than B.C. 114, when it was introduced into Egypt (cf. Greek Est 11, 3). Perhaps it existed before 160, because at that date, when the feast of Nicanor began to be celebrated, the day of Mardochai was already known (2 Mc 15, 36). Nevertheless the commemorative feast could have preceded the editing of the work. The mentality revealed by the work, at once vengeful and triumphant, leads one to imagine an age in which the Jews, having come through a difficult period, allow themselves to hope for the reconquest of their national autonomy. Wherefore, the period which followed the crisis of the Machabean era would be quite apt. In our opinion, the end of the Persian period would be much less apt. It is nevertheless possible that the Book develops a traditional account, of popular origin, which dates back to the Persian period.

§ 5. Canonicity

The Hebrew book had a difficult time entering the Jewish canon. It has not yet been discovered at Qumran. The only allusion, and that indirect and disputable, made of it would be 2 Mc 15, 36. At the synod of Jamnia its admission was still in dispute. It was admitted only during the 2nd century. Probably the principal reason for this hesitation was that it was read on the profane feast of Purim.

The early Christians used the Greek Bible. They found the Book of Esther there and accepted it just as it was. Nevertheless, neither Christ nor the authors of the New Testament cited it. Moreover, Melito of Sardis (171) and St. Athanasius (370) would have excluded it from the canon, and Amphilocus (360) as well as St. Gregory Nazianzen (390) make reservations in the matter. It is also known that St. Jerome, who accepted it, rejected from his Latin translation the fragments which are read only in the Greek. Perhaps he thus wanted to underline the doubt which hangs over the Hebrew origin of these sections. He was unable to find them in any Hebrew manuscript or witness.

These hesitations and shadows notwithstanding, the canonicity of the work is well attested in Church documents well before the Council of Trent's definition (1546).

CHAPTER VIII

DANIEL

BIBLIOGRAPHY

Introductions, translations, commentaries, pp. 25 f. (P. J. DE
   MENASCE, *BJ**; L. DENNEFELD, *BPC**; J. GÖTTSBERGER,
   HSAT*; J. A. MONTGOMERY, *ICC*; S. DRIVER, *CBSC* . . .).
R. H. CHARLES, A *Critical and Exegetical Commentary on
   the Book of Daniel* (Oxford, 1929).
M. GRUENTHANER, "The Seventy Weeks," *CBQ*, 1 (1939),
   pp. 44-54; "The Four Empires of Daniel," *CBQ*, 8
   (1946), pp. 72-82; "The Last King of Babylon," *CBQ*, 11
   (1949), pp. 406-427.
H. L. GINSBERG, *Studies in Daniel* (New York, 1948).
C. LATTEY, *The Book of Daniel** (Dublin, 1948).
H. CAZELLES, "Daniel," *Catholicisme*, III (Paris, 1950), pp.
   447-453.
J. STEINMANN, Daniel* (Paris, 1951).
A. BENTZEN, *Das Buch Daniel*, 2 (Tübingen, 1952).
S. B. FROST, *Old Testament Apocalyptic* (London, 1952).
G. RINALDI, *Daniele**[3] (Turin, 1952).
E. W. HEATON, *The Book of Daniel* (London: SCM, 1955).
A. C. WELCH, *Visions of the End: A Study in Daniel and
   Revelation* (London, 1958).
H. H. ROWLEY, *Darius the Mede and the Four World Em-
   pires in the Book of Daniel*[2] (Cardiff: Univ. of Wales,
   1959).
J. MUILENBURG, "The Son of Man in Daniel and the Ethiopic
   Apocalypse of Enoch," *JBL*, 79 (1960), pp. 197-209.
N. PORTEOUS, *Daniel, A Commentary* (Philadelphia: West-
   minster, 1965).
D. S. RUSSELL, *The Method and Message of Jewish Apocalyp-
   tic* (Philadelphia: Westminster, 1965).

The Book of Daniel stands among the *Ketubim* in the Hebrew Bible, between Esther and Esdras-Nehemias. In the Greek Bible and in all the other versions it follows the three major Prophets, after Ezechiel. The versions have three sections which are not found in the Hebrew canon: the canticle of the three boys in the furnace (3, 24-90); the story of Susanna (13) and that of Bel and the dragon (14). These three deuterocanonical sections will be treated in the following part.[1] Here we will treat only the protocanonical writing, which is composed in two languages: 1, 1—2, 4a and 8—12 in Hebrew, and 2, 4b—7, 28 in Aramaic. This diversity of language has been attested again by the Qumran manuscripts which predate our era.

§ 1. The Biblical Account

The Book of Daniel has a composite literary structure, but the whole is marked by strong conceptual unity.

Literary diversity is very noticeable between the first six chapters, of a narrative character, and the last six, which pertain more to the prophetic genre. We will have occasion to go into greater detail concerning this diversity.

I. THE NARRATIVE SECTION

The author presents his hero, a Judean of noble birth, deported in 597 and introduced, with three other young Jews, into the court of Nabuchodonosor. There they all remain faithful to Yahweh (1).

The fame of Daniel grows in the measure that the young captive reveals a form of wisdom superior to that of the Chaldean Wise Men. The interpretation of a dream of Nabuchodonosor brings him high honors (2).

Meanwhile his companions are thrown into the fire for

[1] Cf. pp. 265 f.

having refused to participate in an idolatrous act. Protected by Yahweh, they are heaped with favors by the king (3, 1-23. 91-97).

The superiority of the true God manifests itself again when Daniel interprets a second dream of Nabuchodonosor. The king will be reduced to the condition of an animal. And that is what happened (3, 98—4, 34).

Later the Prophet explains to Baltassar, during a banquet, the enigmatic words which the invasion of the Persians in Babylonia was, that very night, to verify (5).

Finally, Daniel is thrown into the lions' den, but encounters no harm there. Yahweh sustains him always.

II.   THE PROPHETIC SECTION

Now it is Daniel who recounts his visions, which are four in number.

The first presents four great beasts who ascend from the sea: a winged lion, a devouring bear, a leopard with four heads and the wings of a bird, and the fourth, undetermined, furnished with ten horns, to which is added an eleventh which uproots three of the horns and reveals the eyes of a man. An Ancient of days appears looking like a king. The fourth beast is put to death and the other three reduced to impotence. Some sort of son of man appears; to him the Ancient hands over eternal domination. At his request, Daniel receives the interpretation of the vision (7).

The second vision depicts a ram and a billy goat. The ram has two unequal horns and pushes successively toward the west, north, and south. The goat overthrows the ram, then grows, while his one horn is broken to make way for four horns of which one grows at the expense of the south, of the west, and of the glorious country (Palestine). It goes so far as to attack God, but after two thousand three hundred evenings and mornings the iniquity ends. The angel Gabriel explains to Daniel the meaning of the vision (8).

The third vision, that of the seventy weeks of years, is one of the most famous of the Old Testament.[2] It comprises, in a very tortuous system of computation, a whole series of epochs and events whose end, just as the beginning, has produced various interpretations. In any case, the oracle announces the coming of the kingdom of God (9).

There remains the fourth vision, whose clarity does not leave room to doubt that it views the age of the Seleucids and Ptolemies. Prepared by chapter 10, it projects an immense history film which begins with the undertakings of Xerxes I (486-465) against Greece, describes the conflicts after the death of Alexander the Great between the princes of the south (Egypt) and those of the north (Syria), and ends in the reign of Antiochus IV Epiphanes, the persecutor of the Jews who will, in the end, be persecuted by God (11).

In conclusion the Prophet has left us, without giving it perspective, a tableau in which are interwoven, by means of temporal liberation, eschatological assurances (12).

It is not difficult to reduce the two sections to unity. The whole Book is a solemn affirmation of the transcendence of the true God. A ruling idea emerges: Yahweh will always prevail. Persecutors pass away. The kingdom of God is coming. A message of hope, a source of consolation—such is the character which in the end marks and seals the apparently disparate elements of the writings, reducing them to unity.

§ 2.   Origin of the Work in its Present Form

I. DATA AND DISCUSSION

Until the end of the 19th century, Catholic exegetes generally held that the Book of Daniel was written by its hero who reveals himself a member of the Achaemenian household. At most they allowed certain reservations about some elements which they attributed to a more recent editor.

---

[2] M. J. LAGRANGE, "Les Prophéties messianiques de Daniel," RB (1930), pp. 179-198; Le Judaïsme avant Jésus-Christ (Paris, 1931), pp. 62 ff.

It seemed—and this was their principal argument—that Jewish tradition, both biblical and profane (1 Mc 2, 59-60; Mt 23, 15; Josephus, *Ant.*, XI, 78, 5), and Christian tradition as well, unanimous in their attestations, imposed this opinion. They attempted to confirm it by pointing out the many references in the work to the Chaldean milieu of the 6th century: the importance of magic, the education of young nobles in the palace, the solemnly dedicated, colossal statues of princes, punishment by fire and lions, the agreement of names (Baltassar, Sidrich, Misach, Abdenago: Dn 1, 7) and of certain descriptions (winged animals: 7, 4. 6; plane of Dura: 3, 1) with cuneiform documents. The bilinguism attested the adaptation the Hebrews made to Aramaic in their land of exile. The obvious unity of the work (parallelism of plan between 1—7 and 8—12), the progress and development of the visions and doctrines, the similarity of expression and style were alleged to establish the conclusion, and permitted some authors to include in the original work even the deuterocanonical parts. They were content to answer the objection of the language of the Greek fragments with the hypothesis of a translation.

Meanwhile the critical approach underlined the uneven probative value of these arguments. The place occupied by the Book of Daniel in the Jewish canon, among the *Ketubim* and not the *Nebiim*, proves that the latter collection was closed when the work was written. The postexilic books, especially Sirach in its enumeration of the glories of Israel (49), make no mention of Daniel. The Persian words call to mind an age later than the conquest of Cyrus, and the Greek words, a date later than the Hellenistic invasion of the Orient.[3] The Hebrew of the book by no means contradicts these conclusions, and the Aramaic is a western dialect, whereas one would expect an eastern dialect if the work had been composed in Babylonia in the 6th century, as Wilson has tried to

---

[3] See the lists drawn up by MONTGOMERY in his commentary, pp. 20-23, and cf. H. H. ROWLEY, *The Aramaic of the Old Testament*, pp. 152-156; SCHAEDER, *Iranische Beitrage* I studies many Persian words.

demonstrate.[4] Besides, the writer knew Babylonian history rather poorly: Baltassar (5, 2) is presented as the son of Nabuchodonosor, but he was the son of Nabonidus. This last would have been a better choice in the context of dreams: he was a diviner of dreams. The historical Gobryas is replaced by a certain Darius the Mede (6 and 9) who is completely ignored by history.[5] But the author is very informed about the Machabean period, about which he gives precise details. Finally, the doctrinal developments in the work—angelology, the resurrection of the body, the last judgment and eternal sanctions—relate too closely to the apocalyptic writings which multiplied starting in the 4th century to place the composition of the work in the 6th century.

II.   CURRENT STATE OF THE QUESTION

The debate stimulated reflection which seems today to have reached maturity. It has been rightly observed that the traditional arguments, which are more "recitative" than "doctrinal," have less to do with the author of the work, at least in its present form, than with the hero on stage or the title given the book. Similar references to Josue, Solomon and Job do not suffice to settle the controversies created by the origin of the books which bear their names. On the other hand, the hypothesis of a literary fiction does not in itself contradict the results of internal criticism; it is merely in conformity with the usage of the time. Contrarily, it is necessary to have recourse to somewhat obsolete methods in order to explain away, in the hypothesis of ancient origin, the editorial peculiarities, the historical anomalies concerning Babylonian history, and the quite outstanding details of the Machabean period. Finally, the very doctrinal content of the work dissuades a date earlier than the age of apocalyptic writing. And if the unity of the work is incontestable, it is equally evident

4 "The Aramaic of Daniel," *Bibl. and Theol. Stud.* (1912), pp. 261-305.

5 Cf. H. H. ROWLEY, *Darius the Mede and the Four World Empires in the Book of Daniel* (Cardiff, 1935); cf. *RB* (1936), p. 130.

that if could just as well have been the work of a recent as an ancient author.

Hence the modifications of the older opinions, inherited from rabbinic Judaism, made by modern criticism. There are so many opinions and variations that it is impossible to give more than a brief summary of them here. Some authors decline to hold that Daniel wrote the whole book, but refuse to date the whole work in the Machabean age. J. A. Montgomery attributes the historical chapters (1–6) to an older author (Daniel or some unknown author), and the prophetic oracles (7–12) to a writer of the age of Antiochus-Epiphanes. Others (Baumgartner, Hölscher, Haller) block together chapter 7 with the first six chapters and date this part of the work in the 3rd and 4th centuries. Still others (Riessler) make Daniel the author of the prophetic section, but judge the historical passages of a more recent date. Many (Nikel, Göttsberger, Lagrange) prefer not to determine the elements which an author of the 3rd or 2nd century used to compose the work as we know it now, or even (Junker) restrict the additions of the Machabean author to the visions of chapters 10–12. We leave unmentioned the hypotheses which, exploiting the diversity of language and content, chop the book into fragments, content to break the literary continuity from Aramaic to Hebrew and vice versa, without eliminating the internal anomalies (Lods).

In the end, the question is whether some critical principle does not authorize a conclusion which better appreciates the strong unity of the work. The principle is precisely this, that the incontestable unity demands one author. But Daniel cannot be the author of the whole work, as is proved by the sum of arguments presented in favor of a more recent origin; this conclusion especially emerges from the hypotheses which bring the date of more or less important passages down to the 2nd century. Logically then, the entire work in its present form should be attributed to a writer of the Machabean era.[6]

---

[6] Cf. H. H. ROWLEY, "The Unity of the Book of Daniel," *The Servant of the Lord and Other Essays* (London, 1952).

§ 3. Prior Sources

It would still be an exaggeration to conclude that the 2nd century author was not working with some antecedent material. The unity of the whole, which is ideological, does not extenuate the complexities, which are literary.

The passages of the narrative section could have existed separately before being collected. Their content retains traces of a primitive independence (anomalies of dialect between 1, 1-2. 4a, and 2, 4b–6, 29; of date between 1, 1-2 and 2, 1; the excessively changeable attitudes of Nabuchodonosor in 2, 47; 3, 13-19. 95-96; 4, 34; identity of themes of 2 and 4, and of 3 and 6; no mention of Daniel in 3, while his companions are mentioned in 2, 17. 40). In several cases the seams between the episodes are glaring (1, 21; 2, 1; 6, 1. 29); even their absence attests the prior isolation of the elements.

The visions of the apocalyptic section stand out in a contextual background that is not always even (change from the third person: 7, 1; 10, 1 to the first person: 7, 28; 8, 2. 5. 27; 9, 2; 12, 3), indication of redactional contribution prolonging the narrative character of 1–6. The two languages likewise create a certain disparity between 7, where besides it is a question of a "dream," as in 2 and 4, and 8–12 in which "visions" are recounted. Finally, the purely material juxtaposition of chapters 7–12 (lack of literary connection, bare chronological references to the reigns of Baltassar, Darius and Cyrus) heightens still more the impression of a heterogeneous block.

If one continues the analysis, traces of successive editings appear: 2, 43, in relation to 11, 7. 17, seems to be an addition to 2, 41-42 which is centered on the imagery of the dream; the prayers of 2 and 9 too give evidence, by the manner in which they are introduced, of a similar procedure. We could even suppose a stage in which oral traditions preceded written elaborations and the final editing of the book. This hypothe

sis has now received support from a Qumran manuscript[7]
which contains a narration parallel to Daniel 4, but features
not Nabuchodonosor but Nabonidus. The point of departure
of the work in its present form, then, is to be placed further
in the past: the author used a varied material provided by
popular oriental traditions.

These views seem on the whole to agree with the works of
Bentzen, Rinaldi, Ginsberg, and Cazelles. It is not impossible
to conclude from it to a certain chronology of the composition
of the work, though this point is still an object of serious discussion among scholars.

§ 4. Identity of the Hero

The identity of the hero is currently under discussion. Is he
the same one mentioned by Ezechiel (14, 14. 20; 28, 5), or
does the prophet of the Exile refer to a probably legendary
character known from the documents of Ras Shamra? The
argument drawn from the written form of the name, on which
some have founded the distinction of the two characters, does
not seem absolutely conclusive, since the name Dan-*i*-el, deprived of its *yod* (*mater lectionis*), would be *dnil* in Ugaritic.

It is rather Ezechiel's grouping of Daniel with Noe and
Job, two foreigners to the people of Israel, that leads some
to believe that the Prophet of the Exile is not referring to a
Judean deported to Babylonia. In any hypothesis, it is evident
that the characters of the canonical book are by no means
incompatible with a really existing person. It should especially
be noted that Jewish apocalyptic writings employ real per-
sonalities, sometimes very ancient ones. This is, alongside
the concrete indications of the narration (1, 1. 2; 2, 1; 3,
16; 5, 1; 6, 29), an argument of some weight.

[7] *RB* (1956), pp. 407-415.

§ 5. Aim and Method of the Narration

Greater caution is called for in judging the historical references in the narrative section. It would seem that the second-
century writer used in great measure the midrashic method
and composed a haggada. His purpose was to draw up a spiritual commentary on the events of the Machabean period.

The young Jewish prince would occupy in Babylonia a role
analogous to that which his descendants occupy during the
Syrian persecution. Nabuchodonosor evokes Antiochus, both
of whom profaned the Temple of Yahweh (4 Kgs 24, 13-15;
1 Mc 1, 22-24. 57-62). Babylon, just as Seleucid, set himself
against Jerusalem, the city of the true God. It was a matter
of using this insight and composing a model history, as was
that of Achikar in the pagan world, or better yet, that of
Tobias in Israel.

Daniel and his companions are scrupulously faithful to the
dietary precepts of the Law (Dn 1, 8-16). The three companions of the Prophet refuse to adore the statue of Nabuchodonosor (Dn 3, 12-18). King Darius is not able to overcome the firm resistance of his subject when he decrees that
prayers should be directed only to him (Dn 6, 11). Beautiful
lessons for the Jews faced with the persecutory decrees of
Antiochus!

And here we see that the resistance of the guests of Babylonia makes them capable of contributing by their Wisdom
to the manifestation of Yahweh (Dn 1, 17; 2, 46-47; 4, 34;
5, 14-16). Yahweh works wonders to deliver them from the
evils they willingly undergo for his Name (3, 49-50; 6, 22).
Will this not happen when the persecution of Antiochus will
have exhausted God's patience?

Considering the end to be accomplished, what importance does the change of names and situations have? Nabuchodonosor could be substituted for Nabodinus and Darius
the Mede for Gobryas. The essential was to apply the ancient
traditions in order to illumine, comfort and sustain the Jews

persecuted by Antiochus Epiphanes. And that is the accomplishment of the haggadic section.

§ 6. Nature of the Visions

It is possible that even here the author owes a debt to ancient oracles. But he has impressed on these elements an original form in accord with the spirit of his age. The apocalyptic seed sown by the Prophet Ezechiel (Ez 25–32; 37–39) had blossomed. Several poems of the Book of Isaias (Is 13–14; 24–27; 34–35) mark an important step in this development. Certain parts of Enoch, of which fragments have recently been found at Qumran, are generally accepted as contemporary with the Machabean age: the apocalypse of the seventy weeks, the fall of the angels, and the assumption of the hero would be anterior to 165; the book of dreams, slightly posterior (about 161), projects a clear light on the Book of Daniel. It seems that it is in this line that the author of the canonical work should be placed. It was not alien to him to present history under the guise of prophecy, thus giving prophecy unaccustomed qualities, in order to move the reader's mind to eschatological events, of which the fall of the great empires was a preview. This is the purpose of chapters 7 to 12 of the work.

To this end the oracles of the haggadic section serve as a prelude. The interpretation of the dream of Nabuchodonosor is the leitmotiv which the accounts of the great empires develop. So it is that the visions of the four animals, of the ram and the goat, enlarge and specify the prognosis based upon this key oracle. The whole history of the Orient passes in review, summarized in the princes whom the animals symbolize. The symbols disappear in 10–11, to give way to designations whose anonymity is easily unmasked. But what impresses and at the same time guides the reader is the personality who closes the series, the persecutor par excellence, Antiochus Epiphanes. This eminently reveals the au-

thor's intention. After having proposed the example of Daniel
and his companions to the persecuted Jews, after having emphasized the divine interventions in favor of the deportees,
faithful under trial, he applies to the age in which his compatriots are living the examples he has drawn from another
age. He places before their eyes the action of Providence
which, through the catastrophes of empires, continues to
work for the coming of the kingdom of God, protecting His
people and assuring their survival. There is no doubt that the
Jews of the Machabean era found consolation and comfort
when they read these powerful pages. God's work is accomplished in the midst of trials, but its realization is guaranteed.
The final vision (12), prophetic and therefore less precise,
gives the work a conclusion which forcefully seals its unity.

As for the prophecy of the seventy weeks (9), that is a
problem of its own. It is an example of *pesher*, that is, an
"actualization" of the prophetic Scriptures according to the
midrashic methods. The conclusions of Fr. Lagrange on
the substance and purpose of this prophecy are sound[8]:
". . . . Let us first of all adhere to the meaning, and since it
clearly calls for no calculation, let us cease to search for a
mathematical indication of the year of the birth or death of
Christ in a prophecy which forcefully announces the coming
of the kingdom of God. *The events of the age of Antiochus
and the Machabees* served as a *certain pledge of it.*" The
Messianic interpretation, *in a typical sense,* is today generally
accepted; the Jews themselves already interpreted this prophecy of the age of Antiochus.[9] The principal argument in favor
of the literal Machabean interpretation is the "*Gesichtsfeld,*"
the habitual field of vision of the prophetic section of the
Book of Daniel. In all the visions the same general scheme is
repeated, and the aim is always the age of Epiphanes. There
is no reason to make an exception for chapter 9. A literal
Messianic interpretation has nevertheless had some recent de-

[8] RB (1903), p. 198.
[9] F. CEUPPENS, *De Prophetiis messianicis* (Rome, 1935), pp.
490-521; G. RINALDI, *op. cit.* (Turin, 1947).

fenders.[10] It is to be noted that verse 24 is sometimes considered, even by the defenders of a typical Messianic sense, as Messianic in a literal sense.[11]

§ 7. Religious Meaning of the Work

I. A THEOLOGY OF HISTORY

The Book of Daniel, a haggadic commentary and apocalyptic representation of providential events, is a record whose meaning extends to all ages. Driver rightly noted (*Introd.*, p. 512) that it "traces a religious philosophy of history." But this high purpose becomes incarnate in the decisive thrust which Messianism receives in these pages, vibrant with certain hope in the final triumph of God. In brief, the message of Daniel resumes and passes on the expectation of ages past and future. It is a point of arrival and of departure.

It is a point of arrival. The teaching of Daniel is situated at the end of a long tradition. By crystallizing the struggle between God and evil in the opposition of the empires to the Chosen People, it concentrates the long series of confrontations which history symbolized or described from the beginning (the revolt of Adam, of mankind, of the builders of the tower of Babel) up to the resounding invasions of the potentates of Assyria (Teglath-pilessar III, Salmanasar V, Sennacherib) and of Babylonia (Nabopolassar, Nabuchodonosor). It reechoes the commentary of the Prophets: the pagan nations, even when God uses them to chastise his people, are destined to ruin (Is 10, 5-19. 27c-34; 14, 24-27; Jer 50—51; Is 13—14), while Israel is promised the triumph (Is 10, 20-27ab; 41, 8-20; Ez 36—37). Numerous ideas used by the *nabiim* come up again in the teaching of Daniel: Ezechiel (38, 15-18) and Joel (4, 2. 9-14) envision the last trials of

---

[10] R. P. CLOSEN, VD (1938), pp. 47-56, 115-125; J. LEVESQUE, *Rev. Apol.* 1 (1939), pp. 90-94; J. LINDER, *Commentarius in librium Danielis* (Paris, 1939).

[11] Cf. CEUPPENS, *op. cit., ad loc.*

the people of God; the idea of the judgment of God on the nations is common to all the great prophecies (Am 1–2; Is 14, 24-27; So 1–2; Jer 12, 14; 25, 15; Ez 25–32; Jl 4, 1-17); the resurrection of the dead had already been confusedly mentioned in the apocalypse of Isaias (26, 19) and Ezechiel (37, 11-14). Even Daniel's favorite symbols—the great felled tree, lions, leopards, rams, goats—are not without reference to more ancient books (cf. Os 13, 7-8; Is 15, 9; Jer 5, 6; 49, 19; 50, 17; Za 10, 3). And the stone that breaks up the mountain and shatters the statue (Dn 2, 44-45), might it not be that of Isaias (17, 10; 26, 4; 32, 2) and of Deuteronomy (32, 4-15), that is, Yahweh Himself? The author of Daniel collected all these contributions of the past, developed them and put them to use. The resulting synthesis is the work of a highly original writer. And such is the richness condensed in this body of prophetic history, in which the present situation is buttressed by so many former situations, that one does not hesitate to predict what the future holds.

II. MESSIANISM

Thus Messianism takes here a new beginning. For all ages the reading of Daniel suggests the substitution of the empires symbolized by the animals or designated by anonymous expressions by other empires or other forces, heirs of the monsters of chaos as were their predecessors, and who will oppose the kingdom of God and his Anointed One. The struggle between the City of God which is being built, and the City of the demon, which will experience successive dismantlement, will continue from age to age. The Apocalypse of St. John too, patterning its methods upon those of the author of Daniel, will apply the same rule to the conditions of his time. Enlarging even more the perspective, it will present in the framework of a changed symbolism, which is in many ways a debtor to the Book of Daniel, a vision of the trials of the primitive church, especially of the persecution of Nero and Domitian. The apologists of the future will be able in their turn, if not to adopt the method, at least to extract and apply the lesson. Rather than search in the symbols which clothe past events for concrete images of future situations, they will use the triumphs of God over the powers of evil, in order to strengthen faith, stimulate hope, rekindle charity. In the meantime they await the realization, after an uneven and tumultous history whose full sense will then be revealed, of the triumphal exaltation of God, the universal kingdom of Christ, the happiness of the elect. Let us conclude with Fr. Lagrange: "Daniel was the first to envision world history . . . as the preparation for the reign of God, to join this splendid vision to the hopes of Israel, to carry the plan of God for men to the threshold of eternity."[12]

Let us add to this general appreciation a very important point. With Daniel, the divine ambassador charged with bringing about the kingdom of God here below takes an entirely new aspect: he is not only the king, son of David; he is referred to under the mysterious title of Son of Man coming upon (or with) the clouds of heaven. This transcendent Messianism directly prepares the way to the New Testament. A number of exegetes (Procksch, Eichrodt, Feuillet, Jacob) relate this new conception to Ezechiel's vision (chap. 1) by the River Kobar of the divine glory "as a figure of man." Some bring into play the great developments of the Wisdom writers (Prv 8; Sir 24; Wis 6–9) on divine Wisdom personified. The further development of the Son of Man tradition (Enoch, New Testament) seems to support this view.[13]

---

[12] Le Judaïsme avant Jésus-Christ (Paris, 1931), p. 72.
[13] A. Feuillet, Le fils de l'homme de Daniel et la tradition biblique, RB (1953), pp. 170-202 and 321-346. Cf. in exactly the same sense P. J. de Menasce, Daniel (BJ, 2 ed.), pp. 21-22; R. Laurentin, Structure et théologie de Luc I-II (Paris, 1957), pp. 132-133.

CHAPTER IX

ESDRAS AND NEHEMIAS

BIBLIOGRAPHY

Introductions, translations, commentaries, pp. 25 f. (A.
  GELIN, *BJ**; P. MEDEBIELLE, *PBC**; M. REHM, *EBi** . . .).
C. C. TORREY, *Ezra Studies* (London, 1910).
A. C. WELCH, *Post-Exilic Judaism* (London, 1935).
A. S. KAPELRUD, *The Question of Authorship in the Ezra
  Narrative* (1944).
W. RUDOLPH, *Esra und Nehemia samt 3 Esra* (Tübingen,
  1949).
H. H. ROWLEY, "The Chronological Order of Ezra and
  Nehemiah," *The Servant of the Lord and Other Essays*
  (London: Lutterworth, 1952), pp. 131-159; "Nehemiah's
  Mission and Its Background," *BJRL*, 37 (1954-1955), pp.
  528-561; "Sanballat and the Samaritan Temple," *BJRL*, 38
  (1955-1956), pp. 166-198.
R. A. BOWMAN, "The Books of Ezra and Nehemiah," *IB*
  (1954).
K. GALLING, *Esra-Nehemia* (Göttingen, 1954).
E. BICKERMAN, *From Ezra to the Last of the Maccabees:
  Foundations of Post-Biblical Judaism* (1962).

§ 1. The Book

I. DIVISION

In the beginning the Books of Esdras and Nehemias formed
a single unit with the Books of Paralipomenon whose account
they continue (cf. Esd 1, 1-4 and 2 Par 36, 22). In addition,
Esdras and Nehemias, like Paralipomenon, were not divided

into two books until a later date. The Alexandrian version at first respected the unity of the book (cf. Swete, Rahlfs). It is not known when, nor under what influence, the division took place. The inscription which opens the Book of Nehemias as we have it could have been taken for the title of a distinct work.[1] Once the division had been made, one finds in the Greek translation: Εσδρας α' (the third Book of Esdras, apocryphal); Εσδρας β' (our first Book of Esdras); Εσδρας γ' (our second Book of Esdras or Nehemias). But in most of the editions of the LXX, our two Books, Esdras and Nehemias, continue to form a single unit (Εσδρας β'). The division is in all Latin canons. The Vulgate canonized it, and the Hebrew Bible of Daniel Bomberg (1517) accepted it.

II. CONTENT OF THE BOOK

The general history (pp. 38-47) has already enabled us to date the work of the pioneers of the restoration. The present account, written in the course of the 3rd century, since it is the work of the Chronicler (see p. 503 f.), centers on three principal themes: the reconstruction of the Temple (Esd 1—6 except 4, 6-23), the repair of the city (Esd 4, 6-23; Neh 1—13), the juridical establishment of Judaism (Esd 7—10).

After the edict of liberation, several parties of faithful Jews returned to Jerusalem. Leading the first group was Sassabasar, prince of Juda (Esd 1, 8), perhaps of royal blood (1 Par 3, 18, Greek), who had the rank of *peha* (governor, high commissioner: Esd 1—2). Nevertheless it falls to Zorobabel, of the Davidic line (Esd 3, 2. 8: cf. Ag 2, 23) to restore the altar of sacrifice and to begin reconstruction of the Temple—which work was soon stopped by the Samaritans (Esd 3, 1-4; 5).[2]

---

[1] Cf. L. GAUTIER, *Intr. à l'A.T.*, II, p. 380.

[2] We accept the distinction of Sassabasar and Zorobabel. Comparison of Esd 1, 8 (Sassabasar, prince of Juda) with Esd 3, 2. 8 (Zorobabel, son of Salatiel, therefore grandson of Joachin) is no obstacle to this distinction, considering 1 Par 3, 18 *Greek*, where Sassabasar is listed as *son* of Joachin. The comparison between Esd 1,

After the reigns of Cyrus and Cambyses, given the favorable political situation, the rebuilders went back to work, encouraged by Aggeus (cf. Ag 1, 1-2. 10) and Zacharias (cf. Za 1, 16; 4, 8-10). The work, again hindered, this time by the Persian authorities, was at last completed after the authorities had permitted it. The repatriates celebrated the Passover in the rebuilt Temple in the 6th year of Darius (Esd 5, 1–6, 22).

Then the spiritual community begins to live again. Esdras, with a mandate from Artaxerxes in the 7th year of his reign, regulates cult and suppresses mixed marriages (Esd 7—10).

In the 20th year of Artaxerxes, Nehemias arrives in Jerusalem. He oversees the reconstruction of the walls, impeded until then by Samaritan intrigues (Esd 4, 6-23), works to bring about social peace, decrees security measures, and prepares the way for peaceful coexistence (Neh 1, 1–7, 73a).

We then find Esdras, assisted by Nehemias (cf. Neh 8, 9), proceeding to the reading of the Law, to the feast of Tabernacles and an expiatory ceremony which seals community participation (Neh 7, 73b—10, 40).

Then coexistence is put into effect, followed by the dedication of the wall, and various lists (Neh 11, 1—12, 47).

The *peha*, who had returned to Babylonia in the 32nd year of Artaxerxes, comes back to Judea with imperial authorization and an edict against crying abuses (Neh 13).

5-11 and Esd 2, 2 (cf. Neh 7, 7) would prove that Sassabasar is Zorobabel only if the caravan of 2, 1 ff., which is certainly prior to the reconstruction of the Temple (cf. 2, 70), must be identified with that of 1, 5 ff. Finally, the doubt which rests on the authenticity of the name of Zorobabel in 3, 2. 8 prohibits a valid comparison of these texts with Esd 5, 16 in order to prove the identification of the two persons. The text of Za 4, 9 is not in itself definitive, because Zorobabel certainly assumed the function of builder very early. All things considered, the distinction of names corresponds to that of the persons, and the attempts to impose them on one and the same subject lose all practical interest.

§ 2. Chronological Reconstruction

The biblical account presents striking anomalies. A more
satisfactory chronological order can be conjectured by a critical examination of the sources and their use.[3]

I. Sources

The memoirs of Esdras and Nehemias form the main outline
of the work.

The memoir of Esdras is easy to recognize in the obviously
related chronological indications: Esd 7, 9 (1st day of 1st
month), 8, 31 (12th day of same month), 7, 8-9 (1st day of
5th month), Neh 7, 73b—8, 18 (the first 8 days of 7th
month), Esd 10, 9 (20th day of 9th month), 10, 16-17 (from
1st day of 10th month to 1st day of 1st month). Afterwards
Esdras remains in Jerusalem about a year. The substance of
his report to the Persian authorities can be drawn from Esd
7, 1—10, 44 and Neh 7, 73b—9, 37.

The memoir of Nehemias comprises the first seven chapters of the book, except for two documents inserted there:
the one contemporary (3, 1-32) which preserves, perhaps in
fictional dress, the names of the rebuilders; the other (7,
6-73a), more ancient, enumerates the first repatriates. To this
unit must be added Neh 13, 1-31, the account of the *peha's*
second term, and undoubtedly 10, the last verses of which
(31-40) are connected with 13: Nehemias figures at the head
of the signers of the community pact. Some fragments at the
end of the book also belong to it (Neh 11, 1-2. 20. 25a; 12,
27a. 30-32. 37-40. 43), whereas others (Neh 11, 21-24. 25b-
35; 12, 1-9. 10-11. 12-26) must have been added later.

The Aramaic source is also very obvious. It provides the
account of the Samaritan opposition to the reconstruction of
the wall (Esd 4, 6-23) and of the Temple (Esd 5, 1—6, 18).

---

[3] Cf. A. GELIN, *Esdras-Néhémie*, pp. 13-22 and 49-50.

Within this document are inserted fragments of official Persian documents (Esd 4, 9-10. 11b-16. 17b-22; 5, 7b-17; 6, 2b-12).

A Hebrew source for the first chapters of Esdras (Esd 1, 1-4; 5) could perhaps be admitted. Certain details (Esd 1, 2-4. 8-11) seem to require it.

II. USE OF DOCUMENTS

The Chronicler dismembered the memoir of Esdras by inserting the section which should follow Esd 8, 36 (reading of the Law, feast of Tabernacles, confession of sins) in the framework of the Book of Nehemias (Neh 7, 73b-9, 37). He is generally unobtrusive in his presentation, except perhaps in rearranging the text when the account is in the third person. He probably composed the prologue (Esd 7, 1-11). It is less certain whether he wrote the very biblical-sounding decree of Artaxerxes.

If one keeps in mind that it contains variously dated documents, it results that the memoir of Nehemias has not undergone major editorial retouches. The intense emotional accent that distinguishes it militates against any suspicion of falsification. If the hand of the Chronicler is apparent in 12, 33-36. 41-42, it is precisely because these verses clash with the whole of the account.

The Aramaic source was obviously reproduced after the events. Opposition against the reconstruction of the walls (Esd 4, 6-23) is evidently subsequent to the reconstruction of the Temple: the names of the kings cited sufficiently demonstrate it. There is also a certain clumsiness in the seam between Esd 4, 23 and 5, 1: verse 24 of chapter 4 is redactional.

As for the Hebrew source, it is best to say that if it existed, the Chronicler has absorbed it in his account. There will always be some difficulty in interpreting correctly Esd 3, 2-8 and 4, 1-3: it seems that Zorobabel was substituted for Sassabasar, and the irritation of the Samaritans is expressed prematurely (compare 3, 8 with 5, 2 on the one hand, and 4, 1-3 with 5, 3 on the other). Was not his intention perhaps to excuse the inertia of the repatriates which Aggeus quite harshly reproves (Ag 1, 14-15)?

III. Chronological order

The problem   After the various documents have been identified, a chronological reconstruction of the events would be relatively easy, if there were no doubt about the relative dating of the activities of Esdras and Nehemias.

The problem has generally been reduced to these two postulates: Nehemias supposes Esdras *or* Esdras supposes Nehemias. If Esdras preceded Nehemias, the first stay of the scribe at Jerusalem would have to be dated in the 7th year of Artaxerxes I (464-424) and therefore in 458, and the first stay of Nehemias in the 20th year of the same Artaxerxes, that is, in 445. If Nehemias preceded Esdras, the latter could have come to Jerusalem only in the 7th year of Artaxerxes II (405-359), that is in 398.[4]

The older commentators held the first opinion, and it is still held by many today, notably Eissfeldt, Höpfl-Miller, de Vaux,[5] Fernandez. The second opinion gathers around Van Hoonacker the majority of modern exegetes, among others Touzard, Mowinckel, Rowley,[6] Snaith,[7] Cazelles. There are worthwhile arguments on both sides: appeals to the necessary priority of the legal and cultic restoration of Esdras, or to the necessary priority of the political and social activity of Nehemias; insistence upon certain chronological details favorable to one or the other position.[8]

---

[4] We pass over the abandoned hypotheses of Kaulen, Hoberg and Lagrange (1894). This last adopted the positions of Van Hoonacker, which were treated at length in RB (1890), 151 ff., 317 ff.; (1923), 481 ff.; (1924), 23 ff.

[5] Art. *Israël* in SDB, IV, cols. 764-769.

[6] *The Chronological Order of Esdras and Nehemias.* Cf. *The Servant of the Lord* (London, 1952), pp. 131-159.

[7] "The Date of Ezra's Arrival in Jerusalem," ZAW (1951), pp. 53-65.

[8] In favor of the Esdras-Nehemias hypothesis are: the present order in the Bible; the existence at the time of Nehemias of cultic material, product of the mission of Esdras (Esd 7, 14-22); the shock

A compromise hypothesis We cannot enter into the maze
of the controversy. Faced with the difficulty of making a positive choice, we lean toward the Esdras-Nehemias hypothesis,
observing that the Nehemias-Esdras sequence involves two
Artaxerxes, while Paralipomenon seems to warrant only one.

But we are also tempted to accept a compromise solution
which, despite the objections that it can arouse, has at least
the advantage of breaking the dilemma: Nehemias supposes
Esdras *or* Esdras supposes Nehemias. It is sufficient to place
the mission of Esdras between the two missions of Nehemias.
We would then read the 27th year (Wellhausen, Procksch)
or the 37th year (Bertholet, Albright, Gelin, Rudolph) of
King Artaxerxes I in Esd 7, 8, that is, either 438 or 428. The
choice of the 27th year would have the advantage of explaining the presence of Esdras alongside Nehemias at the time
of the solemn promulgation of the Law (Neh 7, 73b–8, 18;
cf. 8, 9), and why the report of Esdras was dislocated, since
the activity of the scribe was combined with that of the

---

of the Scribe in encountering mixed marriages (9–10), difficult to explain if he had already collaborated with Nehemias to root out this
blight (Neh 10, 31); and especially the preparatory character of the
spiritual work of Esdras with respect to the more politico-social activity of Nehemias.

In favor of the Nehemias-Esdras sequence are: the contemporane-
ity of Esdras and Johanan, high priest in 411-408 (Elephantine Doc.,
Pap. Cowley, 30) and son (Esd 10, 6) or rather grandson (Neh 12,
10-12) of Eliasib, himself high priest and contemporary of Nehemias (Neh 3, 1; 13, 4); the allusion of Esdras to the work of Nehemias (Esd 9, 9), while the memoir of Nehemias makes no mention
of Esdras; the rather tolerant attitude of the *peha* toward mixed marriages, hardly conceivable if Esdras had already taken his draconian
measures (compare Esd 9–10 and Neh 6, 18; 10, 31; 13, 23-27); the
situation at Jerusalem when Esdras arrived (Esd 8, 29; 10, 5), a
consequence of the coexistence policy of Nehemias (Neh 11, 1–2);
the absence of all the families which returned with Esdras (Esd 8,
1-20) from the list of Neh 3; the almost withdrawn role of Esdras
under Nehemias' rule, hardly reconciliable with the high offices he
would already have filled (cf. Neh 8, 2. 4; 12, 35). Cf. V. PAVLOV-
SKY, "Die Chronologie der Tätigkeit Esdras. Versuch einer neuen
Lösung," *Bi* (1957), pp. 257-305; 428-456.

peha. Thus we would answer the double demand: Esdras *and* Nehemias suppose one another.

In this hypothesis, the order of events would be the following:

Between 538 and 520 several caravans of repatriates arrived in Jerusalem, first of all those led by Sassabasar. He sets up the altar of holocaust and lays the foundations of the Temple (Esd 1, 1–3, 13).

From 520 to 515 the work of reconstruction, encouraged by Aggeus and Zacharias (Esd 5, 1; cf. Ag 1–2; Za 2, 5-17), is brought to conclusion by Zorobabel. The Temple is consecrated and the Passover is celebrated in it (Esd 5, 1–6, 22).

Between 515 and 445 the effective Samaritan opposition to the restoration of the walls took place (under Xerxes I, 486-465, and Artaxerxes I, 464-424: Esd 4, 6-23).

In the 20th year of Artaxerxes (445), Nehemias begins his first mission. The walls are rebuilt, arrangements for coexistence are made, the work finished, and the dedication of the walls celebrated (Neh 1, 1–4, 17; 6, 1–7, 73a; 11, 1-20. 25a; 12, 27-32. 37-40. 43). The material order is reestablished.

In the 27th year of Artaxerxes (438), Esdras organizes the spiritual leadership of the community (Esd 7, 1–8, 36). He lectures on the Law (Neh 7, 73b–8, 12), presides over the feast of Tabernacles (Neh 8, 13-18), decides to stamp out mixed marriages (Esd 9–10), and stirs his compatriots to just repentance (Neh 9, 1-2).

In the 32nd year of Artaxerxes (433), Nehemias returns to Susa after twelve years of rule (Neh 5, 14). He nevertheless fulfills a second mission in Judea before the death of Artaxerxes (424). In the course of his second stay, the *peha* has to take measures against abuses, in the tradition of Esdras, in order to defend the legal and cultic code of the community (Neh 13, 4-31). It is in this situation that he submits the document of renewal of the covenant to the leaders, levites, and priests for ratification (Neh 10).

Let it be clearly understood that we are only presenting a hypothesis. One of the other solutions proposed by authorities in the field, equally hypothetical, might be preferred. If

the most common is chosen (Nehemias-Esdras), it will be
easy to arrange the events accordingly and put in more striking relief the mission of Esdras, who came to Judea in 398,
in the 7th year of Artaxerxes II.[9]

§ 3. Historicity

It is difficult to underestimate the historical value of these
books. The Chronicler's sources are certainly trustworthy, and
his handling of them does not affect the substance of their
content. Besides, his explicit or implicit references to Oriental
history leave the best of impressions. The conciliatory measures of the Achaemenids in favor of the Jerusalem community
conform to their customary dispositions for their subject
provinces.[10] And it is only right to point out the exactness of
many details of the work: the administrative system of the
Persian State is correctly outlined, with precise notations on
the relations of governors among themselves and with the
great King (Esd 4, 7-23; 5, 3-17; 6, 1-13). The Samaritan
opposition is completely in conformity with the ingrained
anti-Judean mentality of the Northern Kingdom, aggravated
by syncretism caused by the contributions of the Mesopotamian deportees (4 Kgs 17, 24), which hardens and becomes the schismatic Judaism of Garizim. And the restoration conforms to past prophecies, at the same time that it
agrees remarkably with the contemporary ones (Ag 1–2; Za
1–8 and also Mal 1, 6-10; 2, 1-24). The grand historico-
legislative digest, undoubtedly composed in Babylonia, does
not more than orchestrate the statements of the Chronicler.
How else explain the reaction of the Hasidim and the
Machabean revolt, if the repatriates, spiritual sons of Ezechiel, had not put into practice the burning impulse of the
Prophet of the Exile?

[9] Cf. CAZELLES, "La mission d'Esdras," VT (1954), pp. 113-140.
[10] R. DE VAUX, "Les décrets de Cyrus et de Darius sur la reconstruction du Temple," RB (1937), pp. 29-57.

Still it is right to observe that the Chronicler reveals some of his favorite themes, especially his attachment to the Davidic monarchy, which is apparent in his mention of *Judean* and *Benjaminite* repatriates (Esd 1, 5; 4, 1; Neh 11, 4) and the importance he attaches to "Davidic" institutions: cultic rites, role of the priests, function of the levites (Neh 12, 44-47).

§ 4. Religious Meaning

The restoration appears as a resumption of the salvific will of God. It is a new step in progress toward Christ, after those of the promise, the alliance, the Babylonian captivity. But this stage has particular characteristics which must be discussed.

The almost exclusively religious aspect of the community stands out. One could have believed in a restoration of the terrestrial kingdom of David, the coming of the Messianic prince, the establishment of the universal reign of Yahweh (Ag 2, 4-9; Za 6, 10-17; cf. Is 60—62). It was soon necessary to dispel all illusion. Neither Zorobabel, though a descendant of David (Esd 3, 2) and acclaimed by Aggeus (Ag 2, 23), nor even less Nehemias, not of the Davidic line, will reestablish the royalty. Both fervent Yahwists devoted to the great work of restoration give an example of perfect loyalty to Persian authorities. These latter, in spite of some liberal measures (Esd 1, 7-10; 6, 4b-5. 8-10; 7, 13-26; Neh 2, 4-9), gave evidence of a certain harshness in their administration (Esd 4, 6-23; 5, 3-5), especially in the matter of taxes (Neh 5, 4. 15). Political autonomy could no longer be hoped for. So the repatriates retreat into themselves, around the Temple, in the shadow of the walls. The Law, enriched, meditated and deepened, and recognized besides by Babylon as the law of the land, became the object of their contemplation. Little by little it weaves a net of observances around them. The Jewish community becomes more oriented toward its specific

excellence, Yahwism, than toward the reconquest of civil independence.

A marked isolationist tendency results. "Judaism," the
product of restoration, is on the road to juridicism. It became
a protective barrier, but at the same time a wall of separation
from the Gentiles. And in this way did it not perhaps descend
to the esoteric, rather than opening the door that leads to the
kingdom of God?

Not at all. The prophets sustain Messianic hope. In their
eyes it appears with ever greater radiance. Undoubtedly the
reign of God appears to them centered on the holy city, colored by Judaism. Still they celebrate the conversion of the
pagans (Is 56, 1-8). Religious universalism is constantly affirmed (Is 66, 18-21; 24, 18-23; 25, 6-10; Mal 1, 10-14; Jl
3, 1-4). It inspires the songs which celebrate the nations
streaming to the holy rites (Ps 95 [96], 7-8; 97 [98], 4-6). In
truth, a missionary spirit animates the best sons of Israel.

But is it not precisely from the hardening of their religious
institutions, from their zeal for the Law and their interest in
deepening it by making it interior, that the subjects of Zorobabel, of Nehemias[11] and Esdras draw the strength to re-
spond, despite contradictions of the time, to the urging of
the *nabiim?* No doubt mediocre souls will shut themselves
up in egoism and will blame their harsh situation on God
(Mal 2, 17). Some preexilic disorders will reappear: especially social inequalities with the excesses that follow from
either side (Neh 5; Za 7, 8-12; 8, 16-17). The wound of
mixed marriages will not soon be closed (Mal 2, 10-16), and
cultic frauds will be favored by the poverty of the numerous
offerers (Mal 1, 8. 12-14). Nevertheless, some noble Israelites refine their knowledge of the divine. In the measure
that it becomes more spiritual, their souls come nearer to
God. The Anawim Psalms ring with touching pleas, which
reveal their authors' familiarity with Yahweh (Ps 114-115
[116], 119 [120], 122 [123], 123 [124], 129 [130], 130

---

11 J. Coste, "Portrait de Néhémie," *Bible et Vie chrétienne*
(1953), pp. 44-56.

[131], etc. . . .). Others exalt God, the benefactor of His People, faithful to His covenant, accepting the thankful homage of the residents of Jerusalem (Ps 110 [111], 111 [112], 134 [135], 135 [136]).

When seen in relation with this comforting evidence, the institutions which were born during the Exile grew firm: synagogues in which the Law and the Prophets are read, a corps of scribes faithful to the traditions of Ezechiel and Esdras, the council of the Sanhedrin, which was to assume later an imposing juridical form.[12]

We can at least suppose that it is in this spiritual ascent that the elite of the community progressed, until the terrible crisis that shook it to its foundations, the crisis of Hellenism after Alexander the Great's conquest of the Orient. The Book of Nehemias closes rather abruptly: perhaps it had a sequel which has not come down to us.

[12] J. Touzard, "L'âme juive au temps des Perses," RB (1916), pp. 299-341; (1917), pp. 54-137 and 451-488; (1918), pp. 336-402; (1919), pp. 5-88; (1920), pp. 5-42; (1923), pp. 59-79.

CHAPTER X

THE BOOKS OF PARALIPOMENON OR THE CHRONICLES

BIBLIOGRAPHY

Introductions, translations, commentaries, pp. 25 f. (L. MARCHAL, BPC*; H. CAZELLES, BJ*; J. GÖTTSBERGER, HSAT* . . .).

G. VON RAD, *Das Geschichtsbild des chronistischen Werkes* (Stuttgart, 1930).

A. C. WELCH, *The Work of the Chronicler, its Purpose and Date* (Oxford, 1939).

A. NOORTZIJ, "Les intentions du chroniste," RB (1940), pp. 161-168.

A. BEA, "Neuere Arbeiten zum Problem der Chronikbücher, Bi (1941), pp. 46-58.

A. M. BRUNET, "Le Chroniste et ses sources," RB (1953), pp. 481-508; (1954), pp. 349-386.

W. A. L. ELMSIE, "The First and Second Books of Chronicles," IB (1954).

K. GALLING, *Die Bücher der Chronik* (Göttingen, 1954).

W. RUDOLPH, "Problems of the Books of Chronicles," VT, 4 (1954), pp. 401-405; *Chronikbücher* (Tübingen, 1955).

D. N. FREEDMAN, "The Chronicler's Purpose," CBQ, 23 (1961), pp. 436-442.

W. F. ALBRIGHT, "The Date and Personality of the Chronicler," JBL, 82 (1963), pp. 369-381.

The Books called Chronicles are presented in the Hebrew Bible under the title *"Dibrey hayyamim,"* that is, the events or acts *of the days* (journal), or perhaps *of the years* (annals). In fact their content is no way measured by days or years.

Hence, the name *"Chronicon totius divinae historiae"* given them by St. Jerome, fits better this collection of accounts, if not its literary tendency.

The title "Chronicles" was for a long time overshadowed by that of παραλειπόμενων (LXX), Paralipomenon, usually used by the Fathers in the sense of "things left out" (by the earlier historical books), rather than in the sense of "things handed down," defended by some modern authors.

In the beginning our Books of Chronicles composed one volume. The division dates from the Alexandrian translation. Later versions propagated it. Since 1448, this division has been in use in Hebrew manuscripts. The Bible of Bomberg canonized it (1517).

It is moreover certain that the Books of Esdras and Nehemias are a sequel to the Chronicles. To recognize this it is sufficient to compare 2 Par 36 and Esd 1, 1-4. Similarities of vocabulary, style, and mentality likewise indicate unity of authorship.

§ 1.   General View of the Work

Taking this last remark into consideration, the work of the Chronicler seems to be the most important part of a history, which, beginning with the "Origins," took the reader to the end of, or perhaps beyond, the Persian age. Reduced to the dimensions of the two books of Chronicles this history covers the time from Creation to the beginning of the Exile. Nevertheless, the long period from Adam to David is represented principally by genealogies (1 Par 1–9), whereas that from David to the Exile contains more or less important facts about the Davidic kings (1 Par 10–29: David; 2 Par 1–9: Solomon; 10–36: kings of Juda).

The very presence of genealogies at the beginning of the book is significant. It is well known that Israelite mentality, in conformity with primitive Semitic law, attributed a fundamental value to the group (family, clan, tribe). Responsibility, considered then as collective, obliged the group to keep the genealogical record up to date. And if it is true that the Chronicler is sympathetic to the universalist current, it is just as important to remember that the reform of Esdras and Nehemias had accidentally favored an isolationist tendency. Judaism took on this aspect for a time; it felt it necessary to exhibit Israelite ascendancy.

§ 2.   The Chronicler's Sources

I.   HISTORICAL SOURCES

The work is basically a repetition, in an anthological form, of ancient writings augmented by oral traditions.

The author uses first of all older writings, of which he often reproduces the text, with or without appreciable modifications. Thus it is possible to indicate among the sources he had before him:

1) *Inspired writings.* In the section 1 Par 1—9, the genealogies are taken from *Genesis, Numbers, Exodus, Josue, Ruth.* . . . From 1, 10 to the end, entire passages come from *Samuel* and *Kings* (1 Sm 31—4 Kgs 24). We have here an extensive reuse of past material, which corresponds well to the method of the age (cf. the relations between *Deuteronomy* and the *Book of the Covenant*; the first prophecies of Jeremias and Osee), and especially to its underlying mentality (the cult of Scripture—living meditation of the Scripture sustained itself and provided a principle for interpreting events). Consequently, the Chronicler did not need to cite sources; his readers could not fail to recognize them.

2) *Profane sources.* Here, on the contrary, the references[1] are explicit. They are inserted sometimes in the body, but more frequently at the end, of the passages.

Some of those sources belong to a collection of *historical writings*: the Book of the Kings of Israel and Juda (2 Par 27, 7; 35, 27; 36, 8 etc.); the Book of the Kings of Juda and

[1] E. PODECHARD, "Les références du Chroniqueur," RB (1915), pp. 236-247.

Israel (2 Par 16, 11; 25, 26; 32, 32 etc.); the Book of the
Kings of Israel (1 Par 9, 1; 2 Par 20, 34); Acts of the Kings
of Israel (2 Par 33, 18); midrash on the Book of Kings (2 Par
24, 27). The first four titles are probably the same book.
And the midrash is possibly not a distinct work; the literary
genre is similar throughout. Thus the Chronicler would have
had before him a vast compilation of diverse documents,
which scarcely formed a unit. Besides, it is impossible to
determine whether these documents are parallel to, or identical with, those used by the Books of Kings, or whether they
have been reworked after the pattern of the latter, and
whether, and in what measure, the Chronicler depends more
or less directly on the sources of the Books of Kings or on
the Books themselves.

II. OTHER SOURCES

Other non-canonical sources are attributed to known persons:
Samuel the Seer (1 Par 29, 29); Nathan the Prophet (*ibid.*
and 2 Par 9, 29); Gad the Seer (1 Par 29, 29); Iddo the
Seer (2 Par 9, 29; 12, 15); Semeias the Prophet (2 Par 12,
15); Jehu the son of Hanani (2 Par 20, 34); Hozai (perhaps
hôzim, the seers, or *hôzayw*, *his* seers [of Manasses]: 2 Par
33, 19); midrash of Iddo the Prophet (2 Par 13, 22); the
Vision of Isaias (2 Par 32, 32); Ahias the Silonite (2 Par 9,
29); the relation of the Acts of Ozias written by the Prophet
Isaias (2 Par 26, 22).

By reason of the quality of the personages cited, these
sources are called *prophetic*. It will be noted that they cover
periods of history more or less remote (10th to 8th centuries). It is possible that these writings at one time made up
a single collection, an anthology of prophetic relations (cf.
the reading *hôzim*, suggested by the LXX in 2 Par 33, 19).
Were not the first historical books supposedly written by
nabiim? Still the possibility is far from being a proven fact;
the texts cited are not unquestionably favorable to this hypothesis. But the contrary opinion lacks proof as well. Some
outstanding critics think, moreover, that these writings of

Samuel, Iddo, etc. are presented under names which, according to the custom of the age, are no more than literary fictions. We would in this case be faced with documents of a recent date, much like the Apocalypses and the Apocrypha. Witness what, much later, one finds in the non-canonical literature of the archives of the Qumran sect: the struggle of the children of light, a midrash on Habacuc! So the very character of the sources which the inspired Chronicler used leads us to think that his work is the product of similar methods.

He had, finally, to collect oral traditions: recollections preserved in Judea, passed down by the repatriates after the return from exile, and sometimes associated to more recent events. No doubt these traditions were inserted into the plan of the work with some uncertainty. They were floating elements which the Chronicler fixed according to their frame of reference, and perhaps also according to their relation to the purpose he had in mind.

§ 3.   Purpose and Literary Genre of Chronicles

The Chronicler followed a set plan. To judge by the results of a comparison of his account with his known sources (especially the Books of Samuel and Kings), it is impossible to avoid the conclusion that our author proposed not only to write history, but deliberately set out to put a religious doctrine in plain relief. It is not so much the material likeness of his account to his sources that sustains this conviction, but rather the formal comparison of the two series of writings. A constant tendency is discernible: to justify by history the solutions given to complex problems in the post-exilic community, and especially to refer the fundamental elements of the Jewish community to David, without neglecting, however, the Mosaic origin even of the Davidic institutions.

Now such methods are characteristic of a literary genre much used in that age: the midrash.

I. MIDRASH[2]

The midrash, following the religious sense of the verb *dâraš* (to consult the divinity), is a writing that tries to investigate and use ancient texts in order to explain the present. This research, however, does not heed demands imposed by our western mentality. Our exegesis aims to give the text the meaning required by the objective reconstruction of time and place. Thus we discover the literary genres of the Bible including the midrash. Midrashic research aimed, rather than to discern the precise meaning, to draw from the text numerous and diverse ideas that resulted in maxims of justification and edification. The word of God in putting on the clothing of human language should not lose any of its universal meaning. It remains charged with a volume of knowledge and contains the universality of wisdom. It is to be approached with our own reason, but also it is to be treated with our imagination. Thus the authors of the midrashim proceeded. The midrashim assumed an historical, philosophical, juridical, mystical character. The midrash is then at the same time a form of intellectual speculation and of imaginative development founded on Scripture and in the sense of tradition.[3]

Midrashim assumed multiple aspects.[4] They found their way into all sorts of books. In the Wisdom writings legal ordinances are the occasion for certain language changes; thus in certain proverbs that constitute a type of updating of the Law destined to spread Yahwism. Also ancient accounts give rise to imaginative developments: in this sense compare Wis 10, 15—12, 27 (a recollection of the Exodus) and 16, 1—19, 22 (plagues of Egypt) to the accounts of the Pentateuch. The midrash in this instance in some way amplifies history. In the prophetic genre history is given a meaning, while the future is colored according to the mentality of the age of the nabiim (cf. Ez 16; 40—45; Is 40 f.; Dn 1—6). In

[2] See pp. 173 f.
[3] Cf. R. BLOCH, art. "Midrash," *SDB*, V, cols. 1263 ff.
[4] See pp. 173-177 (French ed.).

the legalist works the ancient historico-juridical texts prolifer-
ate with details and moral applications. Just compare the
priestly code with the more ancient passages (J, E, D).
Finally, in the historical books canonical and non-canonical
sources are used or simply recopied with the fixed purpose of
adapting them, even embellishing them, to support a thesis
according to the common exegesis of an age. Tobias, Judith,
Esther furnish classical examples of midrashic literature.[5]

The Books of Chronicles are to be interpreted in the light
of this literary genre. The Chronicler uses certain objective
facts, and in this way he is an historian. But he sometimes
arranges them to serve his thesis, and in this way he is a
midrashic author. His objectivity is influenced by his interpretation.[6]

II. CRITICAL OPINIONS

Two exaggerated positions are to be avoided: the first is that
of J. Wellhausen. He maintained that midrash is essentially
an idealization of the past. The midrashic authors teach us
only about the historical and doctrinal ideas of their time.
The authors record past centuries exclusively from these
ideas. Thus the Chronicler judaized, in the light of the
priestly code, the history of ancient Israel.[7] In general the
disciples of Wellhausen were less radical than their master.
They held that a certain number of documents used by the
Chronicler have objective value. They did not consider the
facts of the work as *a priori* unacceptable. Nevertheless the
essential positions remained inflexible with Torrey (1909-
1910), Curtis (1930), Pfeiffer (1941). With J. W. Rothstein
(1923) the theory leaned towards granting that the Chronicles have an historical value. The existence of serious sources

---

[5] Cf. A. ROBERT, *RB* (1935), pp. 345-350.
[6] Cf. LAGRANGE, *RB* (1916), pp. 501-504; *Le judaïsme avant
Jésus-Christ*, pp. xv-xx; L. DENNEFELD, *Le judaïsme biblique* (Paris,
1932), pp. 38-56; J. BONSIRVEN, *Exégèse rabbinique, exégèse
paulinienne*, pp. 250-259 and *passim*; *SDB*, IV, cols. 565-567.
[7] PROLEGOMENA VI, 1905, 165-223.

contemporary to Samuel and the Kings, and partially identical with them, was admitted. A first redaction would have arranged these memoirs according to the model of P. A second redaction arranged them according to the Hexateuch. Von Rad[8] (1930) held for these two strata, but accentuated the influence of the Hexateuch and strongly stressed that of D. According to A. C. Welch (1939), the second stratum was the outcome of a compromise in which P prevailed over D, which in effect had principally inspired the first editor. In short, the Wellhausian movement assumed a certain form according to which the influence of P, associated not strictly with that of D, but with the Hexateuch as a whole, would have influenced the Chronicler. This would all the same depend on trustworthy sources of history.

The second position, by way of reaction to minimizing the historical sense of Chronicles, set about explaining the least discrepancies without taking into account the literary genre of the work. This method would easily create in the reader the opposite impression it set out to produce.

Now Catholic exegetes follow a path which, without accepting the extreme opinions of the radical critique, endeavors to take notice of literary method of the age in order to appreciate the exact objective value of the Chronicler's account.

Thus we do not consider all the details added to the Books of Samuel and Kings as purely imaginative. The different sources of these works to which the Chronicler refers are not necessarily unreliable. The very documents used in Samuel-Kings could have contained information not used in these works but which a later historian could have taken up. Moreover, the religion of Israel was rooted in history. The Chronicler then, no matter what his intentions were, could not boldly disregard objectivity without the risk of weakening his thesis by deliberately ignoring the evidence of facts.

The exegete must find the right starting point. In general a

---

[8] G. VON RAD, *Das Geschithtsbild des Chron. Werkes* (Stuttgart, 1930).

number of data proper to Chronicles are held to be exact: cities fortified by Roboam (2 Par 11, 5-12a) and by Ozias (26, 6-15); construction work by Joathan (27, 3b-4); details concerning the burial of Asa (16, 14) and Ezechias (32, 33); details about the death of Ochozias, killed by Jehu (22, 7-9); circumstances of the death of Josias at Megiddo (35, 20-25). . . . Extra-biblical documents have sometime confirmed facts presented by our author: the inscription of Karnak concerning the invasion by Sesac (2 Par 12, 2-11); inscriptions of Assarhaddon and Assurbanipal concerning Manasses (33, 11-13). The reign of Joatham is rightly presented as an era of prosperity and military success (27, 3-6; cf. Is 2, 7-16). The details furnished by Chronicles about the underground aqueduct of Ezechias (32, 30) are more complete than the brief reference in the Book of Kings (4 Kgs 20, 20).

The author does, however, present views that sometimes do not correspond with those of his predecessors. Sometimes he perpetrates important omissions, modifies expressions, inverts the order of events, adds personal glosses, and explains facts in the light of tradition.

Examples of this genre have become classic: David's adultery and homicide are passed over in silence. There is no mention of the bloody drama of the King's old age. If there is a question of the census and the plague, it is because these events are connected with the choice of the Temple site. And David was to prepare for its construction. However, it is not God but Satan who inspires the King with a desire to take the census (1 Par 21, 1; cf. 2 Sm 24, 1).

Solomon is idealized even more boldly. There is no question of competition with Adonias nor of decline at the end of his life. If he offered sacrifice at Gabaon, it was certainly not to conform to the usage of his time (cf. 3 Kgs 3, 2-3), but because there was in that high place "the tabernacle of the covenant of the Lord" which Moses had made in the wilderness (2 Par 1, 3), and here verse 4 justifies David who offered sacrifices in Jerusalem.

Besides, one has the impression that the process of earthly reward is a bit exaggerated. The good kings—those who are in the line of Deuteronomy or the priestly code, destroying the high places, protecting the levites—are showered with blessings (2 Par 14—15: Asa; 17—20: Josaphat; 29—32: Ezechias; 34—35: Josias). Nevertheless the eye of God is on their least infidelity (2 Par 16, 1-12; 20, 35-37; 32, 31; 35, 20-22). One can imagine what is in store for unfaithful kings. Joram of Juda not only loses control over Moab (4 Kgs 3, 4-27) and Edom (8, 20-22); he is subjected to an invasion by the Philistines and Arabians, devoured by a stomach disorder and excluded from his father's grave (2 Par 21, 11-21; cf. 4 Kgs 8, 24). Achaz, already castigated by the author of the Book of Kings (4 Kgs 16, 1-20), receives a double measure of affliction in the Chronicles (2 Par 28, 5-8). In brief, the Chronicler has a way of seeing or not seeing things that is often enough in contrast with the facts presented in Samuel-Kings, the only historical work with which we can compare his. The differences (cf. Vannutelli's synopsis) are sometimes difficult to reconcile (compare 2 Kgs 21, 19 and 1 Par 20, 5; 2 Kgs 8, 18 and 1 Par 18, 17; 2 Kgs 24, 24 and 1 Par 21, 10; 3 Kgs 9, 10 and 2 Par 8, 8. . . .). It becomes evident that the author sacrificed the role of historian to that of the panegyrist, the apologist or the theologian.

§ 4. Religious Value of the Work

We are thus led to define the intentions and objective proper to the Chronicler. His main objective is to present a panoramic view of the kingdom of God in the framework of the Davidic monarchy, past but not destroyed.

The genealogies already betray this plan: the lines of schismatic tribes are not given beyond the Davidic era; those of Benjamin and the Levites, who remained faithful to the dynasty, are continued until the Exile; the genealogy of the holy King's descendants is continued to the age of Esdras and Nehemias (5th century).

In the Chronicles the kings of Israel are only mentioned in their relation to the sons of David. *David himself is the center* and the culmination of the account; it is he who is the principal artisan of the kingdom of God!

Just as Moses was the mediator of the alliance between Yahweh and the Israelitic community of Sinai (the *'edah* of the priestly redaction), thus David was put in charge of the alliance (2 Par 13, 5) which was to associate God and the community (*qâhâl*) destined to live in Chanaan. This covenant, whose effects extended to Davidic kings, truly inaugurated the universal reign of Yahweh. Even after the northern tribes' schism, the frontiers of Juda and Benjamin were opened to different descendant clans of Jacob: people of Ephraim, Manasses, Simeon, Aser, Issachar, Zabulon (cf. 2 Par 15, 8-15; 30, 1-22). Even foreign tribes, including Egyptian representatives, were not excluded. David was made the head of a universal kingdom.

One can understand that the entire historical vision of the Chronicler must adjust to this basic fact whose Messianic coloring is obvious. And so the oracle of Nathan is seen in a new light (compare 2 Kgs 7, 14. 16 and 1 Par 17, 13. 14): it goes beyond the horizon of Solomon. The Temple, the dwelling place of Yahweh, appears as the center of an enriched cult. Does not all the liturgy organized there stem from David? The son of Jesse not only moved the ark from Obededom's house to Sion, he not only prepared for the construction of Yahweh's house, he also arranged the services of the Dwelling. Here we have the levites joining the priests (1 Par 23). The sacerdotal law and the Deuteronomical tradition limited their roles (Nm 1, 50-54; 3, 7. 8; 4, 15; 7, 9; Dt 10, 8; 18, 1-8), but the Davidic liturgy qualified them to function in the sanctuary until they could assume their office definitely in the Temple. In short, David instituted the levites as Moses had instituted the priests. It is he who determined the types and details of both, and provided for the organization of the sacred music. He laid the ground for all the Temple functions (24-26).

This Temple, as it should, had already known a brilliant fame. The entire life of Israel was centered on it. The moral and religious life, the sanctification of souls, took place there through ritual acts, purifications, sacrifices, especially thanksgiving sacrifices and participation in sacred feasts. It is there that one sought and found God, because the Covenant must be renewed after apostasies and become more profound in the measure that revelation is extended. The Chronicler delights in recalling the solemn feasts celebrated with the singing of the psalms and the sound of harps, citterns, trumpets and cymbals (2 Par 5, 11-14; 6, 6; 29, 25-30; 30, 21).

Thus the Chronicler views the religious community in the kingdom of God over which ruled David and his successors, the anointed of Yahweh, the predecessors of the Messias. Should not at least the prestige of the house of David be restored at a time when the restoration of the historical monarchy was impossible? To do this, should not the merits of the dynasty be stressed, against the objections to it, thus maintaining faith and hope in a second David? This faith and hope ran through the oracles of the nabiim and the ardent pleas of the psalmists (cf. Ps 88 [89]).

The fervent religious conviction of the Chronicler is manifested in his historical accounts expanded to benefit the theology of the Kingdom. The work of Ezechiel and the priestly law profoundly influence the spirit of the book and the description of the sacred rites. The legislation of Deuteronomy accentuates, more strongly than in the Books of Kings, the judgment of the kings, and inspires reforms and developments that are at work in the Kingdom (Asa, Josaphat, Ezechias, Josias). The transcendence of Yahweh, more and more acknowledged, maintains in souls a respect for the monotheistic ideal. This ideal is more clearly affirmed and purified in the measure that the spirituality and holiness of the Divine Being are better perceived (the Angel of Yahweh). Yet His love is a cause of joy and happiness. Already the King of peace takes the place of the warlike God. The Davidic kingdom is a kingdom of peace, defended by Yahweh for the faithful, or paternally chastised by the jealous God for those who reject his love.

§ 5.   Date of the Work

The content, language of a later age, influence of the priestly
law on the concepts and terminology of the author make it
clearly impossible to place the redaction of the Chronicles
before the Exile. If one considers the numerous genealogical
lists which contain descendants beyond the return from the
captivity, and especially the Davidic genealogies continued
until the end of the 5th century, then the date cannot be before the year 400. This conclusion must be drawn if the
primitive union of Chronicles and Esdras-Nehemias is considered, as well as the influence of Esdras and the Torah on
the mentality of the author. The choice of Albright to use
this as a *terminus a quo* and put the redaction at the beginning of the 4th century is understandable. If, however, the
one author theory is accepted (contrary to Galling who holds
for two Chroniclers), it seems that the work belongs to a more
recent era. The mention of the high priest Jeddoa (Neh 12,
22) in a list of Nehemias would indicate a date after 330,
since his pontificate was contemporaneous with Alexander the
Great, if Josephus is reliable. True, this pericope could have
been added to the primitive text, but there is also a question
of the daric [Persian gold coin] in the historical Davidic context (1 Par 29, 7). Such a monetary designation would suppose that the connection with Darius had been lost in reference to this exchange. Now the last king with this name was
Darius III Codoman who died after the battle of Hecatom-
pylos in 330. Moreover, the appearance of the work fits well
with a later date in the course of the 3rd century. The author
seems to want to concentrate on the Temple. This would
indicate that his work was composed at a time when Judean
Yahwism risked being wrecked by the combined efforts of the
Samaritan schism that developed beginning in 350 and was
completed by the construction of the Garizim temple, the
collusion of high priest successors of Simon I the Just with the
Tobiades (sister of Onias II, married to a son of Tobias

around 240) and the financial support of Ptolemy III Ever-gete (Joseph's administration about 220). This puts us in the second half of the 3rd century. At least it is known that in 157 Eupolem used a Greek translation of the Book of Chroni-cles. It is equally probable that Ecclesiasticus referred to it in his portrait of David (Sir 47, 2-11) about 180.

§ 6.   Canonicity and Liturgical Use

If the work appeared in such a climate, one would think that it could not please discordant elements, the Sadducean priests, while it did please fervent Jews, the Assideans and later the Pharisees. This opposition delayed its acceptance into the Jewish Canon: it was given the last place, cut off from Esdras and Nehemias which had already been ad-mitted. Undoubtedly it was at the Synod of Jamnia (about A.D. 95) that its canonicity was officially recognized. By that time the Sadducees had lost all authority after the destruction of the Temple (70), and the view of the Pharisees held sway.

Christians, except perhaps in the Syriac Church, accepted the canonicity of Chronicles without difficulty. Moreover, the spirit of the work was easily in accord with that of the first communities founded by the apostles. The authors of the New Testament refer more or less overtly to the text of the Chronicles (cf. Mt 23, 35 and 2 Par 24, 21 and the context Heb 9, 11-12 and 1 Par 16, 1-2; Heb 11, 13 and 1 Par 29, 15). The liturgy uses it sometimes, especially in the canticle of Lauds for the *feria secunda* (1 Par 29, 10-13), in a number of antiphons and responses of the Vesperal and the Diurnal (Christmas, the feasts of the Trinity, Sacred Heart, Holy Angels), and the offertory of the common of the dedication of a church (1 Par 29, 17-18).

PART V

THE DEUTEROCANONICAL BOOKS

by A. Lefèvre

General bibliography

See the general commentaries, p. 25 f.

E. KAUTZSCH, *Die Apokryphen und Pseudepigraphen des Alten Testaments*, I. *Die Apokryphen* (Tübingen, 1900).

L. E. TONY ANDRÉ, *Apocryphes de l'Ancien Testament* (Florence, 1903).

R. H. CHARLES, *The Apocrypha and Pseudepigrapha of the Old Testament*, I. *Apocrypha* (Oxford, 1913), APOT.

W. O. E. OESTERLEY, *An Introduction to the Books of the Apocrypha* (London, 1935).

E. J. GOODSPEED, *The Story of the Apocrypha* (1939).

R. H. PFEIFFER, *History of New Testament Times* (New York: Harper, 1949).

S. ZEITLIN ET AL. (eds.), *Jewish Apocryphal Literature* (New York, 1950).

BRUCE M. METZGER, *An Introduction to the Apocrypha* (New York-Oxford, 1957).

L. H. BROCKINGTON, *A Critical Introduction to the Apocrypha* (1961).

M. S. ENSLIN (ed.), *The Apocrypha²* (1962).

B. M. METZGER, *The Oxford Annotated Apocrypha* (New York: Oxford, 1965).

The books we call deuterocanonical are inspired in the same way as the protocanonical books. But collectively they express a more advanced stage of revelation. Even the deuterocanonical fragments of books found in the Palestinian canon (Daniel and Esther) disclose a different style and mentality. In many respects the deuterocanonical books seem to be a prolongation of the Hagiographa. Consequently we prefer to treat them separately, after the latter. We will recall that the Protestants call them "Apocrypha."

These seven books do not form a homogeneous whole. The variety of literary genres found in the Hagiographa appears here also. It includes edifying accounts, meditations and teachings from the sapiential school, and histories of different tendencies. Yet some characteristics are common to all of them. All were composed at a later date, when the age of spontaneity had died out. They are a reflective type of literature, fruits of a period of maturity, and as such they give us something that is precious. For this reflection on the history and literature of the past advances the tradition of Israel right up to the threshold of the New Testament.

For most of the deuterocanonical works we have only the Greek text in the manuscripts and editions of the LXX.

CHAPTER I

BARUCH

BIBLIOGRAPHY

Introductions, translations, commentaries, pp. 25 f. and 208
(A. GELIN, BJ*; L. DENNEFELD, BPC*; V. HAMP, EB*;
B. P. SAYDON, CCHS*. . .).

HARWELL, The Principal Versions of Baruch (New Haven:
Yale, 1915).

P. HEINISCH, "Zur entstehung des Buches Baruch," Theol.
und Glaube, 20 (1928), pp. 696-710.

A. GELIN, "Tables," DTC (Paris, 1953), pp. 379 f.

A. PENNA, Baruch* (Turin-Rome, 1953).

Following the Book of Jeremias, the MSS of the LXX place
Baruch, Lamentations and the Letter of Jeremias, generally
in that order. We find the same grouping in the lists of the
books declared canonical by the Greek Fathers (Athanasius,
Cyril of Jerusalem) and by the Council of Laodicea. Baruch
is also considered an appendix to Jeremias, and is cited by
that name; so it is in the most ancient citations known
(Athenagoras, Irenaeus).

Our Vulgate adds the letter of Jeremias to Baruch as
chapter six. But this is not too significant since the long title
shows well enough that it is a distinct work. On the other
hand, the good MSS of the Vulgate completely omit Baruch,
as did St. Jerome, haunted by hebraica veritas. It is an earlier
version which is included in the Latin Bible.

§ 1. Composition

After the prologue (1, 1-14), we can clearly distinguish three
sections: a psalm of penitence (1, 15—3, 8), a praise of Wisdom as identified with the Law (3, 9—4, 4), and a discourse
of exhortation and consolation (4, 5—5, 9). These sections
belong to three different literary genres, the psalm-prayer, the
sapiential poem, and the prophetic discourse. Keeping in
mind that the Greek, full of Semitisms in the first part, becomes purer in the last section (which explains the hypothesis
of a Hebraic original in part), and that the final discourse
supposes the imminent return to Jerusalem, while the prologue puts us at the beginning of the Exile, we can understand why the unity of authorship is hotly contested. But
opinions on authorship and the dating of different parts differ
considerably. Some Catholics maintain that the psalm is by
Baruch but, following Heinisch, they attribute the final discourse to a disciple of Second Isaias, and they put the sapiential poem at some undetermined date after the Exile. Others
opt for dates ranging from the 3rd century B.C. to the 2nd
century A.D. In other words, the internal criticism is hard to
handle.

Actually, if Baruch did write the book, it is hard to explain
why the Jewish tradition neglected the original. We know,
however, that pseudepigrapha were admissible, even on the
part of inspired authors (Eccl, Ct, Wis of pseudo-Solomon).
We can rightly inquire whether the same literary fiction
comes into play here. This would not be too surprising since
the pseudonym Baruch is often found in apocryphal literature. An examination of the work will allow us to form an
opinion on the matter.

§ 2. Contents

According to the prologue, the prayer was read in Babylon
on the anniversary of the destruction of Jerusalem, on the

fifth of the month of Ab, during the assembly in which the
Law was read. Pilgrims setting out for Jerusalem to celebrate
the Feast of Tabernacles brought the prayer to have it recited
in the Lord's house during the feast and the ferial days following, since they offered sacrifices there. This all fits in well
with Jewish custom in the Diaspora from the time of Esdras
until St. Paul. We have two prayers analogous to Esdras,
composed in similar circumstances (Esd 8; Neh 9). But the
prologue adds a certain number of facts, dates, proper names,
historical settings, all of which contribute more difficulty than
useful information. We don't know the year for the date of
the tenth of Siwan (1, 8); by contrast the year 5, the seventh
of the month (1, 2) is all the more surprising, as the date
seems to be taken from 4 Kgs 25, 8 with the substitution of
"year" for "month." At any rate, it is hard to envision the
exiles grouping about Jechonias in the fifth year after the sack
of Jerusalem (cf. 4 Kgs 25, 27), and Nabuchodonosor re-
building the ruins of the Temple. The idea of praying for
Nabuchodonosor and his son Baltassar (? cf. Dn 5, 2) far
exceeds the precepts of Jer 29, and is inspired by the practice
held in honor since the Persian epoch (Esd 6, 10; 7, 23). And
last but not least, the supposition that there was a regular
cult at Jerusalem at that time, with a possibility of offering
holocausts, is at variance with history; nothing like this takes
place until the return of the high priest Josue (Esd 3). It
makes more sense to call this prologue an artificial construction, at least from a modern standpoint. In its own era, it is
edifying history. The dates and names insert into the great
religious history of Israel the ordinary occurrence of the annual pilgrimage, which evoked the great dates of return from
exile, while looking forward to the definitive restoration. This
process reveals a late epoch, far removed from the time of
Baruch.

The "Prayer of the Exiles" (1, 15–3, 8) rests its argument
on a humble confession of sins to appeal to divine mercy.
This literary genre, a psalm of collective penitence, is found
in all the books of the Old Testament (3 Kgs 8, 46-53; Ps 79;
Sir 36, 1-19; Dn 3, 26-45). The idea comes from the prophets,

Osee (14, 3-4) and especially Jeremias (3, 22-25; 10, 19-25; 14, 19-22; etc.); the most polished example is Is 63, 11—64, 11. The psalm is closely related to the prayers of Esdras (Esd 9, 6-15; Neh 9, 6-37), and still more to the almost identical formularies of Neh 1, 5-11 and Dn 9, 4-19.

Within such a fixed literary genre, and in the easily recognizable words of Jeremias, seeking his inspiration in the Law of Moses (esp. Dt 28—30) as expressly cited, our author has nevertheless succeeded in creating an original little masterpiece which aroused, as we know, the enthusiasm of good La Fontaine. He knew how to make the prayer progress in successive waves which somewhat overlap and push at one another. A very profound religious sense finds, in the sense of shame for sin, an assurance of being pardoned and of singing God's praises.

To date this prayer, some put it alongside Dn 9 which Baruch imitated. But it is difficult to determine in what sense this influence comes to bear, or if the two prayers don't depend on an ordinary prayer. Besides, the doctrine of Baruch on the last ends, less advanced than in Daniel, indicates an earlier date. It might fit in the beginning of the 2nd century, with Ben Sira, who also provides a good means of comparison (Sir 36).

The section in the sapiential style (3, 9—4, 4) is an exhortation, as the formulae of introduction (3, 9-14) and conclusion (4, 2-4) indicate. The meat of the section is the "Hymn to Wisdom" (3, 15—4, 1). It is beyond all human research. The rich and powerful of the earth, the people of the East who were considered the most wise, did not know it, nor did the renowned giants of the days of old, and that is why they all perished. It is futile to climb up to the heavens to seek it, or to cross the sea to buy it with money; He who has created the world and rules it, He alone knows it, and He has given it to Jacob His servant. This Wisdom has appeared among men: it is the divine and eternal Law, which gives life.

Our author imitates here the hymn to Wisdom of Jb 28, but he continues to draw his religious inspiration from Dt 30 (cf. Dt 4, 1-8). Ben Sira also offers some points for comparison (Sir 1, 1-20; 24, 1-32). We can therefore conclude that this composition also dates from around 200.

The discourse of consolation which ends the book (4, 5—5, 9) is symmetrical to the psalm of penitence in the beginning. In his speech to the children of Israel (4, 5-9), the poet recalls that their woes arise from having offended the eternal God, their Author who has nursed them, and Jerusalem, the mother who reared them. The speech thus passes into the mouth of Jerusalem who recalls the pain she has endured because of her heedless children and the pleas she has directed to the Eternal One for their own good. These cries are heard, and she announces to her children their speedy return (4, 9-39). The Eternal One answers by the mouth of the prophet that the mourning of Jerusalem is over and her children will be brought back (4, 30—5, 9).

The author continues to draw his inspiration from Dt (esp. 32). The picture of Jerusalem sighing her complaint and then consoling her children is borrowed from Lamentations and from Second Isaias (Is 40, 1-11; 49, 14-26; etc.); the elements in the consolation by which God answers her come from Is 60—62 especially. Once again the author's merit lies in his skilful composition. We progress in successive waves from the sense of sin to the joy of salvation. By giving Jerusalem the central place between the scolding of the prophet and the granting of salvation by the Eternal One, the author carefully sets in relief the role of mediator of the city-mother which prefigures the Church.

The last verses of this discourse (4, 36—5, 9) are found almost word for word in one of the apocryphal psalms of Solomon (Ps Sol 11). These psalms may date from the 1st century B.C. and must be later than Baruch, since they speak a more developed doctrine concerning the last things. Aside from more precise data, the connection between this discourse and the preceding chapters leads us to place it also in the first decades of the 2nd century.

There actually is a connection between the various parts of the book. If the consolation at the end is a response to the prayer at the beginning, it is the Law that intervenes to reinstate Israel in her privileges. The formulae of exhortation which permeate the hymn to Law-Wisdom (3, 9-14; 4, 2-4) bring out this connection. The prologue recalls the Festival with octave (1, 14), that is, Tabernacles, the feast of the renewal of the Covenant by the recalling of the Law. This reference can be taken seriously. The ceremonies of the time of Esdras offer a good point of comparison (Esd 9—10; Neh 8—9). Though not a liturgical text as such, Baruch hands down quite well the feelings of a Jew of the Diaspora who unites himself to the feasts of Jerusalem.

§ 3. Doctrine

The teaching of the Book of Baruch forms a drama of sin, conversion, and salvation. Law-Wisdom, a gift of God and source of life, plays the most important role. Revelation, the sheer grace of God, saves man from sin. As for the last things, Baruch has the current doctrine of the Old Testament up to the 2nd century. Since he wrote from a collective standpoint, the problem of the world beyond does not pose an acute problem. On the other hand, he has a quite original title for God, calling Him the Eternal One. He is the only one in the Bible to use this expression; elsewhere we find scores of times "the eternal God," but never the adjective alone. This preoccupation with eternity haunted the author from the start. The psalm of penitence aspired to an eternal Covenant (2, 35), but it rested on the sad thought that we disappear without returning, while God abides forever (3, 3). The remedy was then given in the Law, which likewise endures forever (4, 1), but which leads men to eternal peace (3, 13). Salvation comes finally from the eternal God (4, 8) who has been offended but who reveals His glory first of all in chastising, then in saving the sinner. The Eternal One pervades the couplets of the consolation discourse (4, 10. 14. 21. 22. 24. 35; 5, 2) which announces eternal joy (4, 23. 29; 5, 1. 4). This opposition between changing, ephemeral man and the eternity of God, ever the same, faithful to accomplish His word, is a customary theme in prophetic literature, but the insistence of Baruch gives it new force.

The adjective "eternal" has no equivalent in Hebrew that permits the substantive use, and in fact it is found alone only in works written directly in Greek (2 and 3 Mc). Everything points to the fact that the last part of Baruch was also written in Greek, which confirms the late date assigned to it.

The Fathers of the Church willingly concede a Messianic sense to 3, 37: "Then she was revealed on the earth and she conversed among men." The author clearly says that he is dealing with Mosaic law, identified with Wisdom; he is not thinking of the Messias. The Messianic application is still correct after the revelation of the New Testament: the Word of God, His Wisdom, is the Son of God who became man (Jn 1; Heb 1; etc.).

§ 4.   Appendix: The Letter of Jeremias[1]

All the modern commentaries agree with St. Jerome in admitting that this letter is pseudepigraphic. But that in no way conflicts with its canonicity which is, as is true with Baruch, better attested than that of some deuterocanonical books, since it is admitted in the lists of Athanasius, Cyril of Jerusalem and the Council of Laodicea.

It is admitted today that the Greek text we have is translated from a Hebrew original. The errors by the translator leave no room for doubt. The clearest error, in v. 71, clothes the idols "in purple and marble," while this is a well known formula taken from the parable of the evil rich man "clothed in purple and byssus" (Lk 16, 19); the Hebrew *shesh* can mean precious white cloth (Prv 31, 22) or costly white stone (Ct 5, 15).

The *date* is more difficult to establish. The letter is certainly later than the definitive version of Jeremias, and this

---

[1] A. ROBERT, "Jérémie (letter of)," SDB, IV (1949), cols. 849-857.

puts it in the postexilic period. A rather low date must be
assigned in this period, to the time when pseudepigraphy
was in vogue, starting with the 3rd century. This plea against
idols could well take place within the period of Greek domination. Alexander had rebuilt the Esagil destroyed by Xerxes,
and gave new life to the cult of the Babylonian gods. The
Seleucids imitated him in this work of restoration, and it is
from the ritual of this period that we have become acquainted
with the feast of the Babylonian new year. This renewal of
idolatrous cult is the reason for the letter.

This letter is really a long *satire* against the idols. A short
introduction aims the message at the Israelites living in Babylon, inviting them to remain faithful to the true God. A
short exhortation recurs at the end of each couplet to break
the monotony of the indictment. The writer's art is reduced
to that as he accumulates, with little order and some repetition, all the traits which show the powerlessness of the idols.
But if he lacks the art of composition, he can be cutting and
he chooses traits that are meaningful.

As the other writings of this era, this one is inspired by the
ancient works. Its models are Second Isaias (esp. Is 44, 9-20),
and above all Jer 10, 1-16, which is already a supplement to
the authentic works of Jeremias. But its inspiration is not
solely bookish; its description of Babylonian customs shows
that it knows how to open its eyes. Archeology and secular
documents confirm its documentary value.

From a doctrinal standpoint, the letter adds nothing to the
prophetic sources cited above. It is, at greater length, what
the psalms sing (Ps 115, 4-8; Ps 135, 15-18). The subject
will be treated again later in Wisdom in greater depth
(Wis 13–15).

CHAPTER II

TOBIAS

BIBLIOGRAPHY

Introductions, translations, commentaries, pp. 25 f. and 208
(R. PAUTREL, *BJ**; A. CLAMER, *BPC**; A. MILLER,
HSAT*; F. STUMMER, *EB**; F. DE VINE, *CCHS** . . .).
C. C. TORREY, "'Nineveh' in the Book of Tobit," *JBL*, 41
(1922), pp. 237-245.
H. BEVENOT, "The Primitive Book of Tobit," *Bibliotheca
Sacra**, 83 (1926), pp. 55-84.
A. CLAMER, "Tobie (Livre de)," *DTC*, IV (1946), cols.
1153-1176.
R. PAUTREL, "Trois textes de Tobie sur Raphaël," *RSR*,
XXXIX (1951-1952), pp. 115-124.
G. PRIERO, *Tobia** (Turin-Rome, 1953).

§ 1. Texts

In the Greek manuscripts, Tobias forms a group with Judith
and Esther. The place of this group varies. It comes right
after the great historical books in the Sinaiticus, after the
sapiential books in the Vaticanus, and after the Prophets in
the Alexandrinus. The text differs a great deal from one
manuscript to another. The accepted text (Vat., Alex., minis-
cules) has been somewhat altered, and what the story gains
in edification, it loses in picturesque detail. The Sinaiticus
reflects best the primitive text, and it contains a vivid and
colorful narrative. It was the basis for the ancient Latin versions. The three main texts, Vat., Sin., and Lat., have been
published in full in the great critical edition of the LXX at
Cambridge (1940).

All known versions depend on one or another of the Greek
recension, even the Hebrew and Aramaic texts of the Middle
Ages. But it is generally agreed today that the Greek itself is
a translation from a Semitic original. Although placed outside
the regular canon of the Scriptures, Tobias always was popular
with the Jews. Thus St. Jerome procured an Aramaic text, in
light of the translation given in the Vulgate. He did not begin
this work wholeheartedly, since he did not believe that what
he was translating was canonical. But he did not wish to avoid
the entreaties of Bishops Chromatius and Heliodorus: "I
have satisfied your wishes, not my tastes, and I did the best I
could," he wrote them. Aramaic was not at all familiar to
him, and he translated with the aid of an interpreter. A Jew
read to him in Hebrew the text written in Aramaic, and St.
Jerome dictated immediately to his copyist the Latin translation. The work took only a day (PL 29, 23-26).

Can this ancient Aramaic text be found? Surely the Vulgate does not allow for its reconstruction, for it is too influenced by older Latin versions, as well as by the ascetical
notions of Jerome. An Aramaic Tobias, found and published
in 1875 by Neubauer, cannot be the original; it betrays the
influence of the Greek versions. Until further findings, the
Sinaiticus represents the form closest to the original. Recently
the manuscripts found around Qumran have yielded Hebrew
and Aramaic fragments of Tobias,[1] which can be dated
around the beginning of the Christian era. Their publication
will perhaps require a revision of our point of view. The Book
of Tobias must have been written in the 3rd or 2nd century
B.C.

§ 2.   Contents

In spite of differences of detail, all the recensions are in accord
with the overall story. As a kind of introduction, old Tobias
recounts the fortune and woes of his life up to the time of

[1] RB (1953), p. 86; (1956), p. 60.

the story. An Israelite of the tribe of Nephtali, he was, already in the time of the ancients the only one to practice the Law faithfully. Deported to Ninive with his wife Anna and his son Tobias, he remained faithful there despite all his trials, up to the time when his scruples of righteousness brought down on him the almost blasphemous reproaches of his wife. Ruined, blind, abandoned by all, he turns to God and begs him, in a humble and penitent prayer, to take him out of this wicked world where he has nothing to hope for (1, 3–3, 6).

Now at the same hour, continues the narrator, at Ecbatana, Sara, daughter of Raguel, is suffering abuse from a servant girl who derides her misfortune. She had seen all seven of her husbands die successively as they attempted to espouse her. A jealous demon, Asmodeus, killed them before they could approach her. She also sends forth a cry of anguish to God, asking the Lord to put an end to her days and to her humiliation (3, 7-15).

Both prayers are heard, and God sends His angel Raphael who will direct the play (3, 16-17).

The main actor will be the young Tobias. His father gives him some lengthy advice, which makes of chap. 4 a small collection of proverbs on good works; next he sends him to recover an important sum of money left in deposit with a certain Gabael, in the heart of Media (5, 1-3). It is then that Raphael, under the name of Azarias, offers to lead the young man (5, 4-22). The angel is not only a guide; he teaches the young Tobias what to do in the face of danger, he teaches him the remedies for the blindness of his father and against the wicked works of the demons, he brags about the charms of his cousin Sara, and invites him to ask for her hand in marriage (chap. 6). When he arrives at Ecbatana, Tobias insistently asks for the hand of his cousin, and to the great astonishment of the parents, the first night passes without incident. Fourteen days of rejoicing are none too much to fete the happy couple. In the meantime Azarias himself goes to recover the money and bring back Gabael (7–9). Meanwhile, at Ninive, Anna and Tobias are anxious about not seeing their son return; hence young Tobias is urging his departure, and begins the return journey with his wife, always under the guidance of the angel. The joy of the homecoming reaches its peak when Tobias returns sight to his father, through the cure pointed out by Raphael. Once again there is lengthy rejoicing to fete the young couple (10—11).

Nothing remains but to take leave of the actors. Raphael reveals his identity before disappearing, but not before he gives, in certain proverbs, a new teaching on good works. Finally he invites his hearers to give thanks to Providence (chap. 12). Tobias is eager to fulfill this duty in a hymn which enlarges on the prophetic views concerning the future glory of Jerusalem (chap. 13). The old man's death is like that of the patriarchs. Upon his deathbed he unveils the future to his son, and once again recommends filial piety to him, as well as the practice of good works and the fear of God (14, 1-11). Young Tobias, after rendering his final duty to his father, and then to his mother, moves to Ecbatana to perform the same duties in the declining days of his wife's parents. He dies at a ripe age, after having had the consolation of seeing the realization of the prophecies of his dying father (14, 12-15).

§ 3.   Literary Genre

The Book of Tobias, within its minor genre, is one of the literary jewels of the Bible. Its charm emerges best in the recension of Sinaiticus, or in one of the good translations recently made, such as in the Jerusalem Bible. The liveliness of narration and dialogue, the picturesque observations, the simple but evocative words, the supple and varied composition which joins continuity with suspense, the finely described characters, and especially the beautiful soul, vibrant yet serene, of the inspired and humanistic scribe, all contribute to the irresistible charm of this book which lifts up our hearts with the joy of doing well under the surveillance of God.

In composing this story, the author naturally looked for his inspiration in the tales of Genesis. The story of Joseph and especially the mission of Eliezer (Gn 24) furnished him models of narration as well as themes to exploit. Like the old book of the Patriarchs, Tobias is a book of "benedictions." The benedictions exchanged for greeting or taking leave call down the blessing of God and return it to Him in thanksgiving (9, 6; 11, 17); the prayers permeating the book, cries for help (3, 11; 8, 5-7) or songs of thanks (8, 15-17; 11, 14-15; 12, 6; 13, 1-19), happily begin with the beautiful formula of benediction which appears generally in Jewish prayer even in our own day. The book closes with such a formula, and the author hopes that all nations will some day join their voices to that of Jerusalem to bless the Lord (14, 7).

The benediction is the happiness which comes from God, and praise returns this happiness to its source. The fundamental theme of the book is the *way of happiness*. This way, which is the sapiential teaching, is concretized here in a real journey; but this journey is above all a symbol. Fear of God in the observance of His commandments, a fear consisting of love and confidence, piety full of respect and attentiveness toward father and mother, scrupulous justice and honesty in social relationships, effective concern for all the brethren in need, such is the way of happiness. This will not prevent evil from touching the just man. But this evil will be welcomed as a merited and purifying trial, as a promise of the happiness which God gives without fail to those who allow themselves to be formed in wisdom by Him. Moreover this benediction is awaited on earth, the benediction promised to Abraham, a progeny which possesses the earth (4, 12), and a long life to see this happy prosperity. The question of a reward in the afterlife is not even posed.

§ 4. Doctrine

The book has added new light on another point, or at least more precision about a traditional doctrine: the role of angels, good or bad, is here put in special relief. The names Raphael and Asmodeus are meaningful: the one kills, the other cures. The fumigations that chase out Asmodeus depend on a medicine not compatible with magic recipes, but the main result seems to show that the exterminator only has power against the transgressors of the Law. Sara, as heiress, was reserved for a man within her relationship (Nm 27, 9-11; 36, 1-12), and God punishes with death those who violate the *laws of marriage* (cf. Lv 20); Asmodeus is only the instrument of divine justice. Raphael attends to the servants of God. He trains them through salutary trials, but he upholds them in their troubles and offers their good works and prayers to God (12, 12-14 and *passim*). The teaching couched in these images is already that of the New Testament.

The whole teaching of the book bears the mark of the sapiential books, teaching which is practical as well as profoundly religious. We are not surprised to find there recipes for medicine (cf. Sir 31, 19-21; 38, 1-15), nor to find the wise man occupying important positions near kings (cf. Sir 38, 33; 39, 4). Two collections of proverbs well underline the *didactic end* of the author (4, 3-19; 12, 6-10; 14, 8); we find parallels in Ben Sira, who gives a teaching akin to that of Tobias. The literary genre of Tobias is clear enough and parallel to the sapiential genre. The search for beauty, both literary and esthetic, is an aim of this genre, as is the transmission of moral and religious teaching. In these conditions the question of historicity loses much of its interest. Today no one recognizes strict historicity here. Naturally the occurrence of real events is at the basis of the story, but these events are masked in intentional disguises, under literary embellishments which make them unrecognizable to us. Moreover, we lose nothing thereby, since the intention of the author was not to satisfy the curiosity of historians.

§ 5.   Tobias and Ahiqar

For a long time Tobias has been compared with Ahiqar. The wisdom of Ahiqar has been very successful in the realm of letters: it passed into our language under the guise of the

Life of Aesop, the first of La Fontaine's Fables, after having proliferated into all the literatures of the East. It is readily admitted today that the story of Ahiqar comes from Babylon. Its pagan origin did not prevent it from being relished by the Jews of Elephantine, who have given us the most ancient copy in Aramaic, unfortunately in very bad condition (papyrus of the 5th century). The wisdom of Ahiqar is presented in the form of a narrative lined with a collection of proverbs; the fusion of the two elements is not as well done as in Tobias. In favor at the court of Sennacherib, then of Assarhaddon, Ahiqar was reviled by Nadan, his adopted son, who was quite anxious to take his place. Though condemned to death, he was saved by the executors who held him in concealment. But when the king expresses sorrow at the loss of such a counselor, Ahiqar is brought in alive. He saves Assarhaddon from great embarrassment, while Nadan dies of vexation about this. The author of Tobias has well summed up the moral of this story (14, 10-11, where Nadan has become Nadab); he makes Ahiqar a nephew of Tobias (1, 21-22; 2, 10; 11, 18).

This all seems to rank Tobias and Ahiqar in the same literary genre. Assyriologists think they have found the historical prototype of Ahiqar; perhaps Tobias will have the same luck some day, but that will not change the teaching of the inspired book. A strange variation in the title of Ahiqar is instructive. The Syriac recension, well within the Christian era, entitles it "Proverbs or History of Ahiqar," while the old title of the Aramaic papyrus simply said "Proverbs of Ahiqar." The old authors did not have about the historical value of this literary genre the illusions that the more recent copyists had.

Tobias is already cited in the letter of St. Polycarp to the Philippians (10, 12). The Fathers did not make commentaries on the book, but the personage of Tobias is freely used in examples (as the *De Tobia* of St. Ambrose, PL 14, 759-794). The Roman liturgy only uses it in the recent office of the Archangel Raphael and in the readings for September with corresponding responses; but it is sometimes inspired by its formulae, as in the Introit of the Trinity (cf. Tb 12, 6).

CHAPTER III

JUDITH

BIBLIOGRAPHY

Introductions, translations, commentaries, pp. 25 f. and 208
(A. BARUCQ, BJ*; L. SOUBIGOU, BPC*; A. MILLER,
HSAT*; J. STUMMER, EB*; A. E. COWLEY, APOT . . .).
F. ZIMMERMAN, "Aids for the Recovery of the Hebrew Origi-
nal of Judith," JBL, 57 (1938), pp. 67-74.
A. LEFÈVRE, "Judith," SDB, IV (Paris, 1949), cols. 1315-
1321.
P. SKEHAN, "Why Leave Out Judith?" CBQ, 24 (1962), pp.
147-154; "The Hand of Judith," CBQ, 25 (1963), pp. 94-
110.

§ 1. Texts

The Book of Judith, written in Hebrew or Aramaic, exists
only in the *Greek translation*. The text has not undergone as
serious changes as has Tobias, although one can discover several recensions. The more recent versions (Latin, Syriac, etc.)
all stem from the Greek. The Vulgate gives quite a shorter
text which is the fruit of St. Jerome's revision according to
the Aramaic text. This Aramaic text is lost without a trace,
and we cannot trust the Vulgate to form an idea of it, for St.
Jerome tells us himself that his work on this was done rather
hastily and without real care (PL 29, 37-40). He did not
admit the canonicity of the book, although he had heard
about a decree of the Council of Nicea on the subject. The
Book of Judith was nevertheless used by the Fathers since the
1st century. St. Clement of Rome (1 Cor 55) already cites

Judith with Esther as an example of self-sacrifice for the
common good.

§ 2.   Literary Genre

The genre of this book does not fit in with the historical
genre of Kings, or even of Paralipomenon. The reign of
Nabuchodonosor, called king of the great city of Ninive, is
put a little after the return from captivity; the Temple has
already been rebuilt. We know that Ninive was destroyed in
612, that the Assyrian Empire perished in 610, that Nabuchodonosor reigned in Babylon from 604 to 562, and that he
destroyed Jerusalem and the Temple. We also know that
Cyrus crushed the power of Nabuchodonosor's successors and
ended the captivity in 538, but that the Temple was only
rebuilt under Darius in 515. Could the author have committed the gross error of making Nabuchodonosor responsible
for such disparate events? Not at all. Even though modern
research had great difficulty in discovering the above dates,
no Jew was ignorant of the respective roles of Assur, Nabuchodonosor and the Persians in the destiny of Jerusalem. Only
two hypotheses remain possible. Either the account of real
events is veiled under pseudonyms, or the author writes historical fiction for a didactic purpose, borrowing elements from
quite diverse epochs. In either case, the procedure hides the
intention of the author.

If we are concerned with a real event, it should be possible to determine either the place or the epoch. Every date
before Darius is excluded, since the Temple was rebuilt. This
brings us to the Persian era, unless we must seek an even
later date. Many details fit the Persian era. Holophernes and
Bagoas are Persian names possessed by well-known persons.
Holophernes turns up as head of the armies of Artaxerxes III
Ochos in an expedition against Egypt, where a counselor of
the king bears the name Bagoas (Diod. Sic. XVI, 47; XXXI,
19). Certain details are typically Persian ("preparing the
earth and water," 2, 7; "the god of the heavens," 5, 8, etc.).

Moreover the final chant designates the Persians as the in-
vaders (16, 10). Thus it is that a place for Judith has been
sought in the history of this era. The Chronicle of Eusebius,
in Jerome's version, mentions the reign of Cambyses, and St.
Augustine accepts this date. Sulpicius Severus (*ca.* 420)
seems better informed in placing this episode under Artaxerxes Ochos, who according to the Chronicle of Eusebius deported the Jews to Hyrcania, probably on the occasion of his
Egyptian campaigns. But the Holophernes, of whom Diodorus
speaks, by no means perished miserably. He returns to the
satrapy of Cappadocia laden with honors, with the expectation that his descendants will have there a kingly title. If the
history of Judith has a historical basis in this epoch, it can
only be a very minimal episode. The army which went down
towards Egypt had to protect its flanks. A detachment in
front of the mountain passes must have known the event
described in Judith. But their obscure chief gained renown
and his forces have consequently been enlarged.

According to this hypothesis, the book must have looked
back on the event a long time after its happening. It might
well be dated in the 3rd century. Certain traits come from
Greek usages (crowns, 3, 7; 15, 13), or late Jewish usages
(presabbath, 8, 6). On the other hand, Nabuchodonosor and
Holophernes are not persecutors who wish evil upon Jewish
religious institutions, in the manner of the Seleucids who
force the introduction of Hellenic customs to Jerusalem. The
pretensions of the pagan king to divinity (3, 8; 6, 2) by no
means exceed the swagger of the kings of Assur in the Book
of Isaias (Is 14, 4-21; 37, 22-29). We find ourselves, therefore, before the Machabean persecutions; certain chapters of
Daniel (Dn 1–6) and the Book of Ecclesiasticus seem to reflect the same milieu as Judith.

The author is not writing a historical work. His Nabuchodonosor is a type of the enemies of Jerusalem, or rather a
type of the pagan whose pride must be put to shame. If he
has taken a real episode as a point of departure, our author is
not interested in it for its own sake, but for its symbolic
value. He has little interest in the exact description of places,

persons, and events; so it would be a waste of time to seek to reconstruct the historical event by which he was inspired. Aside from this, it would be vain curiosity, since the narrator does not wish to teach us a particular fact in the history of Israel, but the general sense of this history. This narrator is an artist who knows how to draw out his effects. Judith does not appear until chap. 8; the action has much time to develop. The first seven chapters present the setting of the drama. First there is a description of the distant background, and then the schema begins to center our view upon the exact place where the tragedy is enacted. At the same time that the geographical location narrows, the forces of evil are converging to close in on the tiny people of God. One would have to overlook the too well known denouement, in order to feel the agony from this closing of the vise.

§ 3. Contents

In the background of the canvas looms a colossal Nabuchodonosor (chap. 1). Arphaxad, a rival of his stature, builds before him a city with walls of fantastic thickness. Against such an adversary, Nabuchodonosor calls upon the forces of the entire world, from Elam and Persia to the ends of Egypt and Ethiopia. The entire West scorns this appeal. With only his eastern troops, Nabuchodonosor overthrows Ecbatana as if it were a house of cards. The victory was celebrated on the spot with 120 days of merrymaking; but the western peoples, among whom Jerusalem and Samaria occupied a rather modest position, had nothing but bread.

The action develops slowly. Nabuchodonosor remains thereafter in solemn isolation befitting a god (3, 8). Holophernes assumes the task of waging vengeance upon the rebels (2, 1-3). Near Ninive, a huge army is assembled and armed and advances forcefully to the West. In one strike it reaches the western sea and the boundaries of Japhet, the coasts of Ionia. Suddenly deciding to march to the south it lays waste to Syria and Damascus and forces the entire coast, from Tyre

to Gaza, to submit. The army then heads for Egypt. Already
in the plain of Esdrelon, it must reach the coastal route by
passing over the hills that join the mountains of Samaria to
Mount Carmel. The reassembly in the plain takes a whole
month (3, 9-10).

The time for action has arrived. The invading force is at
the foot of the mountains which defend the access to Jerusalem. The narrator gives us a month of respite in order to
allow us to fathom the tragedy of the situation. Against a
great conquering army, Israel is a poor little people that has
just escaped the bonds of captivity (4, 3). The chief-priest
sends an order to the frontiers to bar the passes, especially at
Bethulia; meanwhile solemn prayer and fasting are ordered,
to beg the Lord not to deliver the house of Israel into the
hands of the impious (4, 4-15).

This resistance throws Holophernes into a fury. But the
astute narrator does not hasten the attack. Holophernes has
called together the local chieftains in order to be informed
on the local situation. An Ammonite, Achior, relates at length
what it is that makes Israel a people different from all others;
their history proves that they are invincible as long as they
are faithful to their God. The whole council laughs at him
scornfully. "There is no god but Nabuchodonosor, says Holophernes" (6, 2). Achior is sent up to the front; let him go
and share the lot of this invincible people. In the city, Achior
reveals the plans and the pride of Holophernes. For those
besieged, as for the reader, the mission of Achior was not
without its function. The issue of the battle is clarified: God
and Nabuchodonosor are present as well as the two armies.
Some see in this an apocalyptic trace as in Ez 38—39 or in the
"War of the children of light and of darkness," found at
Qumran.

Finally Holophernes launches his attack (7, 1-3). The people of Bethulia are shut up within the walls (7, 4-5). On the
advice of the Ammonite and Moabite allies who know the
country, the impetuous general defers the final attack. He
has control of the water supply at the foot of the city, and
those under siege can only surrender or die of thirst. Within

the city, the leaders are ready to hold out. But the populace
would have said with Quohelet that a living dog is better
than a dead lion. They prefer to live in slavery rather than
die of hunger and thirst, along with their children. The head
of the city obtains a delay of five days, through great effort.
Who knows if the Lord will show His power here in favor of
His people? Nabuchodonosor had taken five years to overcome Ecbatana; God has five days to beat the mighty and
victorious army.

It is at this point that the heroine enters the scene. Judith
has been a widow for several years. Although wealthy, she
lives a life of prayer and fasting. As in the case of Daniel and
his companions, this strictness in religious observances only
makes her beauty shine more brilliantly (8, 1-8). She calls
together the elders of the city and reproaches them for treating God like a man, in imposing upon him an ultimatum. He
deserves an unlimited confidence, whether He chooses to
chastise us or to save us. Their duty is to sacrifice themselves
in defense of the frontier and of the holy city. Ozias replies
that in five days God has an opportunity to send rain and to
fill the cisterns. It is useless to wait for a miracle, answers
Judith. Let me go out of the city with my handmaid, and
before the five days are up, you will see what God can do
through the hand of a woman (8, 9-36).

The *hand of God* must accomplish everything; Judith
therefore addresses an ardent prayer to the God of her father
Simeon, before going into action (chap. 9). On these mountains where the patriarch beat down the seducers of his sister,
a seducer of the children of Israel is acting sacrilegiously; may
God help His handmaid to seduce the seducer and to beat
him down. Then, unhurriedly, she can launch into action.
She observes the rites of feminine seduction as well as those
of the Law (10, 1-5). Thus she proceeds before the enemy.
From the outposts to the tent of the general, her beauty
opens the way for her (10, 6-23).

Placed in the presence of the seducer of her brothers, she
leads him astray as much by the charm of her conversation as
by her beauty (chap. 11). But amidst the pagans, she stays

faithful to God. Each night she goes to the stream outside camp; after the ritual ablutions, she sends up a pure prayer to God. During the day, she does not touch the food of the pagans, but eats provisions which she has brought along with her, prepared by her handmaid. Three days of waiting pass in this way (12, 1-9). Finally on the fourth day the bait is taken; the general is ashamed of the respect which this Jewess has imposed upon him (12, 10-12). He invites her to a banquet. She shows up, calm as ever. She is left alone with this drunken ruffian. With one last prayer to ask strength of the God of Israel, she cuts off the head of Holophernes with the sword which hangs from the bed-post. As usual, she is allowed to leave the camp; she goes straight to Bethulia with Holophernes's head in the sack used for the provisions of her handmaid (13, 1-10).

The night ends in *thanksgiving*. Ozias blesses this wise, brave woman, and the God who has guided her action. Achior, overcome at the sight of Holophernes's head, confesses his faith in the God of Israel, and has himself circumcised on the battlefield. When the fifth day comes, it is to make known the triumph of Israel. The enemy is in retreat; Israel comes from everywhere to gather the spoils. From Jerusalem the chief-priest himself arrives with the council in order to congratulate Judith: *Tu gloria Jerusalem*. The new Debora intones the song of victory, which is also a hymn of thanksgiving; then the procession makes its way to Jerusalem to make an offering in the Temple of the spoils of the enemy (16, 18-20).

Judith will live a long life, rich and honored, but refusing to all who offer themselves to break her widowhood. Israel rejoices peacefully until her death, and for long after (16, 21-25).

§ 4.   Theology and Morality

Some moralists have condemned the action of Judith who, to achieve a good end, the liberation of her people, uses bad means, deception and seduction. This condemnation overlooks the fact that the book is not a case of conscience nor a book of an edifying nature, but a page of theology. To his enemies as to his servants, God applies the law of talion. Judith is an instrument of justice in His hands. He who wished to seduce Israel into the ways of idolatry must himself be seduced and led astray. The key of the book is the prayer of Judith (chap. 9). Inversely, those who are faithful to God can count on His faithfulness. Judith acts in the role of a prophet; it is God who has put the words into her mouth. She is a model of observance of the Law and of confidence in God. Those who imitate her can count on the *protection of God*. On the other extreme, that pride which reaches even up to God, leads the imitators of Holophernes into the most abject vice and degradation where they will find the miserable end they deserve. Lightning from heaven does not carry out the *just judgments of God*, but they are shown in the normal consequences of human actions. Through the example of Achior the author even carefully shows that no one is excluded from the salvation that comes from Israel.

Cleverness added to courage, prudence in counsel, and calmness and strength in execution, these qualities embellished with a beauty which shines as much in conversation as in appearance, make of Judith a fine example of the ideal Jewish humanist. The Christians did not cease to admire her all the more, since her chastity in widowhood seemed to them a foretaste of Christian virginity. The liturgy only applies the texts of Judith to Mary in recent offices; but these applications are not devoid of all basis. She who cut off the head of the enemy of God and of His people is well in line with her who is to crush the head of the serpent. The beauty of Judith remains, however, quite pale alongside her who is full of grace.

CHAPTER IV

THE BOOKS OF MACHABEES

BIBLIOGRAPHY

Introductions, translations, commentaries, pp. 25 f. and 208
(F. M. ABEL, *BJ**; M. GRANDCLAUDON, *BPC**; D. D.
SCHÖTZ, *EBi**; W. O. E. OESTERLEY, *APOT* . . .).

E. BICKERMANN, "Makkabäerbücher" in PAULY-WISSOWA,
Realenc. des Alt, XIV (Stuttgart, 1928), pp. 779-800; *Die
Makkabäer* (Berlin, 1935); *Der Gott der Makkabäer* (Berlin, 1937).

E. BICKERMAN, *The Maccabees* (New York, 1947).

F. M. ABEL, "Les livres des Maccabées," *EB* (Paris, 1949).

S. ZEITLIN–S. TEDESCHE, *The First Book of Maccabees* (New
York, 1950); *The Second Book of Maccabees* (New York,
1954).

R. NORTH, "Maccabean Sabbath Years," *Biblica*, 34 (1953),
pp. 501-515.

A. LEFÈVRE, "Maccabées (Livres 1 and 2), *SDB*, V (Paris,
1953), cols. 597-612.

A. PENNA, *Libri dei Maccabei** (Turin-Rome, 1953).

J. C. DANCY, *A Commentary on 1 Maccabees* (Oxford,
1954).

W. H. BROWNLEE, "Maccabees, Books of," *IDB*, III, pp. 201-215.

W. FARMER, *Maccabees, Zealots and Josephus* (1956).

T. W. MANSON, "Martyrs and Martyrdom," *BJRL*, 39 (1956-1957), pp. 463-484.

§ 1. Title and Texts

The Books of Machabees owe their title to the surname of
Judas, the main hero of the story. The meaning of the name

is a matter for discussion. It may derive from *maqqaba*, "hammer" (cf. the surname Charles Martel). It well becomes the man who smashed the horn of iniquity (1 Mc 2, 48; cf. Za 2, 1-4). This surname had become as the proper name of Judas (1 Mc 5, 34; 2 Mc *passim*). The giving of this name to the two books broadens its meaning, for the Church thereby designates the seven martyred brothers (2 Mc 7), the only saints of the Old Testament of whom the Latin rite still makes mention. This imprecise usage entails some risk of misunderstanding. The Latin translator of the *Onomasticon* (ed. Klostermann, p. 133; *PL* 23, 911) is already surprised that the relics of the seven martyred Machabee brothers are venerated in Antioch, since the family tomb (Judas) is in a well-known place at Modin in Palestine (1 Mc 9, 19; 13, 25).

In the Greek MSS of the Bible, the Books of Machabees are quite diversely represented.[1] While the Alexandrinus (5th c.) has four books of Machabees and the Sinaiticus (4th c.) only has the first and fourth, the Vaticanus (4th c.) doesn't have any. The ancient Latin versions contain only the first two books, those which the Church retains as canonical.[2] The Vulgate follows this version, which St. Jerome did not wish to alter; yet the Vulgate is hardly a fair testimony of the Latin text. The best testimonies have been edited by Dom De Bruyne who studied the question for a long time.

§ 2.   Book 1

I. CONTENTS

Mc 1 covers a forty-year period, 175-135, from the accession of Antiochus IV to the throne of Syria to the death of Simon, the last of the Machabee brothers. This is the history of the

---

[1] W. KAPLER, *Maccabaeorum liber I* (Septuagint) (Göttingen, 1936).

[2] D. DE BRUYNE, *Les anciennes traductions latines des Machabées** (Analecta Maredsolana IV) (Maredsous, 1932); *RB* (1921), pp. 405-409; (1922), pp. 31-54; (1930), pp. 503-519; (cf. 1933), pp. 263-265.

first Asmonean generation, unfolding in chronological order.
After an introduction describing the situation at the offset
(1—2), it relates the successive leadership of the Jewish resistance by Judas (3, 1—9, 22), Jonathan (9, 23—12, 54), and
Simon (13—16).

The historian knows the art of composition. His introduction is a diptych recounting the progress of impiety (chap. 1)
and the growing resistance (chap. 2). On one side is Hellenism, personified in Alexander, sending forth a shoot that
grows until it sets the abomination on the altar of Jerusalem;
the wrath has come on Israel. On the other side, Judaism is
incarnated in Mattathias, the chief of the Asmonean dynasty.
He calls for resistance, organizes it, and in dying leaves as his
will an impassioned plea to his sons to fight to the death for
the people and for the Law. The faithful Jews are going to
halt the unbridling of wrath.

The sons of Mattathias fell one by one into the breach, but
each one led the fight with his particular temperament and
his own method.

Judas is the hero of the battles. He fires his troops with an
irresistible force by the religious flame burning brightly in
his exhortations as well as in his prayers before battle (3,
18-22. 58-59; 4, 8-11. 30-33; 7, 41-42). Having beaten the
Syrian army, he returns as a conqueror to Jerusalem, where
he purifies the Temple (3—4). Thence he shines forth to the
farthest boundaries of the territory, everywhere present to
help his persecuted compatriots (chap. 5). Epiphones dies
miserably on a distant mission (6, 1-16); against his successors, Eupator (6, 16-23) and Demetrius (7), Judas pursues
the fight until his brilliant victory over Nicanor. The two
feasts of the Dedication and of the day of Nicanor (4, 59 and
7, 49) will preserve for posterity the memory of his exploits.
The narrator inserts documents concerning the diplomatic
activity of Judas (chap. 8), and then relates his glorious death
in a desperate combat (9, 1-22).

Jonathan does not have the heroic grandeur of his brother.
He is more adapted to rugged guerrilla warfare than to open
battle, and he is a very shrewd politician. Because of these

qualities he "judges" Israel in peace for about seven years (9, 23-73). When the Seleucid throne is disputed between Demetrius and Alexander Balas, the wary Jonathan plays the role of arbiter so well that both attribute to him all the honors of the sovereign pontificate in Jerusalem, even as far as the title of chamberlain of the king. Demetrius capitulates; Jonathan obtains from Alexander the purple robe with the titles of strategus and partaker of his dominion (10, 1-66). After a reign of five years, Alexander is supplanted by his cousin Demetrius II; for fifteen years the throne of Antioch will be in dispute among two or even three pretenders. This embroilment is just the thing for the diplomacy of Jonathan, who succeeds in maintaining his privileges, and has his brother Simon appointed strategus of the coastal province. It is an irony of history that the brothers of Judas, having been made officers of the king, control all of the territory of Palestine for the benefit of the successors of Epiphanes. The shrewd diplomat renewed old relations with Sparta. The two brothers enforced the Jewish position by filling the country with strongholds (10, 66–12, 38). How could the clever old warrior allow himself to fall for the trick of Tryphon? Once captured, he will soon be put to death (12, 39-54; 13, 23).

Simon did not await the death of Jonathan to regain control of the situation. Fighting and negotiating at the same time, he does not succeed in saving his brother, but he chases Trypho from the territory and resumes friendly relations with Demetrius II, who recognizes him as head of the Jewish nation (13, 1-42). This marks the beginning of a new era, the era of liberation: "Letters and contracts came to be dated from the first year of Simon" (the year 170 of the Greeks = B.C. 142: 13, 42). Valorous and shrewd like his brothers, Simon knows also how to deal with clemency; thus he obtains with the least output the surrender of the last isles of resistance, in particular that of the famous Acre at Jerusalem (13, 43-53). In order to eulogize such a savior of the country, the author has no qualms about using characteristics which were employed in speaking of the Messianic hope (14, 1-15). Sparta, Rome and Antioch recognize the sovereignty of Simon, ethnarch of the Jews (14, 16—15, 24). A passing quarrel with Antiochus VII, who reigned during the captivity of his brother Demetrius II, gives the sons of Simon a chance to show their valor (16, 1-10). The renowned old man dies during a banquet from the blow of a mediocre rival. But the book closes with the name of his son John, who was to be the father of the Asmonean kings.

The conclusion of the book imitates the formula which ends each reign in the Book of Kings. This supposes that the author is writing after the death of John Hyrcanus, which took place in 104 after a pontificate of over thirty years. His sons Aristobulus I (104-103) and Alexander Janneus (103-76) assumed the kingly title. This book must have been written under the reign of Janneus to glorify the ancestors of the dynasty.

St. Jerome had seen the original Hebrew text. Origen has given us the early title in a barely readable transcription, σαρβηθ σαρβαναιελ. The Greek version of the LXX is the source for all existing translations: the ancient Latin version preserved good readings throughout, permitting a better reading of the actual Greek MSS.

II. LITERARY GENRE

Living in Palestine and writing in the sacred language, the author imitated the literary forms of the ancient historical books (Judges, Samuel, Kings). But the Hellenistic influence taught him how to compose with a supple style. His accounts are sober, with a dash of enthusiasm. Especially the prayers, songs of thanksgiving, speeches of the leaders, and eulogy of heroes are emotional and all strive for the manner of expression found in the ancient biblical poems.

We must take into account this traditional style in estimating the value of the author's statements: "Not one of them escaped" (7, 46), "Not one perished" (5, 54). Such expressions, as well as large numbers, are not the formulae of a modern statistician, but are the very appropriate testimony of one living close to the facts. This testimony has much value. Numerous official documents are reproduced (10 in chaps. 11–15 alone); they are considered to be of highest quality by specialists of antiquity. Even if the form has suffered in the process of a double translation, we can have confidence in the author when he says he is transcribing a letter or giving a summary of it.

The sacred author emphasizes the religious meaning of events, but he only ties them in according to chronological order. This lack of historical reflection on causal sequence has saved him from the mistakes which Josephus made in trying to do the work of a historian. The chronology is given according to the Greek era of the Seleucids which begins in the autumn of 312.

III. Teaching

The *religious views* of the author are those of the ancient historians, imbued with the theology of Deuteronomy: "Observe the Law and you will possess the earth." The Law is at the center of everything; it is the Law which divides men into two camps. The struggle is not between the Seleucids and the Asmoneans, nor even between the pagan kingdoms and the Jewish state; it is between the observers of the Law and their enemies. The sons of Mattathias have no scruples in dealing with pagan powers as long as this can serve to insure the observance of the Law. But even though they count on the promises of the Covenant, they do not rest in a quietistic fatalism. The author has no praise for those who let themselves be slaughtered so as not to violate the repose of the Sabbath. It is better to fight in order to make possible the observance of the Law. They even go further to the extent of forcefully imposing respect for the religious prescriptions (2, 39-48). The greatest glory is to die, weapon in hand, in defense of the Law (2, 64). This history thus extols human values at the same time as it extols supernatural values: faith gives rise to heroism, and the service of the country is merged with service of God.

Some rather precise political aims are hinted at in this

book. When John Hyrcanus and his sons ran into opposition from the strict observers of the Law, the Pharisees, it became useful to recall that the Asmonean dynasty owed its rise to power to its zeal for the Law. The Asmonean prejudice, felt everywhere, is sometimes emphasized without false timidity (5, 62). On the other hand, the Assideans, the spiritual ancestors of the Pharisees, do not always show common sense in their lofty fidelity to the Law (7, 8-18). These allusions discreetly recall to the Pharisees the fact that their rallying to the Asmoneans would perhaps be the best way to serve the interests of the Law.

Nevertheless, this history leaves the Christian unsatisfied. It appears somewhat excessive to us that deep religious sentiment can go so far as to avoid pronouncing the name of God. But the predominance of the Law and the silence of the prophets are not without danger. The possession of the earth bears the risk of limiting the ambitions of hope; the eulogy of Simon, in Messianic terms, manifests this idea. In fact, even with the Chosen People, the union of the political and the religious does not come about without risk of confusion. Mattathias would never have thought that his sons would have to worry about the favor of pagan kings in order to obtain dignities and functions in their state, even less the function of chief priest. This deviation became more accentuated later, when the sons of John Hyrcanus had taken on the title of king. We know that this dynasty succeeded in putting on the throne of Jerusalem the Idumean Herod: a strange result from an uprising so pure in its origins.

§ 3.   Book 2

Although it recounts in part the same history, the second book is very different from the first in many respects. First of all, it was written in Greek. Since the text is lacking in the most ancient MSS (Vat., Sin.), the old Latin version is a valuable witness here. The author, probably an Alexandrian Jew, tells us he is summarizing a work of five books by Jason of

Cyrene. We know nothing of this Jason and his work. The summary which our inspired author gives us recounts the persecution from its remote beginnings in 175, and then the struggles of Judas Machabee up to his victory over Nicanor in 160.

I. CONTENTS

As a sort of introduction (1, 1–2, 18), two letters from the Jews of Jerusalem are transcribed. They invite their brethren from Egypt to come and celebrate with them the feast of the Dedication on 25 Casleu. The letter is dated 124, the fortieth anniversary of the purification of the Temple by Judas. The second letter is more ancient; after recalling the death of Antiochus the persecutor, it gives a long account of the marvelous deeds which mark the first restoration of the Temple under Nehemias, so as to heighten the importance of the actual feast. These documents, originating from Jerusalem, are translated from the Hebrew.

Then the proper work of the author begins in a preface where he explains his intentions and his method (2, 19-32). He has laboriously deciphered the massive work of Jason, full of numbers; he makes himself derive from it a readable story for the use of cultured people. In order to do so, he had to take liberty with the sources; and yet he is not writing a history in the technical sense of the term. This is a unique case in the Bible; the inspired author himself defines for us what literary genre he will use.

The work develops in five episodes, where the Temple always occupies the center of perspective.

Under the care of a pious high priest such as Onias, the holiness of the Temple is inviolable; Heliodorus learns this at his own expense (chap. 3).

When the office of chief priest becomes the prey of intriguers in favor of Hellenization, such as Jason and Menelaus, the wrath of God weighs heavy on Israel, the Temple is looted and profaned by impure victims. The sacrifice which

faithful Jews make of their life is an expiation which will
stop the wrath of the All-Powerful (4–7).

"The wrath of the Lord having changed into mercy," Judas
overthrows the pagans. Antiochus dies with the realization
that the hand of God has stricken him. Judas purifies the
Temple (8, 1–10, 9).

Under the administration of Lysias, who rules for Eupator,
Judas wages war on all fronts, against the royal troops, against
the Hellenized cities, and against the surrounding pagan
peoples. Thus he obtains recognition of freedom of worship;
Lysias even has sacrifices offered in the Temple, and asks
the neighboring cities not to trouble the Jews (10, 10–13,
26). The intriguer Menelaus is put to death.

Under Demetrius, who has killed Lysias and Eupator, a
new pretender, Alcimus, wishes to become chief priest with
the support of the king. Nicanor, leader of the royal army,
blasphemes against the Temple. He is defeated and slain by
Judas. His head is exposed in front of the Temple, and they
sing: "Blessed is he who has kept his dwelling free from all
defilement." A feast will recall this victory each year (14,
1–15, 37).

Finally, in fine rhetorical style, the writer takes his leave
from the reader, praising his work for its modesty of expression (15, 38-39).

II. Literary genre

Each of these episodes is composed in the *oratorical manner*:
this is a discourse to move and to persuade. With Onias we
have a taste of the peace in the regular service of the Temple;
then we share his anguish when the holy place is threatened;
lastly we share the joy of triumph when the chastised Heliodorus becomes aware of the holiness of God who dwells there.
In the second discourse, impiety and the anger of God progress from Jason to Menelaus and from the plundering of
the Temple to its profanation; by contrast the death of the
martyrs, which is supposed to put a halt to the wrath of God,
leaves the reader with an impression of hope. In the last three

discourses, Judas is exalted while his enemies are beaten
down, Epiphanes, Lysias and Eupator, and finally Nicanor.
Each proclaims in its own fashion the glory of the All-
Powerful who manifests Himself in the Temple. Everything
works together for the glory of God who has set His dwelling
place in Jerusalem (3, 38; 7, 37; 10, 7; 13, 23; 15, 34).

The author pleads his case like a lawyer. He artfully selects
and highlights emotional episodes. Resounding epithets, bit-
ing remarks, and a broad but not bombastic style, all this is
the work of an orator. We find ourselves here in a genre
widespread in Hellenistic literature, a genre rightly called
pathetic history.

With this in mind we are able to size up the statements
of the author. He is concerned with clarifying the meaning
and religious import of the events related; but he neglects
details which a careful historian would demand. Chronological order yields to the demands of oratorical composition.
Within the narrative the orator rightfully may choose and
magnify outstanding traits. The "help from heaven" (1 Mc
16, 3) here assumes the form of heavenly signs (2 Mc 3,
24-26; 10, 29-30; 11, 8; cf. 12, 22; 15, 11-16). These
"epiphanies," apparitions of the gods coming to help com-
batants, were common in the Hellenistic genre of pathetic
history which Jason of Cyrene imitates. The Jewish author
has transposed the process so as to make it conform with
his faith in Providence which governs the world through the
angels. The inspired author has borrowed these tales from
Jason.

In spite of oratorical liberties, 2 Mc remains a *historical*
work. His plea derives its historical value from the historicity
of facts which were not at all remote. Actually a comparison
with the first book allows us to verify the exactness of its
documentation (cf. *below* the table of concordance with the
two books). The documents proper to the second book (letters and decrees: 2 Mc 9, 17-27; 11, 16-38) are presented
with the same guarantee of authenticity as those of the
first. The festal letter at the beginning (1, 1-9) is just what we
might expect from the scribes of Jerusalem. The long re-

minder that goes with it (1, 10–2, 18) has many characteristics of a haggadic construction. Our author had no illusions, and he took care to give a more exact account of the death of Antiochus (chap. 9, cf. 1, 13-17). On two important points 2 Mc happily completes the ideas, brief as they are, of 1 Mc: the part taken by the chief priests in the attempts at Hellenization (2 Mc 4) better explains the origins of the conflict, and the arrangements made with Lysias (2 Mc 11) replace the purification of the Temple in a more realistic historical context.

III.   DOCTRINE

It is especially from the religious point of view that the second book surpasses the first. The cult of the Law is no longer linked with political aims. The struggle is between Judaism (the word appears here for the first time: 2, 21; 8, 1; 14, 38) and Hellenism (4, 13). They are diametrically opposed. Compromise can only lead to disaster (4, 7-17), and there is no question of accepting the office of chief priest through the nod of a pagan king (11, 2-3).

This uncompromising trait of religion stems from its *holiness*. The sacred Law could not be broken (6, 23. 28), even if it were a case of legitimate self-defense (5, 25; 6, 6; 15, 3). The holy Lord of all holiness (14, 36) can allow no stain upon the holy land, in the holy city, in His holy dwelling, and among His holy people. The sword of Judas is holy too, inasmuch as it comes from God (15, 16), and it is no surprise to find the heavenly armies taking part in the fighting.

The stakes of the battle are really beyond this earth. We could even say that Judas is striving for the coming of the kingdom of the saints, which Daniel mentions. Faith in a resurrection transfers to another world the enjoyment of the good things promised (7; 14, 16). But while awaiting this outcome, all the saints strive steadily for the coming of the kingdom. Prayer, ritual sacrifice, and voluntary sacrifice of one's own life have effects which are not limited merely to the present generation (15, 11-16; 12, 39-45; 7, 32-38). Such Judaism does not undergo the risk of being sidetracked into a political movement, since it transcends earthly values.

If there is one distinguishing mark to show the difference between the two books, it is their view of the *martyrs*. In the first book, their death is only a result of the wrath which has come upon Israel (1 Mc 1, 64); it is armed resistance that will turn aside this wrath, and the sword of Judas will effect this (3, 8). In the second book, the pain suffered is indeed a chastisement, but its voluntary acceptance is itself an expiation that stems the wrath of God; if Judas comes off victoriously, it is because his sacrifice has been acceptable (2 Mc 7, 36; 8, 5).

IV. INFLUENCE

2 Mc must have been composed shortly after the reception of the letter from Jerusalem on the Dedication. This puts it before 1 Mc, about 120. The book of Jason, a few years previous to this, is therefore close to the events. In the Jewish milieu, Philo seems to have been familiar with 2 Mc; 4 Mc, a little later, forms a long treatise on the martyrs which derives its inspiration from 2 Mc. But Josephus, who uses 1 Mc frequently, does not seem to have known 2 Mc. In the NT, Heb 11, 35 must refer back to the martyrs of 2 Mc 6—7. Among the Fathers of the Church, the citations begin in the 3rd century. The cult of the seven martyred brothers must have begun in Antioch in the 4th century, for St. John Chrysostom gave two discourses in their honor.[3] Aside from the Scripture readings in the breviary for the month of October, the Roman liturgy does not use the first book; readings from the second are used in the Mass of the Dead, at the Mass for Peace, and on Ember Saturday during Lent.

[3] *PG*, 50, 617-626: cf. H. DELEHAYE, *Origine du culte des martyrs*[2]* (Brussels, 1933), pp. 201-202.

§ 4. Concordance of the Two Books

This table gives corresponding sections of 1 and 2 Mc; it
serves to show the liberties which 2 Mc takes with the
chronological order.

Accession of Antiochus IV		
Epiphanes		
(September 175)		
Hellenism at Jerusalem	1, 10-15	4
Plundering of the Temple		
(169)	16-28	5, 1-20
Misdeeds of the governors	29-32	21, 26
The Acre, stronghold of		
Hellenism	33-40	
Enforced Hellenization	41-55	6, 1-9
The abomination on the altar	54, 59	
Massacre of the faithful	56-63	10-11
Divine wrath	64	12-17
Eleazar. The seven brother		
martyrs		18-7, 42
Mattathias and his sons resist	2, 1-28	cf. 5, 27
Slaughter of observers of the		
Sabbath	29-38	cf. 5, 25; 6, 11
Organized resistance	39-48	
Last will and death of		
Mattathias	49-70	
Judas begins his campaign	3, 1-26	8, 1-7
Epiphanes in the East, Lysias		
regent	27-37	cf. 10, 10-13
Judas defeats Nicanor and		
Gorgias at Emmaus	3, 38—4, 25	8, 8-29, 34-36
Résumé of the other		
campaigns		30-33
First campaign of Lysias	4, 26-35	11, 1-12
Negotiations, tolerance		13-21, 27-38
Cleansing of the Temple,		
Dedication	36-61	10, 1-8
Struggles against neighboring		
peoples	5, 1-67	10, 14-23; 12, 1-45
Timothy killed at Gazara		10, 24-38
Death of Epiphanes (*ca.*		
December 164)	6, 1-16	9, cf. 1, 13-17

Decree of pacification by Eupator		11, 22-26
Lysias remains regent	17	10, 9-11
Attempts of Judas against Acre	18-27	
Second campaign of Lysias	28-54	13, 1-22
Peace obtained, Lysias retires	55-63	23-26
Demetrius acquires the throne (*ca.* November 162)	7, 1-4	14, 1-2
Intrigues of Alcimus, Bacchides	5-25	3-4
New offensive of Alcimus, Nicanor	26-32	5-30
Nicanor blasphemes against the Temple	33-38	31-36
Heroism of Razis		37-46
The day of Nicanor	39-49	15

Only dates (B.C.) verifiable from secular sources are given. The events proper to 2 Mc, put in italics, are outside the series, impossible to date.

CHAPTER V

WISDOM

BIBLIOGRAPHY

Introductions, translations, commentaries, pp. 25 f. and 208
(J. J. Weber, *BPC**; E. Osty, *BJ**; J. Fischer, *EBi**;
C. Lattey, *CCHS**; S. Holmes, *APOT* . . .).

P. Heinisch, *Das Buch der Weisheit** (Münster, 1912).

C. E. Purinton, "Translation Greek in the Wisdom of
Solomon," *JBL*, 47 (1928), pp. 276-304.

Macdonald, *The Hebrew Philosophical Genius* (1936).

J. Fichtner, *Weisheit Salomos* (Tübingen, 1938).

L. Bigot, "Sagesse (Le livre de la)," *DTC*, XIV (Paris,
1939), cols. 703-744.

H. Duesberg, *Les scribes inspirés**, II (Paris, 1939), pp.
441-592.

A. M. Dubarle, *Les sages d'Israël** (Paris, 1946), pp. 187-
235.

P. Skehan, "Isaias and the Teaching of the Book of Wisdom,"
CBQ, 10 (1948), pp. 384-397; "Borrowings from the
Psalms in the Book of Wisdom," *CBQ*, 3 (1941); *The
Literary Relationship Between the Book of Wisdom and
the Protocanonical Books of the Old Testament* (1938).

J. Henning, "The Book of Wisdom in the Liturgy," *CBQ*,
14 (1952), pp. 233-236.

J. Reider, *The Book of Wisdom* (New York, 1957).

R. Murphy, "To Know Your Might is the Root of Immortality (Wis xv: 3)," *CBQ*, 25 (1963), pp. 88-93.

A. Wright, "The Structure of Wisdom 11-19," *CBQ*, 27
(1964), pp. 28-34.

§ 1. The Book

I. TITLE

This book is called Wisdom of Solomon by the Greek MSS of the Bible, which place it just before the Wisdom of the Son of Sira in the group of sapiential books. The Vulgate simply calls it the Book of Wisdom, in order to emphasize its superior quality within the sapiential genre. It is actually the most interesting as far as doctrine is concerned, the closest to the New Testament, and also the most well composed. It was written in Greek by an author who possessed a facility in this language. Already St. Jerome noted this, and for this reason left it out of the canon, in which he only admitted Hebrew books. Nevertheless, as W. O. E. Oesterley puts it (*Introduction*, p. 196), "this book was certainly regarded in the early Church as one of the most important, perhaps the most important, of the books which we list as apocryphal." It is frequently cited or used by the Fathers, and the canon of Muratori (2nd c.) ranks it among the books of the New Testament written by the "friends of Solomon."

II. AUTHOR

The attribution to Solomon is obviously fictitious; St. Augustine knows this as well as St. Jerome and Origen do. In placing his teaching on the lips of Solomon, to whom he attributes an audience of kings, the author heightens the glory of his work according to the custom of the time; by so doing he also gives it a place within the traditional development of Israelite wisdom. The author is unknown, but his emphasis on everything in relation to Egypt leads us to believe that he is writing in Alexandria, or at some important center of Jewish culture. The attribution of the book to Philo, already pointed out by St. Jerome, has found some partisans in our times; but the doctrine, the exegetical methods, the style and the language are too different for one to hold this opinion. The assimilation of Greek culture is much more superficial than that of the Jewish philosopher. The tone of the book would fit in well in the first half of the 1st century B.C., when the Jews of Egypt were exposed to the vagaries of Ptolemy VIII.

§ 2.   Composition

The present work exhibits a unity of composition to which we are not accustomed in the Hebrew sapiential books. Still we would not expect to find here the logic of a modern philosophical treatise. The style undergoes quite obvious variations from one part to another; but this is not necessarily evidence of more than one author. It suffices to say that the book was not all written in one stroke, and that the author was under the literary influence of the sources in which he sought his inspiration. The first chapters (1–5) rely mainly on the Prophets, and their style is quite Hebraic; chapters 6–9, which, just as the Proverbs, use bits and pieces from Greek philosophy, are already marked by a lesser degree of biblical style; the last chapters (10–19), where the history of Israel is quite distant from the canonical sources, have a style entirely independent of the OT.

The divisions which we have just indicated leave us with three main parts of the work: the way of Wisdom, opposed to the way of the impious (1–5); Wisdom itself (6–9); and the works of Wisdom in the unfolding of history (10–19).

I.   WISDOM AND THE IMPIOUS

The substance of the introduction is a hortatory discourse (1, 1-15). "Seek God, instead of running after death. Love justice, which is immortal." *Wisdom is presented as a spirit which comes from God, but which becomes more interior to man than himself.* It is offered in order to guide him along the path which leads to God; as an interior witness of the most secret thoughts, Wisdom brings upon those who despise her an inexorable judgment. To reject her is to deliver oneself up to death. Appearances may be deceiving at times, but reality will appear when the justice of God is revealed.

The following chapters describe this judgment. They unfold in the form of a *trial*. We hear first the impious, who find themselves called friends of death (1, 16). Death is really the only absolute for them, and they judge everything by this criterion. The road appears very short to them, but the certainty of death incites them to take unlimited pleasure in life (2, 1-9). They have only revilement and hatred towards the words of the Just One whose conduct is a reproach to them. May his death make them right (2, 10-20)!

The just do not plead their own cause, but the wise man will explain the true doctrine in a series of images opposed to one another. These madmen are ignorant of the fact that life is a mystery hidden in God (2, 21-24); the death of the just is only apparent (3, 1-4). The *judgment of God* will make the glory of the just appear (3, 5-9), as well as the unmitigated misery of the wicked who have been chastised even into their descendants (3, 10-12). In what does a fruitful life consist? Even there appearances are deceiving. The barrenness of the just (3, 13-15) is blessed, while the offspring of adulterers is destined for evil (3, 16-19); barrenness joined with virtue produces lasting fruit (4, 1-2), while the abundant offspring of the impious perishes into nothingness (4, 3-6). What is a long life? It is the life of the just, suddenly snatched away, but redeemed at the judgment (4, 7-15), whereas the wicked will be struck down due to a long life of sin (4, 16-20).

The judgment also reveals the *true values*. The just man presents himself with assurance, though always silent (5, 1); the wicked come with trembling, forced to admit their mistake when it is too late (5, 2-14). The long confession (5, 3-13) is just the opposite of the insolent speech at the beginning, but does not make up for it (2, 1-20). The just will reign eternally with the Lord (5, 15-16), while the divine spirit becomes a storm which overthrows the wicked (5, 17-23). The warnings in the beginning come true on the last day.

II. TRUE WISDOM

Wisdom has led the just to true royalty; an easy transition leads Solomon into his exposition on *kingly Wisdom* (6—9). He begins by warning the kings to think of the strict judgment awaiting them (6, 1-11). Then he arouses a desire for wisdom in his noble listeners by picturing it in the brightest light possible (6, 12-25). Wisdom goes before those who seek her and brings them to the very throne of God to reign eternally. In his generosity, Solomon finds no greater joy than that of sharing the treasure which he has received as a grace; in order to make known the blessings of Wisdom, he will describe his own experience.

Solomon begins by recalling that he is a man like all other men (7, 1-6). It is only through a gift of God, the answer to his prayers, that he has become wise (7, 7). He esteemed Wisdom above all (7, 8-10), and he was not deceived, for it brought him all good things (7, 11-14). In his discourse he elaborates upon the qualities which give Wisdom such great value: it teaches everything about creation (7, 15-21), for it is the all-pervading harmony at the heart of all existence (7, 22-24); more precisely, *it is the emanation of the beauty and power of God unto all creation*, thus rendering lovable to the Creator the beings in whom He finds Himself, especially in the human soul (7, 25—8, 1). So it is that Solomon sought for and loved this Wisdom, the only object of divine love (8, 2-3), inasmuch as she procures all good things, wealth and virtue, wit and knowledge, and everlasting renown (8, 4-13). Wisdom assists the king in governing men and is with him in his moments of leisure to relax him (8, 14-16). With this in mind Solomon still knows that this Wisdom is beyond all his deserving, in spite of his natural talent. He can obtain it only by prayer (8, 17-21). The prayer of Solomon (chap.

9) is the highpoint of the entire treatise on Wisdom (6–8), in which he summarizes the essential characteristics of it. This is also the spiritual highpoint of the book.

III. THE WORKS OF WISDOM

The last word of the prayer evoked the saving role of Wisdom (9, 18); the remainder of the book will show Wisdom at work in this role. It has saved the patriarchs from Adam to Joseph from all dangers of body and soul; but those who stray from her, such as Cain and Sodom, have brought catastrophe upon the earth (10, 1-14). Wisdom also saved the Chosen People through her servant Moses, whereas she has made her enemies perish (10, 15-21). This entire history, retold without a proper name, is quite clear to one who has read Genesis and Exodus.

The salvation of the people is then resumed and expanded in detail. A series of seven episodes contrast the manner in which God forms His children by salutary trials, to the manner in which He brings the wicked to their ruin with the same means. Seven plagues come into play, thirst (11, 2-14), famine (16, 1-4), animal bites (16, 5-14), hailstorm instead of manna (16, 15-29), darkness (17, 1–18, 4), wretched death (18, 5-25), and the abyss (19, 1-12).

God's course of action could thus seem to be lacking in goodness or in justice. A twofold digression, inserted between the two first episodes, answers the objection. God has shown His mercy even to pagan people (11, 15–12, 27). Idolaters are alone responsible for their ruin: in making creatures their gods, they have made all creation their enemy (11, 15-16). The lengthy diatribe against idolatry brings to the fore the responsibility of pagans led astray by vanity (13–15). It is through their folly that they have lost the blessing that God had set upon all creatures (15, 19).

The conclusion of the book takes up the same idea under a different form (19, 13-22). The elements of creation form a harmony which operates to the disadvantage of those who oppose the divine order, while it is the joy and glory of the people of God.

§ 3.   The Book of Wisdom and Hellenism

In itself, the Book of Wisdom has achieved the harmony of an entirely new genre by uniting *qualities of the Hebraic mentality to those of the Greek spirit*. In spite of some borrowings from Greek logic, such as the outline of a sorite (6, 17-20), the author remains faithful to the parallelism, mainly antithetic, which is dear to the Hebraic style; chaps. 1—5 and 10—19 are entirely built on this model. But the Alexandrian Jew has acquired the Greek art of transition. He passes painlessly from one development to another. The link between chapters 10 and 11 is the masterpiece of the genre. In the seven examples of men saved in chap. 10, Wisdom has been at work (10, 1. 3. 5. 6. 10. 13. 15). In the seven episodes of chaps. 11 to 19 God is at work, and a form of prayer develops which addresses itself to God in the second person, as in the psalms of thanksgiving. The first invocation to the Lord is neatly linked to the end of the eulogy to Wisdom (10, 20), while at the beginning of the psalm of thanksgiving a statement in the third person does not specify whether it refers to Wisdom or to God (11, 1). The artifice is a little too obvious, and a person familiar with the Dialogues of Plato would find our author somewhat crude; however, the veneer of Greek culture gives us a more ready access to him than do the old masterpieces of Hebraic Wisdom, such as Job or Proverbs 1—9.

Greek philosophy has not exercised a very profound influence. Some terms are borrowed from the eclectic philosophy of the age, in which Stoicism was dominant. In general they serve to translate various ideas long admitted into the religious thoughts of the Israelites (πρόνοια 14, 3; διοικεῖν 8, 1; 12, 18; 15, 1; στοιχεῖα 7, 17; 19, 18; συνέχον 1, 7; etc.). The assimilation remains superficial and incomplete. Thus we find that the soul is at times in opposition to the body as in Platonic thought (9, 15), and sometimes it is parallel with it, as in Hebraic usage where either soul or body can be used to designate a living person (1, 4). Likewise justice is sometimes the cardinal virtue of the philosophers (8, 7 end), and sometimes the free gift by which God makes man conformable to divine law (8, 7 beginning), a peculiarly Hebrew concept.

§ 4. Doctrine

The doctrine is indeed that of the OT. It has a Hellenized facade in order to meet the demands of the readers, the Jews of the Diaspora, and through them the demands of the more or less sympathetic pagans. During the Machabean era, Israel had taken on a clearer consciousness of retribution in the afterlife. Daniel and 2 Mc on this matter spoke of resurrection (Dn 12, 2-3; 2 Mc 7); Wisdom avoids this notion which offended the Greeks (cf. Acts 17, 32), and speaks of immortality, a Greek word without an equivalent in the OT. But we are not concerned here with the immortality of the soul which the philosophers demonstrate, although it is presupposed; the immortality which Wisdom gives is the blessed immortality, a sharing in the eternity of God (2, 23; 5, 15; 6, 19). The wealth of revealed truth, of which the prophets give us a glimpse in often obscure images, finds a clear and precise expression in its contact with Greek thought.

A new synthesis, the teaching of the Book of Wisdom is deeply traditional. There would be no difficulty in finding its elements scattered throughout the prophets and the sapiential books. But this presentation answered to the needs of the age and constituted the final preparation of the human spirit for Christian revelation.

There were at that time many doctrines of salvation. Salvation was sought in the mysteries, in philosophy, and in Gnosticism. Wisdom answers this need. The mystique which provides entrance into divine mysteries is Wisdom (8, 4); it is she who teaches all knowledge, including that of nature, of man, and that of pleasing God (7, 21. 27; 8, 5-18). The philosophy of good fortune is too transitory; Wisdom teaches the justice which leads to immortality (1—5). But this justice and this wisdom are not qualities that man can acquire through his own resources, a fact which both Jews and Greeks have a hard time admitting: *encrateia* is a grace one must ask of God (8, 19-21). The road to salvation is justice, but it is a justice that first of all must be a gift of God in order to become a virtue of man.

What then is Wisdom? Nothing less than God Himself in communication with spiritual creation. Already in Wisdom God gives to His creatures a reflection of His beauty (7, 22—8, 1), the internal cohesion making all things subsist (1, 7); but *to man God communicates in a more intimate manner* which assumes an acceptance by a free creature; thus man enters into participation with the divine nature, and with His immortality (1-15; 2, 23). Wisdom enters the soul which is open to her and makes it lovable in the eyes of God (9, 10-12; 10, 16); she leads it along the paths of the service of God to the life close to God, the eternal life (6, 9-21; 10).

We are on the threshold of the NT. St. Paul and St. John use the same formulae in speaking about the spirit which God sends into the heart of His faithful to make them acceptable in His eyes, and to make charity grow in them along with all virtues. The glory of the Word is described likewise in terms borrowed from Wisdom (Col 1, 15; Heb 1, 3; etc.). We must not ask more of our author than what he knows. The Trinity has not been revealed to him. But he has advanced as far as possible the preparation of the human spirit to receive this revelation.

CHAPTER VI

ECCLESIASTICUS (SIRACH)

BIBLIOGRAPHY

Introductions, translations, commentaries, pp. 25 f. and 208
(C. SPICQ, BPC*; H. DUESBERG–P. AUVRAY, BJ*; V.
HAMP, EBi*; G. H. BOX–W. O. E. OESTERLEY,
APOT . . .).

N. PETERS, Das Buch Jesus-Sirach oder Ecclesiasticus* (Münster, 1913).

J. MARCUS, The Newly Discovered Hebrew of Ben Sira
(Philadelphia, 1931).

G. R. DRIVER, "Hebrew Notes on the 'Wisdom of Jesus ben
Sirach'," JBL, 53 (1934), pp. 273-290.

H. DUESBERG, Les scribes inspirés*, II (Paris, 1939), pp.
232-440.

A. M. DUBARLE, Les Sages d'Israël* (Paris, 1946), pp. 147-
185.

L. ROTH, "Ecclesiasticus in the Synagogue Service," JBL, 71
(1952), pp. 171-178.

R. SIEBENECK, "May Their Bones Return to Life!—Sirach's
Praise of the Fathers," CBQ, 21 (1959), pp. 411-428.

L. HARTMANN, "Sirach in Hebrew and Greek," CBQ, 23
(1961), pp. 443-451.

A. DILELLA, "Qumran and the Geniza Fragments of Sirach,"
CBQ, 24 (1962), pp. 245-267.

Ecclesiasticus has in Greek the title "Wisdom of the Son of
Sirach." The author mentions himself near the end of the
book (50, 27), adding that he is from Jerusalem. The Latin
name, Ecclesiasticus, has not yet been fully explained, but it
is in use by the time of Cyprian.

§ 1. Text

Jesus, the son, or rather descendant, of Sirach, wrote in Hebrew. His grandson put the work into Greek for the use of
the Jews of Alexandria, among whom he lived during the 38th
year of Ptolemy Euergetes. He tells us this in the prologue
that he places at the beginning of his translation. Of the two
Ptolemy Euergetes, only the second, Ptolemy VII, has a reign
of over 38 years (170-116); thus the grandson must have
translated the work after 132. We can reasonably suppose
that Ben Sirach himself wrote about fifty years earlier, about
180. In his youth he may have seen the chief priest Simon II,
whose majesty had overwhelmed him (50, 1-21).

St. Jerome had seen the Hebrew text which Jewish authors
cite up to the 10th century; then it falls into oblivion until
our own time. In 1896 some pages bought by chance in the
East produced several fragments of it. Subsequent inquiry
showed that these pages had originated in Cairo from the
geniza of an old synagogue. The source was carefully ex-
plored, the scattered pages were reassembled, and the librar-
ies of Europe and America now possess about ⅔ of the Hebrew text of the recovered book. The fragments come from
five different copies, dating from the 11th or 12th century.[1]

These discoveries gave new impetus to textual study. The
textual tradition of Sir is one of the most complicated. The
Greek is longer than the Hebrew, and the Latin (unrevised
by St. Jerome) is longer still. Yet the Latin is on the whole
the translation of a Greek text, and the Greek comes from a
Hebrew original. Certain additions are of Latin and Greek
origin, but some even stem from a Hebrew text that is already
glossed. Even the specialists have had a hard time unraveling

---

[1] I. Levi, *The Hebrew Text of the Book of Ecclesiasticus* (Leyden, 1951); J. Touzard, "L'original hébreu de l'Ecclésiastique," *RB*
(1897), pp. 547-573; (1898), pp. 33-58; id., "Nouveaux fragments
hébreux de l'Ecclésiastique," *RB* (1900), pp. 45-62, 525-563.

this confusion, but one thing is certain: the successive editors of the text, whether Hebrew, Greek, or Latin, all had the tendency to add explanations of their own.

To heighten the confusion, the Greek exemplar from which all the mss derive had reversed the order of two sections (30, 25–33, 13a changed places with 33, 13b–36, 16a). Through this displacement and the abundance of superscripts there resulted a variation in the numbering of chapters and verses among the various editions, a fact which tries the patience of researchers.

§ 2. Contents

The work of Ben Sirach, by its very nature, could expect such disturbances. It is a collection of sentences without order on the most disparate topics. The Greek has interspersed the book with titles (2, 1; 18, 30; 20, 27; 23, 7; 24, 1; 30, 1. 14. 16; 32, 1; 33, 25; 44, 1; 51, 1); but these titles often concern only short passages and do not constitute a division of the work. Only the title of 44, 1, "The Eulogy of the Fathers," is already in the Hebrew text, and it is at the head of an important section (44–50). Neater divisions are marked by two little epilogues (24, 28-32 and 33, 16-18) analogous to the final epilogue (50, 27-29; 51, 13-30); we can evince from this that the early book was gradually increased by successive appendages.

Within the body of the work a certain number of *poems to the glory of Wisdom or of God the Creator* serve at the same time to divide it up and to link the partial collections to one another. A hymn to Wisdom begins the series (1, 1-10); it is prolonged by a group of statements about wisdom and the fear of God (1, 11-30). Then come the first rudiments of formation in wisdom. A courage made of wisdom and confidence is necessary in order to begin the journey (chap. 2). The first steps are filial piety (3, 1-16), respect for all that exceeds the capacity of a beginner (3, 17-27), and the works of mercy which make the beginning wise man ready, and render him beloved to God and man (3, 28—4, 10). This ends with a eulogy to Wisdom who trains her children for glory, making them pass through instructive trials (4, 11-19).

In the following collection, the disciple learns to *discern true values*, good and bad shame, confidence and presumption, and the advantages and dangers of friendship (4, 20—6, 17). A new invitation to enroll in the school of those wise in the fear of the Lord (6, 18-37), to enter it with both courage and modesty, begins a collection of sayings which usher the disciple into the great task of life in society (7, 1—14, 19). All elements of human society pass in review, the professional and family settings, priests and the poor, the aged and the dead, the hot-tempered, the sot, all temperaments, women, friends, the powerful, the princely. The teacher profits from this in teaching his disciple the just mean, so difficult to maintain in regard to material goods, for death takes away honor and riches alike. Beyond the thought of death, it is the fear of God that sums up this teaching. The eulogy of the wise man who fears God (14, 20—15, 10) and a series of thoughts on man before God (15, 11—16, 21) end with a hymn to the Creator (16, 22—18, 13).

Within the easy-going collection that follows we can see a twofold warning against the excesses of the tongue and against lustful involvements (18, 14—23, 27). After a prayer to obtain the grace of self-mastery (23, 1-6), the series ends with advice on the use of speech (23, 7-15) and on adultery (23, 16-27). The collection ends with a poem in which Wisdom sings her own praises (24, 1-27), in imitation of Prv 1—9 where the eulogy to Wisdom follows the admonition against adultery (Prv 7 and 8).

In the *epilogue* (24, 28-32) the teacher encourages his pupil to drink at the fountain of Wisdom as he did. Thus the handbook of the apprentice wise man ends. Amid its apparent disorder we can follow the progressive initiation into the study and practice of wisdom.

The *first supplement* (25, 1—33, 18) closes with an epilogue analogous to the preceding one but more brief (33, 16-18). The fear of God is the main preoccupation; certain themes recur constantly: women (25, 1. 12-25; 26, 1-18), conversations (27, 4-24) and disputes (28, 8-26), service done to one's neighbor (29, 1-20), peace in the family, in moderation (29, 21—32, 14).

The *last supplement* is like the last will of the teacher. The thought of death forms the framework for it (33, 19-23 and 41, 1-13) and is touched upon several times. The inheritance which the wise man leaves is his long experience which even extends beyond the boundaries of his people (34, 9—36, 19); he has learned much from his dealings with people (36, 20—37, 26), ever maintaining that moderation so conducive to good health (37, 27—38, 23). All occupations are honorable since they serve society, but the role of wise man is higher than any other (38, 24—39, 11). This thought uplifts the old teacher (39, 12-15) and he sings a hymn to the Lord whose works reveal His Wisdom (39, 15-35). From this we naturally pass on to the praise of God in creation (42, 15—43, 33), and then to the eulogy of those who carry on the work of God through the wisdom which He has granted them (44—50). We find in this work, so poorly composed from our point of view, a continuous movement, in successive waves; thereby the reader, or rather the pupil, goes from the practice of wisdom to the contemplation of God as seen through his well-ordered creation, the world and man.

§ 3. Literary Genre

Sirach uses classical literary forms of the sapiential genre. The *mashal* remains the framework, taking on various enlargements and elaborations in the manner of Prv 1—9 or 25—27. One series of sayings is linked together by the repetition of one expression, "the fear of God" (1, 11-30); the *mashal* with number sequence arranges the sayings in a progressive order (25, 7-11). Sirach combines these two forms and obtains, so to speak, a *mashal* of the second degree (40, 18-27). The wise man did not form his pupils in thinking without at the same time teaching them how to express themselves; all the subtle or elegant usages of the *mashal* find their models here. Sirach knows how to paint a character portrait (38, 24–39, 11), although he has not acquired a mastery of the classics (Prv 5–7, cf. Wis 23, 16-27). His eulogies to Wisdom do not, however, achieve the perfection of his models (Jb 28; Prv 8, cf. Wis 1, 1-10; 24, 1-27). On the other hand, he has his own lovely series of historical portraits (44–50). Even more so than the impersonal sayings of the old proverbs (Prv 10–22), it is the exhortation which is predominant in Wis, as in Prv 1–9. Sirach puts his own personality into it (24, 28-32; 33, 16-18; 39, 12-14; 51, 13-30) with the lyrical tenor of the sapiential psalms (cf. Ps 34, 37, etc.), mixing prayers of supplication and thanksgiving with his exhortations (22, 25–23, 6; 36, 1-19; 51, 1-12). This is also the case with his hymns to the Creator (42, 15–43, 33) or his meditations upon the human condition (16, 22–18, 13; 39, 15-35); these recall the poetry of the psalms. The poetry of Ben Sira belongs to an old genre in which the forms and themes have become cliches; at least it is a valuable witness to the activity of the scribes in the working out of the later selections of the Psalter.

§ 4. Teaching

Wisdom is an especially valuable document of the *morality* and *doctrine* of Judaism shortly before the heroic age of the Machabees. This book, and the teaching which it reflects, knew how to form characters opposed to the pressure of triumphant Hellenism. The fear of God is at the basis of everything; this fear consists of respect and obedience, as well as absolute confidence in the God of the Covenant. Sirach is careful to warn his disciples that they will not escape trials; they are indispensable in forming character. Looseness, insincerity and carelessness in morality and education are enemies against which one must ever be on his guard. Forceful yet discreet, he knows how to use the means at his disposal, and he knows how to deal with every sort of person. His *forcefulness* may seem impolite to us, and his *prudence* borders on mistrust, but these were hard times. Sirach is, at any rate, healthy in mind and body, full of good humor; although he stands for forceful methods in education, he has no admiration for old prattlers and grumblers. He does not look down on good food, and music is a pleasure to him. This honorable man of Judaism is in general quite congenial, and it is always profitable and enjoyable to converse with him.

The *religion* of Sirach is as sturdy as his humanism, from which it is inseparable. Everything rests on faith in the God of the Covenant. This faith must show itself in works, works of worship certainly, but above all in the practice of justice and mercy towards one's neighbor. This picture of Palestinian Judaism in the 2nd century, just before the rifts which divided the Sadducees and Pharisees, gives us an idea of the soul of the pious Jew, aside from sectarian groups, up to the time of Jesus.[2] Not everything here reaches the heights of the Sermon on the Mount, but we find various traits already present. We learn how to pray to God as a father (23, 1. 4), and we already know that this father will only pardon us if we ourselves know how to pardon (28, 1-7).

§ 5. Limitations and Influence

On one point the theology of this book seems rather restricted: the destiny of man and of humanity receives no illumination from above. The pious man awaits his reward on this earth, in his own person or through his children. Israel hopes for salvation on this earth. The thought of death often recurs in this book as an obsession, but the answer will not be fully elucidated except through the death of the Machabean martyrs.

Must we also reproach Sirach for too narrow a view in his

[2] J. TRINQUET, "Les liens 'sadocites' de l'écrit de Damas, des manuscrits de la Mer Morte et de l'Ecclésiastique*," VT, I (1951), pp. 287-292.

identification of Wisdom with the Law of Moses? Perhaps less than it seems at first glance. In continuity with Dt 4, 5-8, the Prophets (eg., Is 2, 3; 51, 4) and the Psalms (19, 119, etc.) find within the Law a manifestation of the word of God which harmoniously orders the world as well as the conduct of men.[3] There is certainly a risk of declining into slavishness to the letter, but this is also a continuity in development of revelation which culminates in the theology of the Logos in St. John.

The liturgy of the synagogue must have used the Wisdom of Sirach for a long time. We know that even in the 10th century there were copies of it provided with the reading signs ordinarily reserved for the Bible.[4] Christian liturgy makes frequent use of it as does the teaching of the Fathers. Clement of Alexandria cites it so abundantly that he serves as a textual witness on a par with biblical MSS. Christians will always profit from a visit in the school of this wise man. This even-tempered, serious and good-humored teacher knows how to inculcate the practice of solid virtue. He wonderfully unites in his teaching the depth of revealed religion with a sane, down to earth *humanism*.

[3] Cf. A. ROBERT, "Le sens du mot Loi dans le Ps 119," *RB* (1937), pp. 182-206.
[4] C. ROTH, "Ecclesiasticus in the Synagogue Service," *JBL*, LXXI (1952), pp. 171-178.

CHAPTER VII

SUPPLEMENTS TO THE
BOOKS OF ESTHER AND DANIEL

BIBLIOGRAPHY

See the Books of Esther (p. 155) and of Daniel (p. 163).

§ 1. Supplements to Esther

The Book of Esther is accepted by the Church in two different forms. The Hebrew narrative, admitted by the Vulgate (1, 1–10, 3) and by the Peshitto, is shorter. Before St. Jerome, in Latin as in Greek, a longer narrative was used. When St. Jerome had translated the Hebrew narrative, he added as supplementary the principal elements of the narrative admitted up to that time which were not included in his version. Thus separated from their context, these "supplements" (10, 4–16, 24) became difficult to use. We find them in place in the edition of the LXX; but the editors have not adopted a uniform system of reference. We present below the series of supplements, with the mode of reference, 1) of the Vulgate, 2) of Swete, followed by the large edition of the LXX of Cambridge, and 3) the mode of Rahlfs, followed by the Bible of Jerusalem.

	Vulgate	Swete	Rahlfs
1. Dream of Mardocheus	11, 2-12	A, 1-11	1, 1a-b
2. Conspiracy against Assuerus	12, 1-6	A, 12-17	1, 1m-r
3. Edict for the extermination of the Jews	13, 1-7	B, 1-7	3, 13a-g
4. Prayer of Mardocheus	13, 8-18	C, 1-11	4, 17a-i
5. Prayer of Esther	14, 1-19	C, 12-30	4, 17k-z
6. The appeal of Mardocheus to Esther	15, 1-3	4, 8	4, 8

If we pose question of the origin of these appendices, one thing is certain: they were not produced for the Hebrew text. Thus 12, 1-6 already appears in 2, 21-23 with irreconcilable variations; the decrees are duplications of the résumés (3, 13 and 8, 11-12), and the gist of the second (16, 1-24) does not correspond to its résumé (8, 11-12). These are not, properly speaking, actual supplements, but we are dealing with two different editions of Esther.

What connection is there between the two editions? Many Catholic scholars have long admitted that the lengthier edition, originally in Hebrew or in Aramaic, was the original edition of which we only have the Greek translation; the Hebrew Massoretic text would then be an abridgment, purged of all allusion to religion because of the profane character of the feast of Purim. Inversely, St. Robert Bellarmine thinks that the Massoretic Hebrew represents the original edition, and that another author started with it to write a *longer account* which is the basis of the Greek text. This hypothesis is more in line with the midrash development, well known in later Jewish literature.

We also tend to admit more and more that the Greek of the appendices is not a translation Greek: the decrees were certainly composed in Greek, and they are an essential part of the long edition. The question is complicated by the fact that the Greek text is handed down to us in three quite different states. The common text, represented by the large uncials and already used by Josephus, seems to be a compromise between the original Greek text and the Hebrew; this may be the work of a certain Lysimachus (11, 1), who was brought to Egypt in the fourth year of Ptolemy and Cleopatra (B.C. 112 or 47). The Lucianic text, represented by four minuscules, is a much later revision. But the text which the old Latin witnesses, notable both for its coherence and its important omissions (12, 1-6; 9, 1-2. 5-19; 11, 1), seems to be the most ancient. Schildenberger finds here proof of a Greek account at the start; this solution, although it does not solve all the difficulties, seems to be the most probable. The value of the old Latin as proof of the oldest Greek text has good parallels in the Books of Tobias and Machabees.

The *literary genre* of the "supplements," or rather of the Greek edition, is the same as that of the original Hebrew, a story freely treated in order to teach. The new developments introduced by our Jewish Hellenist are well summed up by St. Jerome: "He has improvised, as one does in a school exercise, to underline the sentiments of one undergoing an injustice or inflicting it upon someone else" (*PL* 28, 1433).

Thus the author pursued a precise end, for he offered to the Jews of the Diaspora something more readable in the Hellenized milieu, more genteel thanks to the suppression of characteristics too inimical to pagans (9, 5-19), more religious also, and more demonstrative of the action of Providence and the efficaciousness of prayer. The doctrinal contribution of deuterocanonical developments does not seem very great.

§ 2. Supplements to Daniel

The Greek appendices in the Book of Daniel form two distinct groups. Within chap. 3 (the three Hebrews in the furnace), the *prayer of Azarias* and the *canticle of Azarias* and his companions are inserted; a few narrative verses link these to the context (Vulgate: 3, 24-90). At the end of the book have been added two tales about Daniel, the *judgment of Susanna* and the old men (at the beginning of the book in Theodotion; after chap. 12 in the LXX; Vulgate: 13), and the episodes of *Bel and of the Dragon* (at the end of the book in the two Greek versions; Vulgate: 14). These appendices come from Semitic originals, either Hebrew or Aramaic; but they may have been reassembled and rearranged only in the Greek version.

I. SUPPLEMENTS TO CHAPTER III

The pieces inserted in chap. 3 must have been written in Hebrew. The prayer of Azarias (Vulgate: 3, 26-45) is like the one in Daniel (9, 4-19); it is the people's confession of sin to obtain the mercy of God, that is, deliverance from present calamities. See above, p. 212, about this genre as regards Bar 1, 15–3, 8. Here we find a reflection of the condition of the Machabean martyrs; the prayer develops the same themes as does the discourse of the martyrs (2 Mc 7, 32-38): we suffer because we are sinners, but our sacrifice will appease the wrath of God, and we will be glorified while our persecutors will be chastised. As always, it is the just man who utters this confession in the name of the guilty people from whom he would not think of dissociating himself; such is the way with Jeremias (14, 7-19), Esdras (9, 6-15), Nehemias (1, 5-11), Daniel (9, 4-19) and the martyrs (2 Mc 7, 32). This prayer, composed of common cliches in a form widespread throughout the Psalms and elsewhere, derives its originality from the situation which it reflects. The offering of oneself as an expiatory sacrifice (3, 39-40, used in the Offertory of the Roman Mass) takes on a particular emphasis when compared to the one of the young martyr (2 Mc 7, 37-38). By inserting this prayer here, the inspired author makes of these three young persons of the ancient account a type of the martyrs of his era.

The canticle of the three Hebrews in the furnace consists of two parts. The first (3, 52-55) is in the style of blessings popular in Jewish prayer: *baruk atta* . . . (rare in the Hebrew Bible: Ps 119, 12 and 1 Par 29, 10; more often we find: *baruk adonay*). The second part adds to the hymn of praise of all creation (3, 56-87) a hymn of thanksgiving on the part of the Hebrews delivered from danger (3, 88-90). These hymns, less energetic in their makeup than the psalms that served as their models (esp. Ps 148), are well adapted to common recitation; the Christian liturgies of the East and West have always made use of them.

The introductory verses (25 and 51) serve as titles. The account of verses 46-50 borrows its elements from the Aramaic text; on the one hand, the gist of verses 22-23 is resumed and somewhat emphasized, and on the other hand, we are prepared for the mention of the angel in verses 92 (25) and 95 (28). Since Rothstein,[1] many see in these verses a vestige of the early Aramaic account, which would fill in the gap between verses 23 and 24 (91). It remains to be seen whether the abrupt transition, without psychological preparation, enables the reader to share more fully in the surprise of the king. It is a matter of taste, says Montgomery,[2] who sees in verses 46-50 an awkward filling-in of the compiler. Everything seems to indicate that he is right. In any case, the actual state of the Aramaic text is attested to near the beginning of the Christian era by a fragment found in grotto I of Qumran.

II. CHAPTERS 13—14

The accounts of chaps. 13—14 belong to the cycle of Daniel, from which Dn 1—6 also borrows; they likewise belong in the category of edifying tales (*fabulae*, according to St. Jerome), but they are far superior in literary worth. The story of Susanna is one of the lovely tales of the Bible. The Babylonian context is artificial. The teaching is that of the later sapiential literature, saturated with the piety of the psalms: calumniated innocence obtains divine help through prayer, and wisdom is not the privilege of old people but of the virtuous (cf. Ps 119, 22-23. 100). Primitive Christian art has pictured Susanna as a lamb among wolves; this image is already suggested by Ps 119, 176.

The stories of Bel and the Dragon are full of satirical spirit which contrasts with the tone of Dn 6. These tales illustrate

[1] In KAUTZSCH, *Apokryphen* (1900), p. 175.
[2] *Daniel*, ICC (1927), p. 9.

the struggle which the Letter of Jeremias preached (cf. p. 215), in reaction to the pagan renewal of the 3rd century. The story of Susanna can also be dated from this period. Origen (PG 2, 41-86) already defended the existence of a Hebrew or Aramaic original. This is also the general opinion today.

These picturesque stories have had great success in Christian iconography since the first centuries.[3] They furnish lessons for the Masses in Lent.

[3] Cf. Dom LECLERCQ, "Cappella greca," "Daniel," "Suzanne," *Dict. d'archéol. chrétienne et de liturgie.*

CONCLUSION

THE FORMATION OF THE
OLD TESTAMENT

by P. Grelot

BIBLIOGRAPHY

P. HEINISCH, *History of the Old Testament** (Collegeville: Liturgical Press, 1952).

H. H. ROWLEY, *The Growth of the Old Testament* (London, 1950).

While the present volume is not concerned with a doctrinal examination of the Old Testament (see the following pages), the following are some of the important books treating of this aspect of Old Testament study.

W. EICHRODT, *Theology of the Old Testament*, I (Philadelphia: Westminster, 1961).

P. HEINISCH, *Theology of the Old Testament** (Collegeville: Liturgical Press, 1952).

O. PROCKSCH, *Theologie des Alten Testaments* (Gütersloh, 1950).

P. VAN IMSCHOOT, *Theology of the Old Testament*. Vol. I: *God* (New York: Desclee, 1965).

E. JACOB, *Theology of the Old Testament* (New York: Harper, 1958).

G. VON RAD, *Old Testament Theology*, I (New York: Harper, 1962).

T. C. VRIEZEN, *An Outline of Old Testament Theology* (Oxford, 1958).

PRELIMINARY REMARKS

§ 1. The Genesis of the Bible

The various parts of the Old Testament have been studied in the preceding chapters. After having traced as a whole the history of Israel from the patriarchal period to the threshold of the New Testament, each of the biblical books was analyzed in the framework of the broader category in which it is now present: Torah, prophets, hagiographers and deuterocanonical books. It will be profitable now to take up again from a new angle the results of these analyses, in order to present as a whole the development of the Old Testament from an essentially *literary* point of view. It is not as though this were the principal aspect of the Bible; its doctrinal value is infinitely more important. But in order to realize what was, in its concrete reality, the progress of divine revelation linked to the spiritual education of Israel, it is necessary to follow first of all step by step the genesis of the collection of books, which, in each period, testify to it. The historical framework of its formation henceforth is known and each book or book fragment has been the object of a critical and doctrinal exposition; it is fitting to show groupings, linkings, influences, and subordinations which could not be the object of the preceding studies since they separated for practical reasons works deriving from the same time or the same milieu. If, in this perspective, it sometimes happens that a side-glance is cast upon some works foreign to the Bible, it does not follow that they are being put on the same footing as the Bible. What we are trying to retrace here is not a history of Hebraic and Jewish literature, but only the gradual formation of the inspired books.

Thus conceived, the literary history of the Old Testament affords a solid point of departure for biblical theology, in order for the latter to be something else than a repertory of themes, presented independently from the historical development which, from the faith of Abraham, leads to the Judaism contemporaneous with Christ. That is to say that this development itself will constantly be sketched on the background of our study. We will avoid, however, attempting on the sole plan of the Old Testament a doctrinal synthesis which could seem desirable to more than one reader. It is because, first of all, the Christian study of the Bible cannot separate the two Covenants; the theological meaning of the Old Testament, which we must uphold, reveals itself only in light of the New Testament. The first constitutes an ascent toward Christ; but it still carries with it, on the level of institutions as well as of ideas, provisional materials which must either be surpassed or rethought. Christ, in His person, His acts and His words, clarifies, in retrospect, all that precedes Him; He is, by that very fact, a principle of interpretation and a criterion for choice. We will therefore reserve the synthesis of biblical theology for the time when the New Testament will allow us to define the meaning of the Old Testament, since in its original novelty, it will be a fulfilment of the Sacred Scriptures.

Furthermore, it seems useful to us not to confuse two aspects of the Old Testament which despite the fact that they are closely united, are yet quite distinct: the books where biblical revelation was crystallized and the complex of institutions where these books were born. God, by various means, spoke to a people whom He was calling to the faith. The people not only preserved His Word in the form of a written collection which grew with time, but also in its living tradition, much more elusive, even though the writings which it left us find their roots in it. In order to be complete, a history of revelation should evoke this living tradition which is the echo of the Divine Word in the history of a human community. One would then have to go beyond the framework of the Bible and give a place, for instance, to the literary productions of Judaism during the last centuries before Christ and during the time of the New Testament: is it not in relation to this concrete milieu, broader than the canon of the Scriptures shows it to be, that Jesus preached and lived, that the Gospel was announced, and the Church founded, in short that the New Covenant relieved the Old? So be it; but our present intention is more restricted; we are studying the Sacred Scriptures and them alone; we are trying to realize how their collection was made. This undoubtedly requires close attention to the life of the Chosen People, in all the meanderings of a complicated history, but only as a term of reference without which the genesis of the Bible could not at all be understood.

§ 2. Limits and Divisions of this Sketch

Useful as a genetic study of the Bible is, it nonetheless entails a measure of uncertainty. Not only because our information on Israelite and Jewish literature is sparse: it is understood that we are limiting our study only to the preserved works which appear in the canon. But, even for these, how many precise details are lacking! The localities, the authors and even the periods cause problems. Next to assured critical conclusions, there are times when we can only count upon probable or possible solutions. A tableau like the one we are undertaking here can only be presented therefore as a provisional plan. If it allows a better view of the organic unity of the Bible, it is certain that the future will bring corrections, and more precise and perfect details to it. It is important to understand it with this reservation of principle, which from the outset establishes its limitations.

As to the great literary periods of the Old Testament, they coincide in a way with that of the history of Israel. The period of preparation which precedes the reign of David is very important from the historical and religious point of view, since it sees revelation born with Abraham, become more precise with Moses, and implanted in Chanaan after the conquest and at the time of the Judges. But on the literary level, it is much more difficult to capture because, in a certain measure, its productions were incorporated into vaster syntheses, done during the royal period. With David and Solomon, Israelite literature soars under its written form, when Jerusalem becomes an important cultural center (10th-9th centuries). After the schism, this literature develops in a parallel fashion in the two kingdoms of Juda and of Israel; but primarily, the two traditions meet when the "remnant" of Israel takes refuge in Juda after the ruin of Samaria (9th-8th centuries). The humiliation of Juda during the apogee of Assyria coincides with an apparently slack literary period; then, during the last fifty years of the Judean State, there is a renewal which continues at the time of the Babylonian captivity, while the theocratic organization of Judaism little by little replaces the former political institutions of the royal period (7th-6th centuries). The Persian period sees Judaism becoming established; at the same time, collections of the ancient books become a body and new literary currents are developed (6th-4th centuries). Finally, the conquests of Alexander place Judaism opposite the Hellenistic civilization, and its literature suffers the shocks of this confrontation (4th-1st centuries). We will thus distinguish six successive periods, while recognizing that such a schema comprises its share of artificiality.

CHAPTER I

AT THE ORIGINS
OF THE BIBLE: MOSES

§ 1. From the Age of the Oral Tradition to the Written Civilization

If revelation occurs at a time when the Near East has for a long time already reached a written civilization, the human community which receives it accedes to it only little by little. The fact is elucidated by the Bible itself. The Hebrew patriarchs which Genesis describes to us still belong to the nomadic or semi-nomadic age where oral traditions reign. Subsequently, Exodus evokes the use of writing at the time of Moses (Ex 17, 14; 34, 28). But one must surely not exaggerate its extension for if at the time of the Judges, the art of writing seems spread even to the common people, it is only with precise and defined ends of an altogether practical order (Jgs 8, 14). Finally, one enters fully into the domain of the written civilization when Israel becomes master of the urban centers and especially when David establishes his monarchy in Jerusalem.

It is therefore normal to place oneself first of all in the perspective of this historical framework when one wants to study the birth of sacred literature in the people of God, and from that point of view, to cast a glance on the preceding centuries to draw a balance sheet on them, without trying to trace their literary history in detail. The point of view of the royal scribes is then seen; these latter were interested in collecting all the inheritance of the past and transmitted it to us in their books.

It must also be noted that the oral tradition did not end at the moment when written literature was in full sway. It was

born first and had served as a cradle for the archaic works
established before the royal period. It then continued subsequently to feed literature from century to century, thanks to
its partially autonomous development. For example, with respect to the Pentateuch, the priestly narrators drew materials
that had been previously unexploited. Likewise, one must not
represent the oral tradition and written literature as two do-
mains foreign to one another from the point of view of the
means of expression used. Solomon's contemporaries must
not have seen any appreciable difference between the narratives spread orally (as had been the immemorial custom) and
the narrations put into form by the court scribes, for the
art of the latter proceeded from that of the ancient storytellers and the transition from the one to the other was ef-
fected rather imperceptibly. However, an important turn of
events took place at the moment when there was fixed in
writing what up to then had been entrusted to the living
memory of men.

§ 2.   The Traditions of Israel[1]

Israelite traditions, at the time of the monarchy, appear under extremely varied aspects as to their origin, their aim,
their form and their atmosphere. The internal unity of the
nation is already an established fact, but from social groups
which, though conscious of a certain original relationship, yet
have had various historical experiences. Each of these groups
(clans, tribes and groups of tribes) has its own traditions.
Thus, Gn 38 is peculiar to Juda, while the wars of Josue apparently refer to the battles of the Benjaminites and in Gn 4
a Kenite origin is discerned.[2] Other traditions are bound up
with places: burial places or battlegrounds, former tribal rest-
ing places (such as Cades) or venerated shrines (such as

[1] Cf. p. 187 ff., Vol. One.
[2] Cf. pp. 189, 199 and 252, Vol. One.

Sichem).[3] Each institution, finally, has its own traditions, especially the shrine of the Ark of the Covenant, which since Exodus has a whole history, and the Aaronite clergy, guardian of a tradition of worship formed at Cades.[4]

It would be a mistake to look in these traditions only for memories of history. Their aims differ profoundly according to each case. Often, it is actually a question of preserving the memory of ancestors and of their accomplishments: military leaders such as the Judges and most recently Saul; religious leaders, such as Samuel; Moses, founder of the nation and its legislator; the fathers of the race, Abraham, Isaac, Jacob whose tradition subsists in the places where they have lived. But it happens also that the adventures of the groups are hidden behind the exploits of eponymous heroes (Gn 34) or that the religious causality is brought out in preference to secondary details (as in the Exodus from Egypt). Furthermore, with the help of hindsight, history has become schematized. The most important elements still emerge next to a large number that are forgotten; they center around a few very living figures which animate an anonymous mass: it is thus that popular memory can narrate the past. However, many traditions have a purpose of an entirely different order: they explain the how and the why of present customs (cf. the rite of the paschal lamb), names of places (Jgs 2, 1-5), the state of the tribes (Gn 49); they tell the origin of groups, institutions and tribes, frequently resorting to the procedure of eponyms, organizing them into genealogies, which is a popular way of explaining with simplicity the origin of things.[5] It also happens that these traditions tend to give rules of conduct, either by conveying juridical or ritual material which is imposed to be practiced by the Israelites (Gn 32, 33; Ex 12, 21-22), or by introducing moral or religious lessons about the history of former heroes (the story of Joseph): this is a feature of popular wisdom known in all countries. It is con-

[3] Cf. p. 243, Vol. One.
[4] Cf. p. 220, Vol. One.
[5] Cf. art. "Généalogies,"* Catholicisme, IV (Paris, 1956) 1811 ff.

stantly this Jewish conception of God, of the world, of man and of history which is thus concretely expressed in order to be transmitted from one age to the next. The traditions contain practically all the baggage of national culture before the creation of a written literature.

As to the forms in which they are presented, some are already fixed (we will come back to them later), but most are still fluctuating. They are canvasses in prose, more or less precise in their details. Their genres[6] vary, from the very short etiological narrative to the more developed episode which tends to be transformed into a "short story." On this point, it is difficult to distinguish what belongs properly to the traditional sources used by the chroniclers of the royal period and what was actually done by them. It is possible, however, to hold as probable that as a whole they respected the manner of the materials they had at hand.

Let us add that the atmosphere of the narratives differs considerably from one to the other. The story is realistic and down to earth in the miserable adventure of Abimelek; but the story is treated as a religious epic in the exodus from Egypt. The harsh enthusiasm of the war of conquest contrasts with the rustic calm brought about by the memory of Abraham and Isaac. The pilgrimage to Sinai is very closely linked to notions of worship, while the stories of Joseph and Samson, each in its way, serve to inculcate a lesson of wisdom. There is no doubt that these variations already existed in the ancient traditions when they were still being transmitted orally. It would be wrong therefore to consider the traditions as formless, pre-literary or infra-literary materials. At the time when they are going to be collected, they already constitute a true literature whose genres are a prelude to those of written literature.

It is even likely that, from the time of the Judges, they tended to group themselves into *cycles*. Either according to their historical origin: cycles of conquest and of Judges, cycle of Saul. . . . Or, according to their geographical roots: cycles

6 Cf. pp. 132, 136 (French ed.).

of Bersabee, of Sichem, of Cades, of Bethel (of shrines, most of the time). Or finally according to the institutions that preserve them: traditions of the Aaronite clergy, traditions around the Ark of the Covenant, tribal traditions. . . . Better still, as national unity becomes a reality, not only in fact but in the consciousness of men, particular groups of memories and customs also tended to become interpenetrated to become the common good of all Israel. Thus, the state in which the royal scribes find them is the result of a more or less long, more or less complicated evolution. On the whole, they make up a rich treasure, both cultural and religious.

§ 3. The Most Ancient Written Texts: Moses

In the framework of the oral traditions, Israel also possesses the first elements of a written tradition. In fact, the specimens of archaic texts that the Bible has preserved are perhaps only the remnants of a much more extensive literary production, for the poetic texts allow us to see, starting with the 12th century, the existence of an art which far surpasses its first stammerings. In this regard a remarkable difference is observed between the refrains of the nomadic times, brief and short-winded, and the war-chants of the conquest, like those of Josue (fragmentary) and of Debora: Israel had quickly assimilated the culture of the conquered lands. Let us notice again, in the order of worship, the refrains of the Ark; in the prophetic "genre," the oracles of Jacob, Balaam and Moses; with the sapiential literature, there are the apology of Jotham and the parable of Nathan; finally, the two elegies of David, prior to his reign in Jerusalem. We even know the title of two collections of works of this type used by Hebrew historians: the book of *Jashar* and that of "The Wars of Yahweh";[7] but it is difficult to say if they are ancient or if the initiative is that of the Solomonian scribes. These first manifestations of the Israelite literary genius make it rather probable that certain

[7] Cf. p. 191, Vol. One.

traditions had been put into written prose relatively early, although on this point the texts do not bear up under scrutiny. It is known, however, that several pages attributed by critics to the Elohist or to the Yahwist traditions contain a very definite archaic flavor; moreover, it is likely that certain prayer formulae in more recent recensions existed before in some way in the Israelite shrines from the time of the Judges.

But it is especially in the matter of law that the existence of ancient written texts is solidly attested by the Bible. Moses' activity in this field is too strongly affirmed by Hebrew tradition for us to deny him any literary activity, even if it is difficult to circumscribe it. There is agreement on the earliness of the Book of the Covenant (Ex 20, 22–23, 33), despite the trace of certain refinements, and of the ethical *Decalogue* (Ex 20 and Dt 5), probably enlarged by its later revisors, and there is no stringent reason which could oblige us to deny to Moses what remains the core of the Mosaic Law. But one would unduly restrict Moses' part in the Torah, if one attributed to him only these few writings: around them is centered the common law which largely overflows its limits and which is Mosaic just as they are. Finally, one can say that with Moses the Bible, as an *inspired book*, was born at the same time as the people of Israel was itself born by contracting a covenant with Yahweh. At the time when Hebrew literature begins to develop in a more tangible way, thanks to a concurrence of providential circumstances, the personality of the founder of the nation already dominates it, not only by the texts which derive from him, but by his religious message which will entirely impregnate it.

CHAPTER II

JERUSALEM, CULTURAL CENTER

§ 1. Hebrew Culture at the Beginning of the Monarchy

Saul's monarchy prolonged in many ways the period of the Judges; David's finally transformed the nation. It created the Israelite State by superimposing upon the former framework of the tribes, a specifically Chanaanite institution: centralized urban kingship. At the same time that Israel is peacefully absorbing independent populations, it takes on structures that are mostly inspired from contemporary monarchies: those of Phenicia and even, all things being equal, of Egypt. In keeping with this social and political development, the religion of Israel finds a new balance. Victoriously overcoming the crisis of the time of the Judges, it finally incorporates what could be assimilated from the Chanaanite cults in matters of rite, concepts and phraseology.

Two facts mark this change. First of all, kingship is henceforth part and parcel of the religious charter of the nation: the monarch, the anointed of Yahweh, becomes a part of theocracy and the promises of the Covenant are personally renewed to him, for himself and for his race (2 Sm 7). In the second place, with the transfer of the Ark to Jerusalem, the old confederational shrine of the tribes, formerly located in Sichem and Silo, is now located in the royal capital, which becomes the holy place par excellence, the one where "Yahweh makes His name dwell." In the preceding ages, a first form of hope had developed; that of living happily in a land "flowing with milk and honey," and of ruling over the peoples "who do not know Yahweh." To these fundamental elements are added henceforth those that have been introduced by a most recent history; the king and the holy city and soon the Temple enrich the tableau of the marvelous future which Israel expects from its God. Let us add that in Jerusalem there is realized a sort of synthesis between two currents of cults which both issued from Hebrew origins: that of the North, linked to the shrine of the Ark, which thus reflects in a very direct way the tradition of Moses and of Josue; and that of the South, coming also from the tradition of Cades, which had already been able to open to independent worship elements by assimilating them. This duality is found, it seems, in the two priests attached to the person of David: Ebiathar, a descendant of Eli, who will be dismissed under Solomon; Sadoq, whose genealogy ties him to the lineage of Aaron and who finally will prevail alone.

Such is the framework in which Israelite culture is affirmed. Once the urban kingship is created, a whole people of scribes tends to the affairs of the palace: it is charged with keeping the annals of the reign, preserving the archives, writing the correspondence, administering the goods of the royal house, collecting the taxes.[1] Schools furnish the training for this personnel; along with the sons of functionaries, the royal princes and the members of the aristocratic families receive there a more perfect education; naturally the clergy of the royal shrine profit from this movement. These institutions take on unequaled scope under Solomon;[2] thus, everything is ready for the flourishing of a literature of learned men, still rooted in popular tradition, but wearing the stamp of the literate caste whence it emanates.

To create this cultural foyer, the Hebrew state does not start from scratch. On the one hand, the preceding periods (Moses and the Judges) have left to it institutions where the first elements of the national culture have already been developed in an embryonic manner. On the other hand, while absorbing Jerusalem and the other Chanaanite cities, David incorporated into his state and transferred to the religion of

---

[1] Cf. p. 294, Vol. One.
[2] Cf. pp. 307 ff., Vol. One.

Yahweh the indigenous institutions of a much more ancient origin: scribes, cantors, etc. . . . Finally, as the political and economic horizon of Israel becomes wider, especially under the reign of Solomon, the country is introduced into an international traffic of ideas and of artistic tastes which is favorable to the flourishing of letters. It is not astonishing in these conditions to see Hebrew literature reach its classical period in the 10th century, without always being able to distinguish the origin, national or foreign, of the elements which are narrowly fused in it.

§ 2.   The Vestiges of an Administration

The archives and the administrative and juridical documents do not properly speaking belong to literature; however, they constitute for historians a source of information of the first order. The Books of Samuel and of Kings have preserved a certain number of them which come either from the royal chancery or from the archives of the Temple. This is sufficient to allow us to see an essential aspect of the activity of the royal scribes.

Given the profound evolution of the institutions which marks this period, one would expect to find also in the texts the trace of a juridical activity directed toward a legislative reformulation. But on this point investigations prove to be rather disappointing. The Book of the Covenant[3] presupposes a more archaic economic and social state, and the Yahwist Decalogue (Ex 34) deals essentially with worship. It seems therefore that, in the time of David and Solomon, royal law is exercised only in the framework of ancient customs, partially codified, without yet attaining a reformulation of Mosaic law. The adaptation to new circumstances of the texts and customs of yesteryear is thus left to the appreciation of those who fill the positions of judges, and this flexibility guarantees a living law always dominated by the authority of Moses.

[3] Cf. p. 190, Vol. One.

§ 3. Around the Worship

We would like to know in detail the transformation and the development of the rituals, which took place after the removal of the Ark to Jerusalem and especially after the building of the Temple of Solomon. The state of the evidence does not allow us to satisfy our curiosity: this is because the rites and religious customs are much more easily transmitted from one generation to the next by the simple operation of the existing institutions than by dead documents. Texts such as Ex 13, 3-10 and 34, 10-26 (except for Deuteronomist additions) can preserve in a succinct form old Yahwist rituals brought from Cades by the Aaronite clergy. But to these archaic rites, the Yahwist Decalogue (Ex 34) adds others which are more easily understood as adaptations to Yahwism of agrarian rites long since implanted in Chanaan (especially the three agricultural feasts of the annual cycle). One could therefore think here of a composition during the royal period, which would also have left traces in some places in the Book of the Covenant (Ex 22, 28-29; 23, 14-19). Finally, one must look for the collections of customs done during the periods of David and Solomon in the late priestly compilations made in "Sadoqite" milieus. The conservative spirit of the religious centers assures us that these texts substantially reflect the ancient tradition; but one should not overlook the part played by more recent adaptations: ritual conservatism is not necessarily fixed. From the point of view in which we place ourselves here, these compilations are therefore utilizable only with some difficulty.

In Chanaanite and Aramean centers, prophetism was linked with worship,[4] such as, it seems, Hebrew prophetism at the time of the Judges. Thus, in David's service one finds two accredited seers, Gad and Nathan, and the texts give us some idea of the oracles performed by these religious coun-

---

[4] Cf. p. 341, Vol. One.

selors of the king in the exercise of their official capacities. Furthermore, their personality already breaks through the framework of professional prophetism, both by the authentic inspiration which is manifested in them and by their freedom of speech with regard to the king: they thus announce the grand-style prophets of the following centuries. The oracle of Nathan[5] preserved in 2 Sm 7 (with Deuteronomist glosses) is of first-rate importance: it is at the origin of dynastic Messianism. The question of the two "royal psalms" is more difficult: these are Ps 2 and 110 which contain prophetic oracles.[6] The first apparently alludes to 2 Sm 7; but some authors see in it rather a late literary imitation.[7] On the other hand, the archaic origin of Ps 110 is often retained, because there are rather strong arguments in favor of it.[8] Some even see here a Hebrew adaptation of a royal enthronement psalm of Jebusean origin; whence would come the mention of royal priesthood, actually exercised by David (2 Sm 6, 17-18) and by Solomon (3 Kgs 3, 15) and of Melchisedech, king-priest of Salem, whose inheritance would have been received by David. The hypothesis cannot be considered as demonstrated.

These two texts introduce the problem of the psalms.[9] One should not be surprised that a large number of them are attributed to David. He was a poet and musician himself as is shown in his two elegies on the death of Saul and of Abner. The king surely must have played an important role in the development of worship lyricism. The genre existed before him, both with the Hebrews and with the Chanaanites, and especially in the city of Jerusalem whose personnel he incorporated into his service. The transfer of the Ark could have given him the opportunity of organizing a guild of cantors which must have become increasingly important after

[5] Cf. p. 285, Vol. One.
[6] Cf. pp. 57 f.
[7] Cf. A. ROBERT, "Considérations sur le messianisme du Ps. 2"*, *Mélanges Jules Lebreton*, I (RSR, April-October, 1951), pp. 88-98.
[8] E. PODECHARD, *Le Psautier**, II (1954), pp. 168-183.
[9] Cf. p. 31 ff.

the building of the Temple. It is hardly doubtful that originally Chanaanite hymns were then adapted to the liturgy of
Yahweh; in any case, the style of the native poetry did not
fail to influence the new compositions. Unfortunately, in the
present state of the problem, it is difficult to say what part
of the psalter dates from this period. For example, the following are generally placed among the ancient psalms: 18
(royal *Te Deum*), 20 and 21 (prayers for the king), 24,
7-10 (processional of the Ark), 29 (with heavy Chanaanite
coloring), 72 (retouched later on). . . . But in fact there are
as many questions as there are psalms. One can admit that
from the very beginning of the royal period, most of the
genres and literary canons now present in the psalter[10] were
already fixed and their place in the liturgy was determined
by usage. However, a literary current such as that one is
bound to be developed normally with time; there should be
no hurry in wanting to reconstitute a whole "royal liturgy"
on the basis of the internal criticism of the psalter and the
analogies offered by the other Semitic religions. There are
certainly relations, but they are not easy to pinpoint and in
particular the existence in Israel of a "New Year's day" similar to that of neighboring religions remains problematic.

§ 4.   Wisdom Literature

With the schools for scribes Wisdom literature[11] also takes
hold in Israel. The Bible honors Solomon with it, and attributes to him considerable literary activity (3 Kgs 5, 9-
14). One must take hyperbole into consideration, but there
is no reason for doubting this testimony. In fact, Wisdom is
at that time an international fact, and traces of it are found
from Egypt to Mesopotamia; if the Chanaanite documents
are lacking on this point, the fact is probably accidental (cf.
3 Kgs 5, 11; Ez 27, 8-9 and 28, 3-4).

[10] Cf. p. 44 ff.
[11] Cf. p. 84 f.

Wisdom is first of all the concern of the king: the art of governing well and of succeeding in temporal matters. But this art concerns also many people in the royal administration: every scribe must be a wise man; that is why the education he receives strives to impart this knowledge to him. Doubtless a practical wisdom; but from the knowledge of man and of the world, full of refined psychology, is easily developed a reflection which, altogether empirical at its origins, rapidly tends toward speculation, especially when it blends in the data of religious thought. With respect to this, one can say, for example, that the ancient oriental myths[12] which were vivid expressions of a conception of the human world in its relations to the gods, bordered on the sapiential genre.

In Israel, this literary current crosses immediately on its way a religious tradition solidly anchored in the minds. Surely it is first of all receptive to maxims of all kinds, similar to those collected in the Book of Proverbs (10, 1—22, 16; 25—29). A large portion of these, especially those which appear to be the "mirror of the king's people" (Duesberg), can date back to Solomon, but the later development of the genre must be reckoned with.[13] But from the very outset, wisdom, knowledge, and discernment are considered as a privilege of Yahweh who alone can give them to men (2 Sm 14, 17 and 20; 3 Kgs 3, 9; cf. Gn 3). Thereby, all the moral ideal of Yahwism, its conception of the world and of man seem to be one of the areas of the sapiential field; there is no frontier between it and religious reflection. We will not be astonished to find trace of the sapiential current in a good number of writings which theoretically depend on altogether different literary genres.

[12] Cf. pp. 127-129 (French ed.).
[13] Cf. p. 87 f.

§ 5.   Memorialists and Historians[14]

Such are the intellectual components of the milieu in which
a very important historiography is going to develop by leaps
and bounds; in Jerusalem from the reign of David and especially from that of Solomon, a well-organized clergy, a caste
of scribes and an already ancient prophetism are so side-by-
side that their fields overlap. Born at their crossroads historiography will reflect in variable proportions their respective
preoccupations. The work of the annalists precedes historiography properly speaking and opens the way for it. We no
longer have the official chronicles of the kings; but in their
dryness, certain indications give us some idea of them (2
Sm 8). As to the work of the memorialists and the historians,
this directly outclasses all that oriental antiquity has left us
in this genre. In Assyria, the royal annals are dithyrambs in
praise of the monarch; in Egypt one particular event of the
reign is recounted, but without yet creating a continuous
historiography; with the Hittites, religious causality in history
is not ignored, but one does not rise to broad views embracing
whole reigns or even longer periods. It is difficult to say in
what measure the knowledge of the former stimulates the
genius of Israelite scribes; they nonetheless draw from their
faith a concept of man and of history which allows them to
catch a broader glimpse of the events. With them, all the
actors of history, even the greatest, remain subject to a divine
law which surpasses them, judges them, commands their destinies because, consciously or not, they are the artisans of
Yahweh's design. Whence come both breadth of outlook and
remarkable impartiality.

From the reign of David, it seems that a long narrative
retraces already the origins of the Israelite monarchy, from
the anointing of Saul to the capture of Jerusalem (that is,
during the whole duration of the wars of independence). A

[14] Cf. p. 277 ff., Vol. One.

history of the Ark of the Covenant perhaps has to date from the same period; it traces its history from its capture by the Philistines to its transferral into the royal city. The masterpiece of this genre, probably written under Solomon, is the history of David's succession (2 Sm 10—20 and 3 Kgs 1—2). Then there is a history of Solomon (where the author of Kings drew the matter of 3 Kgs 3—11); without counting the remarks devoted to particular episodes or to the exploits of David's paladins (2 Sm 21—24), but their date is more doubtful. All these pieces treat of contemporary events, whose actors or witnesses are often still living. Recourse to oral tradition is discernible in some places (David's youth); and this is normal for the matter treated. As for the style, it prolongs and brings to its perfection the art of ancient storytellers: all the popular vim and vigor passed into these productions of literate men.

§ 6. A Synthesis of Sacred History[15]

But the traditions of Israel allow us to go much further back into the past; by drawing abundantly from this trove, the Israelite scribes are going to achieve a large work of religious history. These traditions, as has been seen, were already becoming interpenetrated and were beginning to take form from the time of the Judges. Now, after the establishment of the monarchy and the foundation of the empire, their total meaning becomes more evident, in a broader perspective. The Israelite historians discover the profound unity, underlying both their expansion and their diversity: the unity of a *sacred history* directed by God; of a history whose point of departure is the promise made to Abraham, whose heart is the Covenant and whose justification and purpose is the glory of Yahweh present in His Temple and triumphant by the victories of the Anointed One. This is not merely a simple human

[15] Cf. p. 191 ff., Vol. One.

reconstruction, but a view of faith which becomes explicit under divine inspiration.

Since all the traditions preserved in the various parts of the nation are thus convergent, it is the duty of historians to stress the link which united them around memories of the Exodus and of Sinai, which are as it were their center of gravity. On the other hand, they underline, from the earliest centuries, the cohesion of all the Hebrew groups called to live in fateful solidarity inside the people of Yahweh: these groups are members of the same family. Whence the importance of the genealogies around which will be centered the sacred history; more than extracts of civil-status, they will be a concrete translation of the profound idea which polarizes all of history: that of the divine choice which singled out men called to make up the people of God.

That is why, contrary to the ancient traditions of India for example, which dealt essentially with worship and were independent of time, those of Israel are fixed in the framework of a history. It is a real history but told with the help of the most diverse of materials; it is a very human history, but its religious significance is much more important than the precision of the details. It is this history which drains all the other components of the national tradition (law, customs, worship, folklore) and establishes them in the perspective where they derive their profound meaning. Furthermore, this history will go back beyond the patriarchal period, beyond even the oriental empires and the faraway neolithic age, the rather imprecise memory of which hovers in chapters 4–11 of Genesis. It will even incorporate sacred cosmogony which Israelite monotheism contrasts to the pagan myths, whose images it does not fear to use again for its own doctrine. Moreover, creation is the point of departure of the divine design which was little by little revealed with the call of the patriarchs, the deliverance from Egypt, the Covenant at Sinai, the gift of the "promised land," the installation of the monarchy, the promises made to David and the choice of the Temple at Jerusalem as the residence of Yahweh among men. . . . And if Yahweh had thus painfully and gradually to form this people called to serve Him and to procure His glory from a barbarian human mass by giving to it little by little the rules of conduct capable of making of it a wise people, is it not because at the beginning, at the origins, a mysterious catastrophe had disturbed the order of a world that had issued from His hands in perfect condition? By explaining on the one hand the present condition of man and on the other the meaning of the historical work of God, the inspired book thus introduces into the picture of the origins the fact of human sin which right from this period interferes with divine will and from century to century continues to place obstacles before the unfolding of Yahweh's design.

Such is the grandiose plan of this work which, for lack of knowing exactly its author or authors, we call the holy Yahwist history (J). It is of little importance if it was realized in one stroke or by one author; if it contained or not in a continuous story all of past history up to the period of David and of Solomon; if it used, next to pieces drawn from the oral tradition, certain bits of more ancient writings (J¹ or L of the critics); if certain pieces, where theology is more closely allied, were added after the event to the primitive collection. It is sufficient to notice that it existed at least virtually in a whole collection of accounts related by doctrine and by the editorial procedures used. Just as diverse as the materials that serve as its base, it sometimes borders on religious lyricism (the flight from Egypt), sometimes on sapiential teaching (Gn 3; the story of Joseph); sometimes on historiography (the story of Gideon) and sometimes on juridical teaching (Mosaic Torah and certain etiological accounts). On the whole, it is a literary monument without parallel in the history of religions, because it condenses in it what is specific and irreducible in Yahwism: a theology of history based on the theology of the Promise. As to its composition, it is difficult to suggest precise dates: we would ascribe the whole work to the reign of Solomon; but, for many authors, the work would have spread itself over the following century in the cultured centers of the court and of the Temple. There is no doubt that it then played a role in the training of the elite just as did in Egypt sapiential literature or with the priests of Mesopotamia the Sumero-Akkadian myths; but what a difference in intellectual and religious climate!

Thus, at the cultural and political climax which marks the first century of the Israelite monarchy, in a certain sense the Bible can be said to have a literary structure. Around this nucleus of sacred texts dating back to the Mosaic period, the traditions of God's people were crystallized in written form. They nonetheless continued to be transmitted orally; so, other crystallizations will subsequently appear analogous to the first. But the fundamental ideas of the Yahwist writer— or school—first synthesis of a revelation started long ago, will continue to assert itself to similar syntheses attempted in slightly different perspectives. The New Testament itself, by fulfilling the revelation of the secrets of the mysterious plan of God, will show in Christ the crowning and the completion of this age-long work, the first outlines of which were being shown by the Yahwist.

CHAPTER III

THE PARALLEL KINGDOMS

§ 1. The Tradition of Israel and that of Juda

From this schism which follows the reign of Solomon on, the kingdoms of Juda and of Israel find themselves in rather different situations.[1] In Jerusalem, the continuity of the Davidic dynasty assures a certain internal stability; but, on the religious level, the kingdom experiences alternately rises of Chanaanite paganism and Yahwist renewal, according to the attitudes of its kings. Nonetheless, the Temple remains a stronghold for the religious traditions of the nation; it is the place where "Yahweh roars" (Am 1, 2), and from this place will be prepared the revolution that will overthrow Athalia; Isaias also receives his vocation here. In its shadow, the literature inaugurated during the reigns of David and of Solomon continues to develop (worship lyricism, rituals, common law, wisdom, religious historiography, archives and annals); it is not possible to follow this development closely. The permanent armor of this intellectual activity is made up of three fundamental institutions: scribes (or wise men), priests and prophets (Jer 18, 18; cf. 2, 8).

In Israel on the contrary, if the secession is upheld by the country populations tired of tributes that are too heavy, by the clergy of the provincial shrines, whom Jerusalem risks offending, and by the prophetic bodies hostile to innovations in the name of ancient tradition, it is virtually the merchant class and the landowners who take the gain of it to their profit. Thus the monarchy leaning on this class will withdraw from primitive Yahwism more than the Judean monarchy. Following the schism and especially after the founding of

[1] Cf. pp. 50 and 299, Vol. One.

Samaria, a second center of culture, emulator and rival of
Jerusalem, grows in the court of the kings of Israel; its light
falls on rich classes, on the clergy of royal sanctuaries created
in order to compete with Solomon's Temple, on the caste of
the officials. But the kingdom of the North is too open to
foreign influences, especially those of Tyre, causing the nation's religious tradition to suffer. One may notice it in particular when Omri marries his son Achab to the Tyrenian
Jezabel: the political fortune of the "house of Omri" and the
relative cultural expansion which accompanies it then are
tied to the renewal of Chanaanite paganism. The cult of a
national God, in the measure to which it subsists, tends to be
no longer anything but a syncretized Yahwism; from the reign
of Jeroboam I, the sign of the golden calf was an unequivocal
indication of this falling away. Thus it is not surprising that
the literary productions of the time left only a few traces in
the Bible: the fervent Yahwists to whom we owe the holy
books had no choice but to let them fall into oblivion. The
happy exception of Psalm 45, if one were to interpret it as a
royal epithalamium, would be due to an allegorical reinterpretation which would define its biblical sense. However, the archeological documentation hints at a certain administrative (ostraca) and artistic (the ivories of Samaria)
activity, which was fairly intense during the 9th and the 8th
centuries.

In Israel during the 9th century, the attachment to authentic Yahwist tradition is, with exceptions, true more of
strangers to the cultural movement: the "sons of prophets"
who gravitate around Elias and Eliseus give no evidence of
preoccupations of a cultural nature, not considering the
Rekabites or an old soldier like Jehu. The literary consequence: the speeches of Elias and Eliseus have not come down
to us in original MS, though the oracle of Micheas, son of
Yimla (3 Kgs 22, 1-28), is an exception to this. The religious
consequence: the Yahwism of the North, reacting against a
syncretism which seems tied to modern institutions, remains
more archaic, and closer to what it had been at the time of
the Judges in the shrines of the country. The Mosaic tradi-

tion is present there, it would seem, though less well developed than at Jerusalem, or rather, it develops along another line, more conservative regarding the ideas and the rites of Chanaan, and in more direct relation with the form it had assumed in the ancient shrine of the Ark. It is symptomatic to see Elias pilgrimaging to Horeb to renew his faith or to rebuild the altar of Carmel in the ancient manner (cf. Ex 20, 24-25). It is true that at the same time local shrines of the same kind also exist in the Judean countryside; but the Temple of Jerusalem already initiates a centralization which is soon realized.

§ 2. The Prophetic Influence in Israel

The revolution of Jehu (841), however, allows the prophetic influence to gain ground in cultivated circles; even kings seek the counsel of Eliseus. Thus one may glimpse the formation of fervent circles whose members also belong to state institutions: priestly colleges and scribes of the administration. United by a common attachment to the spirit of Elias and Eliseus, they end the current of reform in literary works, quite similar in their form to those which appeared in Jerusalem in the 10th century when the same spirit of religious fervor moved the scribes of the court and the Temple. There is first of all the collating and the fixing in writing of traditions relative to Elias and Eliseus. The cycle of Elias may have been edited toward the end of the 9th century; that of Eliseus at present mixed with a history of Aramean wars, around 750. Next to popular tales which bear the mark of their origins, one may find beautiful pages worthy of the best historians, such as the story of the revolution of Jehu (4 Kgs 9, 1–10, 27).

There is much evidence supporting a relation of the Elohist material of the Pentateuch (E) to the same milieu, as well as several narratives found in the "early prophets," from the wars of Josue to the history of Saul. This recension of ancient traditions is comparable to Yahwist sacred history, to which it is often related in matter and sometimes even in literary expression. It may have included written documents edited much earlier: probably certain tales waxing an archaic flavor (E[1] of the critics); certainly the Decalogue of Ex 20 and the Book of the Covenant. But on the whole, one would surmise rather the shaping of an oral tradition which was still alive, with the added influence of the work edited in Yahwist circles. But whereas for the historians of Jerusalem sacred history culminated in the establishment of the Davidic monarchy and the Solomonian Temple, those of Israel show a greater reserve with regard to modern institutions. Their more conservative point of view, which is explained as a re-action against the abuses of the time, prolong the tradition of the shrine of the Ark into the time of the Judges. The Yahwism which they dream of seeing revived is less that of the Davidic epoch than that of the Exodus, of the desert, of the conquest: here is their ideal. With them this is not an archaism of poor quality but rather a desire to remain faithful to the most essential values of the national religion. Besides, they feel the needs of their time; proof is that in retracing past history they bring it up to date to find in it rules of conduct to be used by their contemporaries. Hence an em-phasis on the "prophetic" side of the great ancestors (Abra-ham, Joseph, Moses, or Samuel); from this also come certain polemical jabs against the worship of the golden calf (Ex 32) or of the Chanaanite Baal (Jgs 6, 25-32) and against the institution of monarchy itself (1 Sm 8 and 12).

Certain of these traits may be more easily understood if one admits that the Elohist collection was made in the course of the 8th century, under the brilliant and prosperous rule of Jeroboam II, as a salutary reaction against the social and re-ligious disorders which were only too apparent. In fact, a similar spirit, sometimes even identical themes, are found in the preaching of Amos and especially of Osee. The first of these two "writer prophets" (a very poor expression) has no ties with the fervent circles of the North: he is a Judean, whose hard and vigorous poetry bursts directly from popular sap. Putting these oracles into writing seems to have been in part his personal work (cf. 7, 1-4; 8, 1; 9, 1), in part that of disciples spontaneously grouped about him; but it is with the Judeans, Isaias and Micheas, that one will afterwards have to look to find the trace of his influence. On the other hand, the work of Osee, deeply rooted in the religious tradition of the North, noticeably enriches the current of thought in which it buries itself. Though it takes certain characteristic themes from it (moral decalogue, attachment to the Covenant and to the ideal time in the desert, memories of the ancestor Jacob, the preponderance of Ephraim, and the hostility to the golden calf and even to the institution of royalty), it introduces into it other themes which reappear later (love of Yahweh for His people, affective religion, comparison of the Covenant to an espousal, announcement of a new Covenant after the purification of guilty Israel). With Osee, the sacred history, from now on prolonged until new times yet to come, assumes the appearance of a drama of love in which Yahweh and Israel are partners: an original interpretation which is a direct prelude to the revelation of the love of God in the New Testament.

In the atmosphere of the prophetic movement, a juridic reform is preparing itself, parallel to the historico-religious work of which we have just spoken. When Osee alludes to "articles of law" (8, 2), he is thinking, undoubtedly, of the ancient legislative compilations (Moral Decalogue and Book of the Covenant). But in the 8th century, this written law no longer corresponds exactly to the practical needs of an evolved society: its rule is surpassed by the facts. It must be adapted to the circumstances, completed, and on certain points, remade, so that it may present an effective barrier to the abuses of power of the royal administration, to the extortions of the rich, the venality of the judges, the moral and religious laxity, which, from Elias to Osee, were unceasingly denounced by the prophets. Such a work presupposes first an evolution of customary law before becoming crystallized into a code. The prophetic preaching, completely in the service of the authentic tradition, indicates in what sense the reform must be directed. Now fervent circles influenced by this reform include levite-priests, guardians of customs and laws, called on more than once to practice law in trials (Dt 17, 18-20). Such is the jurisprudence which, by completing existing texts, prepares the constitution of a new code. This will come in its time, probably after the ruin of Samaria, when the rooting of a foreign aristocracy in the country makes spiritual resistance an urgency if one wishes to save the threatened tradition. Further, the fall of the kingdom of the North will then invite reflection: it will show the necessity of the reform to which the prophets have been vainly exhorting the nation for a century and a half. But on what basis could it be wrought except on the Mosaic Torah itself, enriched by a recent prophetic contribution and readapted to the needs of the time? This is, it would seem, the state of mind which will preside over the edition of the Deuteronomist Code (Dt 12, 2—26, 15), which we would prefer to relate to the tradition of the North rather than to Judean circles, though it may have been written down in the South (see *below*).

§ 3.   The Prophetic Influence in Juda

While this work is being done in original priestly circles of Israel, the kingdom of Juda is won over, in turn, by the influence of prophetism. Amos, the Judean, preached in the North in about 750; his preoccupations and several of his themes reappear in the following decades in Isaias and Micheas, although one cannot clearly define the relation of the latter with the group of disciples which preserved the oracles of the shepherd of Teqoa. The connection is probably closer with Micheas, a man of the country, apparently without culture. But we know that at the time of Ezechias, this preacher, in his crude syntax, deeply impressed minds and hastened the religious reform of the country (Jer 26, 17-19).

The personality of Isaias is more typical of the tradition of Jerusalem. No doubt his supernatural inspiration and his native genius enjoy a profound originality. But he does not stand out in his century as an erratic fragment; rather his work can be situated at the juncture of various literary and doctrinal currents which we have noted in the Judean capital. He is connected with the Sadoqite ministry by his knowledge of its technical vocabulary and by his echoing of certain aspects of its theology: the glory of Yahweh, the holy God in His royal majesty; the essential role of the Temple, His abode. On the other hand, some of his major ideas recover themes dear to "Yahwist" historians: the doctrine of the "remnant," directly related to the Yahwist interpretation of the Deluge; attachment to the Davidic dynasty, which is supported by the oracle of Nathan. Finally, the prophet did not misuse a literate education: he practices the *mashal*, a sapiential genre *par excellence*, and when he denounces a false wisdom impregnated with pride, it is to contrast it to a true wisdom, pierced by a religious spirit, a gift of the divine Spirit. Although a messenger of punishment, as were Amos and Osee, Isaias is no less attached to the national hope; but, like Osee, he carries it forward to a "second time." The comparison of this eschatology with that of Osee is instructive, however. The latter sought the golden age of Israel at the time of Exodus and the desert; Isaias finds it in the Davidic and Solomonian epoch, the purified image of which he projects into the future in order to evoke the reign of the future "son of David." On both sides, the concept of the end of the world takes on the air of a Paradise regained, but the historical experience associated with this wondrous evocation does not exactly cover the same period: for Osee tied himself again to the tradition of the North, which reappears also in Deuteronomy, whereas Isaias endorses the doctrinal development peculiar to the sanctuary of Jerusalem. The fundamental dualism of the nation will thus be found even in the prophetic milieu; but it would be useless, however, to oppose two complementary currents each attentive to different aspects of the divine work: the unique revelation progresses on both sides, along lines which will, in the end, be united.

There is yet another point on which the Book of Isaias gives us a valuable piece of information. It shows us the prophet surrounded by a circle of disciples. In their "hearts," that is, in their living memories, he "binds his testimony and seals his teaching" (8, 16). Thus the prophet appears with the unexpected traits of a master of wisdom who concentrates his care on the formation of a restricted group. One grasps in the raw the existence of one of those faithful groups which gather the words of every inspired man and prolong his activity. Such is the distant origin of pietist groups called to play such a great role in the formation of Judaism. The Isaian circle preserves the oracles of the master, which have already been set down in writing under his dictation; it also preserves the memory of a few important facts of his life (cf. 7; 36–39). One will be indebted to it for the making of his collection, a compilation which through the care of new inspired men allied with the same school, will increase in time.

§ 4.   After the Fall of Samaria

After the fall of Samaria, the remaining devout Israelites in a country decimated by deportation, seek support in the South. At the same time, Jerusalem is reforming itself. From this a double literary activity results. On the one hand, Ezechias tries to gather the cultural and moral if not the political heritage of the North, in order to rebuild around Jerusalem a sort of national unity. His scribes make a collation of Solomonian proverbs (Prv 25, 1). Above all, they revise and complete the collections of ancient traditions formed during the course of preceding centuries in the Judean capital (a Yahwist collection) with the help of materials which Israelite refugees have brought with them (Elohist collection). Such at least is the hypothesis which, in the actual state of our knowledge, would best explain the origin of the J-E compilation (sometimes called Jehovist compilation) used in the Pentateuch.[2] The Book of Judges could have received in the same manner its almost definitive form (except for additions

[2] Cf. p. 215, Vol. One.

due to later revisions).[3] It is interesting to thus see the traditions of the North and South converge once again, as at the time of the conquest and at the beginning of the monarchy, to form a wholly Israelite *Tradition:* the people of the Covenant remains attached to its internal unity in the midst of historical troubles in which it is steeped despite itself.

An autonomous survival of Elohist traditions in circles of Israelite origin, in refuge in Jerusalem, must not however be excluded: the Deuteronomist literature will constitute its direct prolonging. It is exactly in these circles that the Deuteronomist code seems to us to have been edited, probably during the very reign of Ezechias, on the basis of ancient material of which we have spoken.[4] If finally the levite-priests, to whom it is due, deposit it in the Temple at Jerusalem, where it will be rediscovered a century later, it is because the Ark of the Covenant is located there. Behind the royal Temple, they see the ancient federal shrine of the tribes, the same one which an ancient tradition, mentioned in Deuteronomy and the Book of Josue placed at Sichem and at Garizim (Dt 11, 29-30; 27, 4-8 and 11-26; Jos 8, 30-35; 24, 1 and 25-26). In order to cut short the liturgical deviations of the high places, they dream of making it the only legitimate sanctuary of Yahweh in Israel. But for the time being, Sichem is occupied by the semi-pagan Samaritans and the Ark is in Jerusalem; because of this fact, it is Jerusalem which will finally inherit the traditions of the North. One more century will have to pass before the code which synthesizes its religious and social requirements will receive official sanction and will start to become a reality.

In fact, the reign of Ezechias was only the beginning of a reforming movement which does not survive his death. The campaigns of Sennacherib spell the end of the political fall of Juda. Under Manasses, the double influence of ancient Chanaanite paganism (the eternal temptation of Israel) and of Assyrian forms of worship provoke the gradual degradation of

[3] Cf. pp. 264 ff., Vol. One.
[4] Cf. G. Ricciotti, *Histoire d'Israël*, I, 485 and 513.

official Yahwism, which has become more and more syncre-tized (4 Kgs 21, 1-9). The resistance to national apostasy re-mains the work of fervent circles resulting on the one hand from milieus where Deuteronomy was born, and on the other hand from the disciples of Isaias. These groupings which are without a defined status, and are the distant ancestors of Jew-ish pietism, struggle against the meddlings of the powers, but we cannot exactly determine the extent of their influence. However, in order to feed their religious faithfulness, they preserve as a treasure the books willed to them by previous centuries and use them as spiritual sustenance. The Mosaic Torah, written and oral, is their rule of life; sacred history is the object of their meditations; the oracles of the prophets teach them at the same time the fear of Yahweh, the need for a conversion of the heart and for an unfailing hope. Di-vine revelation which is the basis for their faith is thus pres-ent to them under the form of books which they become used to considering as sacred because they find in them the Word of God.

CHAPTER IV

THE ORIGINS OF JUDAISM

§ 1. The Deuteronomist Movement

The weakness of Assyria allows the kingdom of Juda to enjoy a certain amount of glory from the time Josias takes over the reins of power (*ca.* 630). From that time the progressive elimination of Assyrian cults, the first manifestation of nationalism, prepares from afar a much deeper reform. This was provoked in 622 by the discovery in the Temple of the Deuteronomic Code, which had been left there 100 years before. Converging witnesses showed that a profound renovation was about to take place. For Josias, in order to restore his kingdom on the basis of the Covenant and of the Mosaic Torah, immediately applied the Law at the cost of radical measures (4 Kgs 22—23).

This religious policy marks a date in literary history. In fact, with the recognition of Deuteronomy as the law of the state, the northern tradition is fully sown in Jerusalem. At the same time, the work of synthesis undertaken by the scribes of Ezechias is resumed and completed, resulting in a theological and historical literature of great depth. On the one hand, the code that was adopted during the renewal of the Covenant (cf. 4 Kgs 23, 1-3) is completed by parenetic discourses which structure it and sharpen its impact; the doctrine and the spirituality of the pietist circles of the North flourished there in long periods charged with religious emotion. On the other hand, all the historical material accumulated during the preceding centuries is methodically assembled and organized at the cost of glosses and revisions which are easily recognizable by their style. On the whole, the work covers our canonical books, from Genesis to Kings, but not in their present state because the passages of priestly origin are added later. The Deuteronomist additions are rare in Genesis, Exodus, and Numbers; whereas the end of Moses' story (E) is linked up with Deuteronomy; the Book of Josue is given rather important amplifications, while the Book of Judges takes on its profound meaning by the addition of chapter 2 which clarifies its general thesis; finally the Books of Samuel and Kings, composed of various materials, retrace all the events from the Philistine wars to the renewal of the Covenant by Josias. The method of Deuteronomist historians has already been explained. Usually, in their works, the sources are juxtaposed rather than blended, and they are respected not only in their essential meaning but also to the letter; thus, they are still discernible through analysis. This manner of compiling documents did not prevent great theological theses from underlying these books of religious history: the doctrine of the Covenant is verified in all its facts. The teaching which comes from it is related to that of the parenetic discourses of Deuteronomy; it is like a concrete teaching which seeks to awaken in hearts the desire to love Yahweh, to keep His Covenant, and to obey His law in order to live in peace in His holy land. There is something else to note. In adapting itself to Jerusalem, the Deuteronomist tradition becomes enriched. Its concept of national hope, surpassing what it had been in the 8th century with Osee, entails from then on a profound attachment to the Davidic dynasty (cf. 2 Sm 7) and to the Solomonian Temple (3 Kgs 8).

Unfortunately, the reforming activity of Josias ended with his tragic death. Though the code sanctioned by him still kept its official value, its application left much to be desired. The Deuteronomist movement subsisted, nevertheless, in the circles which had previously supported it. As keepers of its writings, they perpetuated its spirit; and much more, they completed them and brought them to light to make of them, in the midst of the national disaster culminated by the destruction of Jerusalem, the charter for future restorations. Thus Deuteronomy and the Book of Kings were enriched in their new editions, with pieces which assumed the death of

Josias, Jerusalem destroyed and the people dispersed. It is generally estimated that a work of this kind was carried out during the restoration of the 6th century. In the meantime, the legislation of Josias, which had remained the official law in the country conquered by the Babylonians and connected by them to the province of Samaria, was introduced under this title even to the Samaritans, for whom Jerusalem had become the only possible place for the worship of Yahweh since Josias had destroyed the high places in the North. This situation was to have important consequences later on: God leads history through unexpected detours.

§ 2. Rebirth of Prophetism

It would be impossible to affirm with certitude that the prophetic spirit ever completely ceased to be manifest, even under the reign of Manasses; but it was at least dormant. When it reappeared in full bloom under Josias it reestablished ties with the two pietist currents noted above: the one grouped around the disciples of Isaias, ends with Sophonias; the other, which depends on the tradition of Osee and the North, reappears in Jeremias. It is not known to which of the two should be related Nahum, the announcer of the ruin of Ninive (shortly before 612), and Habacuc who, toward the end of the 6th century, sketched on an evocation of the Chaldean invasion his sorrowful reflections, his curses on the aggressor, his song of faith. The two works have some affinity to liturgical poetry; but this does not suffice to make of their authors "cultic prophets," a corporate body which Jeremias has shown us in a very poor light; no doubt they imitated its literary genre as Jeremias himself does on occasion.

The long ministry of Jeremias was concerned not only in having us relive in spirit the last decades of Judean history. It informs us rather fully on the religious personality of the prophet himself. Not only do we see him struggling against a crowd of enemies who have vowed to destroy him: nationalist politicians, priests and official prophets; but we also know what echoes the events of his painful mission awakened in his soul. The same affective spirituality, which in his discourses caused him to present Yahweh as a father and a spouse, colors the passages in which he reveals the dark rooms of his soul: this is the intimacy of an incessant dialogue with Him who called him and who continues to give him an extraordinary strength of soul during a ministry full of disappointments.

Although a diffident man, Jeremias maintained a surprising prestige among his diverse listeners; but he hardly had disciples. A faithful friend remained close to him: Baruch, who seemed to belong to Deuteronomist circles, if one can judge by his style, was his secretary; he collected his sayings and read them publicly at the risk of his life. When after the destruction of Jerusalem and the murder of Godolias the governor, the old prophet was dragged to Egypt by fanatic Jews, Baruch followed him there. After his death he gathered the scattered pieces of his work and added biographical chapters which are the apology of a persecuted man of God: had not Jeremias been right in the face of everyone, as evidenced by the recent catastrophe? But Jeremias also left a message of hope to his dispersed compatriots. He explained it in terms which recall somewhat the Messianism of Isaias (23, 5-6) but, in a stronger way, that of Osee. Like the Deuteronomist scribes, he constantly had in mind the thought of the Covenant at Sinai and the entry into the holy land. Through Israel's fault, this plan of divine love sketched in the past ended in failure. But after purifying His people, Yahweh will begin again; this will then be a new Covenant inscribed in all hearts (31, 31-34) and a return to the holy land under the guidance of the Shepherd of Israel (23, 1-4; 31, 1-22). By this updating of ancient history, Jeremias managed to stress its religious significance, which had been exploited in another manner, more moralizing, by Deuteronomist historians: without Israel's knowing it, the events through which it had lived since the Exodus bore prophetic weight.

Probably framed in Egypt, Jeremias' collection must have been brought to Palestine fairly early during the Exile (after 570). It was apparently edited there in Deuteronomist circles. When it was communicated to the Eastern Diaspora, it was enriched by new additions (notably chaps. 50–51), so that toward 520 it had taken the shape it was to preserve in the Hebrew Bible; still the Greek Bible has it in a slightly different form. Isolated and misunderstood during his lifetime, the prophet thus exercised a profound influence in Judea as well as in Babylonia after his death.

§ 3. The Priestly Tradition

The name "priestly" is given to the tradition which is proper to the clergy of Jerusalem. This expression consecrated by the use of exegetes is useful but a little ambiguous, for the Deuteronomist code is also probably of priestly origin; but it is our opinion that it comes from the shrines in the North. We have already seen how, after the royal period, this tradition of the Temple of Jerusalem is linked also to the very origins of Israel in many ways.[1]

The introduction of the Deuteronomist tradition in Jerusalem as the law of the Temple was not accomplished without provoking some struggles. Certainly the exclusive privilege recognized in the sanctuary, whose task it is theirs to guard satisfied the Sadoqite priests; but they intended to maintain their privileges. That is why 4 Kgs 23, 9 remarks that Dt 18, 7 remained a dead issue. The levitical priests of the provinces did not receive the right to officiate in the national shrine. However, the event also provoked, as a counterstroke, an original development of priestly customs and doctrine. The result of this work was crystallized in a little collection which, however recent its writing, no less expressed very ancient concepts: the "code of holiness" (Lev 17–26, with the exception of later additions).[2] Undoubtedly all the critics do not agree in assigning this date to the work in question; however, it seems to us to be situated between Deuter-

[1] Cf. p. 284.
[2] Cf. p. 220 f., Vol. One.

onomy and Ezechiel. Throughout this booklet there appears
a sensitively different spirituality from that of Deuteronomy,
all centered around divine greatness and sanctity. What is
most profound in the liturgical service, the spirit of religion,
appears in it as the supreme motive of all human action. All
obedience to the Law of Yahweh is assimilated to a sort of
liturgical service: in all circumstances the "holy" people works
to the glory of its God just as the priests do in the Temple.
Such is the core of the doctrine of the milieu out of which,
towards the same period, issues forth a very original prophetic
figure: Ezechiel.[3]

Even once seized by the prophetic spirit, Ezechiel remained profoundly affected by his original association with
the priesthood of Jerusalem. There is discussion as to when
he was deported to Babylon: 597 or 586; the question is of
secondary importance. It is more important to notice his dependence on the code of holiness, his contact with Osee, the
Deuteronomist and perhaps Jeremias; this shows what his
readings were. For Ezechiel is clearly a "man of the book."
When he first saw his vocation, the Word of God was present
to him not in the form of an oral message (cf. Is 6, 6-7; Jer
1, 9) but of a written volume (Ez 2, 9–3, 2). It is a sign of
the times. Furthermore, his work shows him to be erudite:
he is not ignorant either of the data of Phoenician mythology
(Ez 28), nor of certain characteristics of Mesopotamian art
(Ez 1); especially he displays a deep knowledge of the laws
and rituals used in the Temple.

His message of conversion, prior to the ruin of Jerusalem,
no doubt echoes the preoccupations of the Deuteronomist circles, but he reinterprets them in a way in keeping with the
Sadoqite theology. The doctrine of individual retribution is
affirmed in it, but as a datum rather badly coordinated to
the whole of the system; this could be a development of the
doctrine of the "remnant" (cf. 9, 1-4) which recalls the message of Isaias. As for the plans for the future which the
prophet draws up after 586, by mixing eschatological evoca-

[3] Cf. p. 417 ff., Vol. One.

tions and practical data, once again we can trace there the priestly tradition: the purification of hearts in the new Israel has a ritual aspect about it (36, 16 ff.); the holy city and the Temple, the priests, sons of Sadoq, to whom are joined the other levitical priests, and the fulfilment of the ceremonies according to the prescribed calendar occupy stage-front; on the contrary the prince of Israel (*naśi*) is reduced to a subordinate position, subordinate to the priesthood. Ezechiel thus sketches the picture of a new theocracy which introduces in its own manner the state-like organization of the royal period. In fact, the Judaism which will issue from the test of Israel will resemble this picture rather closely, with the exception that no prince will be able to maintain himself next to the high priests, who have become the undisputed leaders of the nation.

The manner in which the Book of Ezechiel at present appears, allows us somewhat to see extensive editorial reworking produced after the death of the prophet, in the schools of priestly scribes which had inherited his written work and his spirit.[4] These schools must be looked for in the Eastern Diaspora, and it is this same milieu and in this same atmosphere that the priestly traditions give birth to a vast historico-judaic *corpus* where Mosaic legislation is readopted in a more specifically ritualistic manner. The circumstances of the priests exiled far from their Temple obliged them to accurately collate the customaries and the rituals, with an eye toward the day when they will return home; furthermore, they must outline for the deported Jews rules of conduct to protect them against the contagion of paganism. The fundamental writing called the Priestly Code[5] seems to answer this double purpose. But, as always in Israel, the Torah thus edited on the basis of the ancestral tradition is presented in a living manner in the framework of a holy history. Taking up again the plan of the Yahwist and systematizing it even more, the priestly scribes show how the plan of the Covenant

[4] Cf. pp. 420-424, Vol. One.
[5] Cf. p. 221 ff., Vol. One.

of Yahweh was realized during the course of the ages in four
stages: creation, the covenant with Noah, the patriarchal
covenant and the Mosaic Covenant. In each stage, God gave
His laws to men until He founded, through Moses, the Israelite theocracy centered around the liturgical service to
Yahweh in the Sanctuary of the Ark. At the top of the hier-
archy of the holy people thus set apart from the other nations, Yahweh placed at the same time Aaron, Moses'
brother, the ancestor to the line of high priests. This is not
profane history written with the preoccupations of modern
critics; it is a theology of the Chosen People presented in an
elaborate doctrinal synthesis. In the concrete framework of
the sojourn in the desert, the authors draw up the ideal prototype of the institutions about which they dream. Archaic in
certain respects, their work assimilates everything acquired
during the previous centuries to present a program for the
future. It thus prolongs the sketch of Ezechiel and gives to
Judaism its charter.

§ 4. The Consolation of the Exiles

Thus once the institutions created by the Davidic monarchy
are ruined, the people of God finds the means to survive in a
form that is both very new and very old: after the royal period it reestablishes ties with the sacral community born on
Sinai. However, it preserves an important inheritance from
the royal period. First of all there are the sacred books: the
Mosaic Torah represented by several collections, from the
Book of the Covenant to the Sacerdotal Code, to say nothing
of a customary law which will not be late in becoming established; history books re-edited several times: at the beginning of the monarchy, under Ezechias, under Josias, and
since the destruction of Jerusalem; psalms, the number of
which is impossible to judge; and finally the wisdom maxims
preserved by the royal scribes. This collection of works gives
witness to a revelation profoundly united in its essential principles, but varied, however, in its expression as much as in

the currents which are manifested therein. Israel not only possesses a religious wisdom which sets it apart from its neighboring peoples; the national hope which arose from the Sinaitic Covenant took on at this time an unequaled breadth thanks to the contribution of prophetic eschatology. The dispersed people draws from it a reason for living in the midst of difficult conditions imposed upon it. The whole experience of its past is now projected into the future and it thus continues to feed its hopes.

During the Exile, the Jews regroup in local communities and thus escape assimilation. Each community has its natural functionaries: the heads of families and the elders, the levitic and priestly caste which is hereditary, and finally the literate laymen, former civil servants who will find new markets for their talents as scribes. Schools are little by little founded, as the Jews become adjusted to their new ways of life and find the means to improve their material condition. The heirs to the former pietist groups, disciples of the prophets, members of the Deuteronomist or priestly circles, are the soul of this nascent Judaism. If Judaism finds in its natural functionaries a support to *last*, it is thanks to its most fervent members that God causes it to become conscious of itself. In the "remnant of the just" which escaped the disaster, the people finds spiritual guides capable of orienting it in a manner consonant with the wishes of Yahweh.

In Palestine there remains a restricted worship, for which the Temple of Jerusalem continues to be the center despite its shabby condition; it is likely that the Lamentations were composed in this framework, on the occasion of a solemn mourning celebrated on the anniversary of the ruin of the Temple.[6] It is probable that some psalms were also born in similar circumstances. In Babylonia and in other lands of exile, the religious practices must be adapted to the new living circumstances. Certain exterior rites take on then an increased importance: the Sabbath, prohibitions, circumcision, and fasts on the traditional dates. Furthermore, the local

[6] Cf. p. 139 ff.

communities habitually meet on determined days to pray together: this is a distant origin of synagogal worship. From the ancient worship of the shrines, all possible elements were preserved: recitations or readings of the Torah and of sacred history (written or only confided to traditional schemata), exhortation, prayer and the singing of hymns and the blessing of the assembly.

These meetings undoubtedly play an important role in the constitution of the sacred books. Already established texts are used—and thus is explained in part the preservation of ancient works. In second place, the synagogal liturgy can be considered as the *Sitz im Leben* of a certain number of new works. For example, the same meditation on Exodus, which allows one to suppose a previous reading, is found again in the penitential liturgy of Is 63, 7–64, 11, the exhortations to confidence of Is 43, 16-21, the meditation of Ps 78, 105 or 106. In the second case would not this look like a sermon for Easter time, in which the past would have been updated in order to draw from it the hope of a new deliverance? It is in this manner that *midrash* was born,[7] from a reflection on the Scriptures which are now the consolation of Israel in its time of trial. Naturally the schools of priests, of cantors or of scribes are narrowly linked to the communities of the exile as to their places of worship meetings. The ancient books are collected there, copied, edited and enriched with glosses which complete them and apply them to the needs of the times. The young scribes learn there their trade at the same time as their hearts and minds are trained. Therefore, in the works which flow from their pens, there are multiple allusions to and a systematic re-use of expressions consecrated by usage (what is called the anthological style).

Such is the milieu in which can be best explained, in our opinion, the composition of the great prophetic work which reached us through the Book of Isaias. In a circle where is perpetuated the tradition of the disciples of the prophet, an author who has remained anonymous addresses to the exiles between 547 (the first victory of Cyrus) and 538 (decree of

---

[7] Cf. p. 195.

emancipation of the Jews), a message of consolation[8] wherein can be distinguished, despite the very pronounced literary personality of the author, numerous references to the pre-exilian books: Isaias, Nahum (cf. Is 52, 7-10), Sophonias (Is 49, 13), Jeremias, Deuteronomy, the ancient traditions of Israel and certain aspects of the priestly tradition, without considering a certain affinity with the style of the Wisdom writings. The author is truly literate, as well as a very capable poet; his message especially constitutes one of the peaks of the Old Testament. Not only the eschatology with which his book is completely impregnated is purified of its political elements in order to be centered on the reign of Yahweh in Jerusalem, His holy city, in a perspective of complete universalism; not only the people of this kingdom, beneficiaries of eschatological salvation, is represented in the image of the 'anawim: a people seeking justice, which has the Law of Yahweh in its heart; but to the royal Messias, either peaceful or warlike, is substituted the high figure of the Servant, mediator of a new covenant and spiritual saviour of the multitudes by his suffering, which is a new sacrifice of expiation. This *Gospel* surpasses by far the doctrinal import of several anonymous works almost contemporary to it such as Is 13—14 or Jer 50—51.[9]

Did the prophet of the captivity come back from the exile with the first repatriates and did he then pursue his ministry, so that the last poems of the Servant would take place in the bitter context of the year following 538? There is discussion on this point. In any case, his collection, composed through his own care or that of his disciples, exercised a profound influence in Jerusalem in the first quarter of the 6th century, in a parallel manner to the Deuteronomist, to the books of Jeremias and, perhaps to a lesser degree, of Ezechiel. But with this quarter century there begins the period of the second Temple. Once the shrine is rebuilt, Judaism refinds its center. In the midst of new political difficulties, it will acquire its definitive equilibrium.

[8] Cf. p. 434 ff., Vol. One.
[9] Cf. pp. 382 and 406, Vol. One.

CHAPTER V

JUDAISM DURING
THE PERSIAN PERIOD

§ 1.   Prophetism at the Time of the Second Temple

During the Persian period, it becomes more difficult to follow the chronological order of the formation of the collection
of sacred books. On the one hand, data to retrace the history
of Judaism are lacking more than once, especially between
the years 515 and 445 and from 398 to Alexander. On the
other hand, the biblical works themselves do not date themselves very easily, witness to the diversity of opinions shared
by the exegetes. However what appears more clearly is the
development of the different currents which give expression
to the Revelation. They will therefore serve as guidelines.

Around the reconstruction of the Temple, we notice first
of all a certain prophetic activity.[1] But while Aggeus, Isaias
34–35 and 56–66 (whose unity of authorship is problematic)
extend especially the line of the message of consolation, the
visions of Zacharias 1–8 follow rather the footsteps of Ezechiel by their recourses to all sorts of complicated symbols.
In a general way, the prophetic genre moreover manifests a
tendency to evolve. It is less spontaneous, closer to the written style than to the spoken word. The new authors have
attended the schools for scribes; they are aware of the works
of their predecessors and sometimes point them out (cf. Is
35). The various preoccupations of an ill-known period conflict in juxtaposed pages whose exact historical framework is
often unknown to us (especially for Is 56–66); whence, next
to one another, there appear fires of religious nationalism (Is
63, 1-6) and proclamations of universalism (Is 56, 1-8). The

[1] Cf. p. 450 ff., Vol. One.

repatriates are re-established in their country at the cost of a thousand difficulties; the South is invaded by the Edomites, upon whom the Jews call down the divine wrath (Is 34; 63, 1-6; Abd).[2] Their hope is exalted however at the sight of their reconstructed city (Is 60–62).

As time goes on, a sort of disassociation of prophetism takes place. On the one hand, the role of the prophet as preacher and guide to consciences is being assumed by the wisdom master; on the other hand, eschatological oracles undergo an autonomous development, often at the hands of anonymous authors, in a style where conventional clichés and obscure expressions abound. We cannot, for example, exclude the fact that Ez 38–39 was added to the book of the prophets at about this time in the circles where it was being preserved.[3] According to other critics, Is 24–27 would be ascribed the date of 485 at the time when Babylon was laid to ruin by the armies of Xerxes. But these are only hypotheses, for the works of this type are difficult to date. If the collection of Malachias[4] (only slightly affected by this development of prophetism) can be placed rather accurately around the time when Nehemias came to Juda (middle of the 5th century), Joel escapes the grasp of the historians.[5] Finally, the second part of Zacharias (9–14),[6] contemporaneous with the conquests of Alexander, presents an enigmatic aspect despite the frequent re-use of images drawn from the ancient prophetic works. It is a work for the initiated rather than the echo of a public action. Furthermore, the book foresees the extinction of a decried prophetism (Za 13, 2-6). Soon the combination of the former eschatological oracle and of the prophetic vision (already frequent in Ezechiel and Zacharias) will give birth to a new genre: the apocalypse, a revelation of the divine secrets manifested in dreams or in symbolic vi-

[2] Cf. pp. 455 ff. and 470 f., Vol. One.
[3] Cf. p. 431, Vol. One.
[4] Cf. p. 462, Vol. One.
[5] Cf. p. 468, Vol. One.
[6] Cf. p. 471, Vol. One.

sions. The anguishes of fervent souls, who desire to understand the meaning of a deceitful present, and to be enlightened on the future realization of the plan of God, will all pass into this strange literary form, which during the next period will undergo a growing development.

§ 2.   The Development of the Wisdom Current

The Wisdom current does not date from the Persian period. We have seen it take root in Israel at the time of Solomon. Imbued even at this time by the Yahwist ferment which, in the biblical framework, already gave a peculiar twist to the wisdom of nations, it developed all during the royal period in the circles of the scribes, ending in collections of maxims and exercising its influence on certain other sectors of literature, such as historiography. With the captivity its former literary creations took their place in the treasure of national traditions. As for the scribe, he will no longer be only a functionary who edits acts or annals, but rather a pious man who will enrich the sacred books by meditating upon the ancient texts.

Henceforth, the Wisdom current will experience a great development, at the same time as the religious influence of Yahwism presents itself in a clearer and more direct fashion. It overflows even into the prophetic collections (Is 40, 12-26) as it did in some of the most recent Deuteronomic chapters. But, in general, it preserves the same exterior appearance, affecting a language accessible to every upright man; however, in this apparently neutral expression, it systematically transposes the data of Mosaic and prophetic revelation. Its very method allows it to do its deed with everything, retaining the assimilable elements which foreign literatures can offer (these include Edomite, Phoenician, Egyptian and Assyrian literatures); but, in the final analysis, its essential sources show up: the sacred books, with which the anonymous scribes nourish their thought to the point that they impregnate their vocabulary with the expressions that they find in them. Under this sapiential form, the doctrine of the Covenant takes on a less specifically national character, and this effort at adjustment corresponds to one of the tendencies which, from the Exile onwards, are manifested inside Judaism: next to a strict nationalism, a current affirms itself, one that is more universalistic and more missionary. Wisdom literature will be for it an instrument of penetration even in the pagan circles where it will recruit proselytes, for, in its framework, there is elaborated a doctrine on human life parallel to that reflection which in Greece towards the same period gives birth to philosophy.

At the chronological point of departure of this literature there is the collection of Proverbs.[7] Comprising several ancient collections, it is furnished with a substantial introduction by its editor (Prv 1—9) whose theological scope is much larger. The dates assigned to the work by critics vary from the beginning of the 5th century to the end of the 4th; the time around 480 can be held if we admit that the work precedes Job (Robert). Treating the problems of the righteous and happy life and of divine retribution, the Proverbs serenely repeat a resolutely optimistic traditional thesis: the way of justice is that of life, that of sin leads to death. To this thesis the poet of Job (ca. 450: Dhorme) offers a contrary factual argument. The suffering of the just is a painful problem! Mesopotamian thought had not ignored this problem and we can admit at least an indirect literary influence on Job from the works that this literature had produced on the subject. But finally it is by virtue of specifically Yahwist data that the dialogue of Job and of his friends is elaborated; if it ends with no firm conclusion on the level of theoretical reflection, it is at least noticeable that biblical revelation does not grow in a rectilinear fashion, but through a process of *sic et non:* divine light will not be manifested to man except at the end of a painful experiment where he will have fathomed the mystery of his condition. The timeliness of the problems treated by Proverbs and Job appears even more

[7] Cf. p. 79 ff.

when we relate these books to a certain number of apparently contemporary psalms, which treat the same problems.

§ 3. The Development of Religious Lyricism

It is known that the problem of the psalter is resolved by critics in radically different ways, whatever be their sectarian allegiances. Some tend to appeal to the royal period for almost all the psalms; others place a large number of them (if not the majority) after the Exile. In fact it would be very strange if the religious lyricism of the preexilian period left only a few traces in the Bible, when it is known what care the scribes used to collect the other literary works prior to the destruction of Jerusalem. However, account must be taken of two facts: the readaptation of ancient psalms to new perspectives of Jewish life and thought, when they are reconsidered after the Exile, and the natural development of genres from the past in the corporations of cantors created around the second Temple. The result is that the solution of the problem of the psalms can only be complex. If it is evident that some are ancient (those who clearly speak of the king or come from the Israel of the North), it is possible to hesitate for a number of others. Practically speaking it is their literary and doctrinal situation with respect to the prophetic texts which, very often, constitutes the principal element for their dates.

Critics gladly relate to the postexilian period several categories of works whose dependence upon the prophets seems assured: wisdom psalms such as Pss 1, 34, 37, or legalistic psalms, such as Pss 19, 8 ff and 119; the suffering psalms, born in the circle of the "poor"[8] which prolong certain themes of Jeremias, even though the genre of individual or collective lamentation is ancient; the psalms of the kingdom of Yahweh, at least when after Second-Isaias they present the kingdom in an eschatological perspective; the "historical" psalms; and the psalms into which pass the spiritual decep-

---

[8] A. Gelin, *Les Pauvres de Yahvé* (Paris, 1953), p. 41 f.

tions which are accumulated in the Jewish soul during the Persian period. These general indications leave intact the question raised by each individual psalm; they want only to show how the study of the psalter allows us to penetrate further into the interior drama lived by Judaism after the great dream of the returning years (538-515) is dissipated. At the same time, it is possible to discover how the Scriptures are then for the believers the only reliable source of hope; their prayers feed on them so much so that the theology of the Prophets, of Deuteronomy or of the priestly current passes entirely into its inspired expression.

The Canticle of Canticles can be linked to religious lyricism, and a good number of interpreters give the end of the Persian period as its date. But this is as far as their agreement goes. We have read[9] that some see in it a collection of human love songs with the marriage ceremonies being their framework (*Sitz im Leben*); others consider them as symbolic poems, more or less allegorized, which would sing the spiritual marriage of Yahweh and Israel. Perhaps these theses are not as removed as they first appear, if one realizes that the introduction of the Canticle among the sacred books read publicly in the synagogal liturgy could not have been done without this book being jointly interpreted in relation to the prophetic texts where the Covenant was compared to a marriage (Osee, Jeremias, Ezechiel and 2nd and 3rd Isaias). It could be an allegorical reinterpretation of ancient marriage poems or a lyrical composition hiding a secret meaning behind the sumptuous images of a refined art: in either case, the Canticle testifies to the ingeniousness of the Jewish scribes, skilled at exploiting the prophetic writings and at using an apparently hermetic language to translate the revealed doctrine.

[9] Cf. p. 116 ff.

§ 4.   From History to Midrash

Ancient Israel was not unaware of the historical genre under, however, extremely varied forms. Nonetheless, it has been seen that the literary form of *narrative* was not always used for the purpose of historical teaching, even without taking into account the diversity which could affect it in itself (epic narrative, etiological narrative, popular tradition, historiographical narration, etc. . . .). All sorts of teachings could be translated in them in a concrete manner: juridical, moral or theological. Generally reflection on the historical traditions of Israel or the texts which testify to the past led even to a higher plane than history: that of doctrine and spirituality as in the works of the Deuteronomist school. In the priestly current, the genre tended to become even more stylized; it did not fear to reconstruct the past in a systematic manner by inextricably mixing the data of tradition and the theological concepts of the narrators. This method of developing history with an essentially didactic purpose, with a view to seeking in it a religious significance capable of teaching and edifying souls, is nothing other than one of the forms of midrash. The priestly holy history already obeys the fundamental laws of the genre. After the Exile, it will experience a greater and greater development, without sacrificing a parallel persistence of historiography.

For example, the sources used by the Chronicler in the Books of Esdras-Nehemias[10] are clearly situated on the historical side of the narrative genre: memories of the return, anti-Samaritan dossier, and remembrances of both Nehemias and Esdras. On the other hand, it is the essentially didactic narrative which is developed in the Book of Jonas,[11] and the delightful "novella" of Ruth, even if in fact this latter rests on a valid historical tradition (the genealogy of David).

[10] Pp. 178 ff., Vol. One.
[11] Cf. p. 465 ff., Vol. One.

Midrash, however, does not always take on a narrative form. Thus, the so-called "historical" psalms (78, 105, 106) are also *midrashim*, which flourish in meditation and prayer instead of only ending in stylized narratives of the past. So also, when later eschatological texts, which are generally anonymous, repeat, while developing them, themes and expressions drawn from the prophetic writings, this systematic reinterpretation of ancient material is still in a way midrash: the texts were carefully studied and their meaning was clarified in the light of other passages; finally their explanation gives birth to a new Scripture. Since the discoveries of Qumran, the name *pesher* is given to the exegesis of prophetic texts which tend to bring them up to date in order to clarify the meaning of present events and of "what will happen later on." The Jewish tradition itself has called *halakha* the exploitation of the Scriptures to find in them rules of conduct and *haggada* the free development grafted upon the Scriptures with a view only to edification, especially when it includes narrative materials drawn from the popular tradition or from the imagination of the interpreters. It would be wrong to see in these, literary genres foreign to the Bible: they are the natural result of its reading by the Jewish people. We believe that the first traces of those genres can already be found in the inspired books of the Persian period.

§ 5. The Fixing of the Torah

The center of Jewish thought is neither the Wisdom current nor religious lyricism, or even the prophetic teaching: it is the Torah. In the Persian period, it is fixed in its definitive form. It has been seen how, as early as the Mosaic period, it was the charter of the Covenant; then, in the royal period, it tended to become crystallized into two parallel currents: that of the North, represented by the moral Decalogue and by the Book of the Covenant; and that of the South, attested especially by the cultic Decalogue (Ex 34). At the end, these two currents, while intercrossing several times, experienced their own development, the first giving rise to Deuteronomy, the second to the code of holiness, to the Torah of Ezechiel and to the fundamental writing of the priestly code. Next to these written recensions there remained furthermore a customary law and rituals whose transmission could be accomplished orally without injuring their faithful preservation. During the captivity, it seems that the spirit of the Deuteronomist current dominated the intellectual and religious center that Judaism preserved in Palestine, while that of the priestly current was perpetuated in the Babylonian schools imbued with the influence of Ezechiel. Upon their return from the exile, the Sadoqite priests who came back with Josue brought back with them not only oral traditions, but written works which, for them, enjoyed an authority equal to the books already legally sanctioned in the prior period: ancient juridical compilations and Deuteronomy. Furthermore, from the return onwards, the ancient customaries of the Temple are put back into force, now that the worship service is started anew. It seems that it is in these circumstances that several codes drawn at this time from the Pentateuch are edited, on the basis of preexilian traditions readapted to the needs of the times: code of sacrifices, code of purity, various tariffs.[12]

Whatever be the solution to these very controverted problems, when Nehemias accomplishes in Judea his mission so important for the future of Judaism, the situation of the Torah is complicated. On the one hand, a certain number of texts are probably already recognized by the Persian authorities as the *law of the state* in Israel: these are the archaic codes and Deuteronomy. Undoubtedly there must be added local customs, but it is impossible to say what is their official status. It is rather likely that the priestly compilations are an object of dispute between the repatriated Jews from Babylonia and the "people of the country," especially the Samaritans. In fact, these latter also claim the worship of the "God of heaven" and Jerusalem became their center of

[12] Cf. pp. 225 ff., Vol. One.

worship since the time when Josias had destroyed all the high places of the former Northern Kingdom. It seems that it was to avoid this opposition of two groups that the Persian authorities undertook at this time to fix once and for all their laws and their status. Such seems to have been the mission of Esdras, which could preferably be placed in 398 (some propose the 5th century).[13] To prepare the unification of Jewish laws into a *corpus* officially sanctioned by the state, jurists, belonging to the "priestly" schools (of Babylon such as Esdras himself, or of Palestine) would then have added to the prior texts supplementary articles destined to make them harmonious among themselves and to adapt them to the needs of the times. Finally the historico-juridical entirety of the Pentateuch seems to have come from this work, by blending the two great currents which inherit all the Israelite past: the Deuteronomist and the priestly.[14]

In the present state of our knowledge, this presentation of things seems the most satisfactory *salvo meliore judicio*. On the one hand, it assigns to the fixation of the Torah a set of circumstances which allow us to understand its motive and its importance; on the other hand, it shows how the work accomplished at the time of Esdras did not have as its object to create anew nor to sanction the result of a juridical evolution completely ordered by factors external to the religion of Israel, but on the contrary to collect in a reasoned compilation the proliferation of texts issued from Israelite tradition, such as it had been developed throughout the ages.

Even if there enters into the hypothesis a share of disputable conjectures, it is certain that, well before the Persian period, the Torah is fixed. Samaritans and Jews will preserve it under the same form after their separation (which is preferably placed toward the beginning of the Greek period, even if the prodromes date back to preceding decades). Inside Judaism, the divergences will henceforth bear only on its practical interpretation: harmonization of apparently con-

[13] Cf. p. 186.
[14] Cf. p. 227 f., Vol One.

tradictory passages proper value of the non-written customs, and of the solutions proposed by the private doctors. On this point, the various tendencies will continue to be confronted, opposing especially the priestly circles with the lay doctors; but this no longer concerns the formation of the holy books.

CHAPTER VI

JUDAISM IN THE HELLENISTIC PERIOD

§ 1. The Development of Genres in Palestinian Judaism

Documents are almost completely lacking to retrace the history of Judaism during the 4th and 3rd centuries. However, it is at this time that the Jewish institutions find their definitive equilibrium after the fixing of the Torah. Fixed through the cares of the priestly legists, the Torah is confided first of all to the clergy, divided into 24 classes followed by the levitical orders, among which the cantors have henceforth taken their place. In order to interpret it, the priests intend to hold only to the letter; on the contrary, the literate laymen, the Wise Men, who attribute in their study and in their teaching a large place to other ancient writings, give equal attention to the written Torah and to customs (called "oral Torah"). The gap between the two tendencies will widen with time to end in the sects of the Asmonean period.

With the conquests of Alexander, the Hellenist civilization invades the East, but Judaism does not immediately conflict with it. The most noticeable repercussion of the political changes which took place around 330 seems to be, for Palestinian Judaism, the definitive schism of the Samaritan community which was already virtually realized during the preceding decades but was consummated only with the construction of the temple of Garizim (at an uncertain date). Various institutions compete at this time for the preservation and explanation of the ancient books, as well as for the composition of new ones: priestly circles of the temple and the corporation of cantors, schools for scribes, and the synagogal liturgy. The communities of the Diaspora also have their schools and their synagogues, but we have very little information on their operation and on their real influence in the constitution of the biblical collection. We can only suspect the Eastern origin of the traditions which are at the basis of Daniel, of Tobias and of Esther; but the transmission of these materials until their actual writing remains out of reach.

The fixing of the Torah leads as a counterstroke to that of the prophetic collections. But here, it becomes difficult to assign dates. The last pages of the Book of Isaias seem to be chapters 24–27; certain critics place them around 485, while others place them around the Greek period. The content and the order of Jeremias are considerably different in the Hebrew and the Greek: it is possible to see in this a rather late final draft. For Ezechiel, a certain affinity to the supplementary laws of the Pentateuch is noticed in some passages; while also the date of chapters 38–39 remains under discussion, certain critics place them during the Greek period. In the group of the *Prophetae priores* the priestly rewritings seem more numerous for Josue than for the other books; but it may not be necessary to suppose an editorial work later than the fixing of the Torah. Finally, in the collection of the twelve minor prophets only one characteristic ensemble brings us back to the Greek period, toward the last quarter of the 4th century: Za 9–14. But even these chapters are added as a supplement to the already formed book, just as Is 24–27 is added to the Book of Isaias; it is possible to envisage in these two cases an insertion later than the formation of these collections, as though these were enlarged editions. All this allows one to see a rather large work of collating and editing, realized in these schools for scribes in the 5th and 4th centuries. The collection of the Ketubim then includes several important works: the Proverbs and Job, the most ancient of the Megillot (Lamentations, Ruth, and the Canticle of Canticles which can be brought into this period), but the canonical grouping of the five books does not as yet appear achieved. As for the psalter, it is not known to exactly what date its cloture is to be assigned. Perhaps we must go as late as the beginning of the Hellenistic period, but the existence of Machabean psalms is very problematical.

It is in this group of Ketubim that we must look for the few works composed after Alexander. The great work of the Chronicler (1 and 2 Par, Esd and Neh), seems to have as its framework the reaction of orthodox Judaism to the schismatic Samaritans; in this perspective, it would be easy to explain its insistence upon the legitimacy of the unique sanctuary of Jerusalem and of the unique Davidic dynasty, from which will come the Messias. Using ancient materials, the book (at present divided into four volumes) could well have been born towards the end of the 4th century or during the 3rd). As it has for its purpose to justify through history a theological thesis, it resorts more often to midrash techniques than, for example, to works of history resulting from the Deuteronomist current; but already, on this point, the priestly sacred history has already opened the way. With the Book of Esther whose date is unfortunately not clear, we are fully into haggadic midrash, even if the story told has its point of departure in facts. Linked to the feast of the *Purim*, the work has, furthermore, an orientation to worship.

In the category of the Wisdom writings, Ecclesiastes[1] manifests a certain knowledge of Greek thought, but this contact is without depth; his literary activity can be placed in the 3rd century. Tobias[2] (toward the same time) could rather be tied to Eastern origins (especially in what concerns its angelology), but the place of its composition is a subject of discussion. In any case, this book is distinguished by the way in which it narrowly unites wisdom teaching, the narrative techniques of the *haggada* and the recourse to lyricism: in the lower Jewish literature, the ancient literary currents are thus readily joined. The same mixture reappears in the collection of Baruch,[3] whose most ancient sections could go back to the 3rd century and be of Palestinian origin. Finally,

[1] Cf. p. 145 ff.
[2] Cf. p. 217 ff.
[3] Cf. p. 209 ff.

toward the beginning of the 2nd century, Ecclesiasticus (Ben Sira),[4] master of a school at Jerusalem, in his composite collection makes the inventory of Wisdom in his time: the data from the Torah, from the prophetic teachings and from the more ancient wisdom writings appear in it as closely united. Less creative than in the past, Judaism thus feeds upon what it has acquired, waiting for the Day when the prophetic oracles will be realized, when Yahweh will reign and where the Messias will be at the head of His people.

§ 2. The Confrontation between Judaism and Hellenism

The first contacts between Judaism and Hellenism, at the time of the domination of the Ptolemies over Palestine, did not lead to any crisis. On the contrary, the creation of a large Jewish community in Alexandria led little by little to the translation of the essentials of Jewish ideas into the Greek language; during the course of the 3rd century, the Torah was translated, then other sacred books, at dates more difficult to establish.

The conflict breaks out in Palestinian Judaism, under Antiochus Epiphanes. The Machabean crisis is located at the outset of a rather abundant non-canonical literature, which we cannot deal with here. It is necessary to note only the development at this time of the apocalyptic genre; the oldest sections of the Book of Enoch could be assigned a date around 170. These are the circumstances when the traditions of Daniel perhaps already edited in part, start to take shape, serving as a framework for the only apocalypse properly so-called which appears in the canon of the Old Testament.[5] The book seems to reflect the thought of the *hasidim*, who had been rallied to Judas Machabee toward the beginning of the holy war. A similar spirit, although more nationalistic,

4 Cf. p. 255 ff.
5 Cf. p. 163 ff.

is found again in the *haggada* of Judith,[6] which seems to echo the climate of the Machabean wars. Under the Asmonean dynasty the history of the war of independence finds a good narrator (1 Machabees)[7] whose work intimately joins to the traditional techniques of Hebrew historiography a recourse to those of Greek historiography. As for the work of Jason the Cyrene, who related the same events, we only have a Greek summary of it, composed in Alexandria;[8] there again, Hebrew historiography readily mingled with *haggada* evolves toward the genre of pathetic history, similar to the one practiced by contemporary Hellenism.

Finally, it is in the framework of Alexandrine Judaism that the confrontation of Judaism and Hellenism is resolved, not by a conflict or an absorption of the first by the second, but by a victory of biblical Revelation, which had become capable of assimilating certain elements of Hellenism. The fact is not yet very felt in the recent parts of the Book of Baruch; chapters 4, 5–5, 9 which give the appearance of a sermon delivered in a synagogue and which perhaps were written in Greek, only echo the prophetic Scriptures.[9] The "Letter of Jeremias" is a diatribe against idolatry, which gives us some idea of Jewish apologetics.[10] The deuterocanonical additions to Esther and Daniel contain nothing specifically Greek.[11] We must wait for the Wisdom of Solomon (during the 1st century)[12] to see the inspired literature express itself in a Greek terminology. Still we must remark that this terminology is put into the service of a perfectly traditional doctrine. We know that since the 5th century, the Wisdom current agitated the problem of individual retribution. At the time of Antiochus' persecution, the Book of Daniel had, in our opinion, shed light on this problem in revealing the resurrection of

[6] Cf. p. 224 ff.
[7] Cf. p. 232 ff.
[8] Cf. p. 238 ff.
[9] Cf. p. 213 ff.
[10] Cf. p. 215 ff.
[11] Cf. p. 263 ff.
[12] Cf. p. 247 ff.

the just, called to share the kingdom of God at the end of time. This is this participation of the just in beatific immortality that the Wisdom book explicitly teaches, transposing an essential datum of Jewish apocalyptic into sapiential language.

Judaism continues therefore to enrich its inspired literature at a time when its non-canonical productions start to become more and more numerous. But very often these productions represent less the great traditional current than the spirit of the sects which, as early as the Machabean period, are more and more opposed to one another. Without talking about the Samaritans, three principal sects are distinguished at the end of the 2nd century: the Sadducees, who support the Asmonean dynasty; the Pharisees, who refuse to recognize the legitimacy of the non-Davidic royalty; and the "Sadoqites," whose exact origin remains still a problem and who lead to Essenism. This tableau of a divided Judaism is instructive. It shows how difficult it is at this time to define Jewish orthodoxy on the sole basis of Scripture and oral tradition. On both sides, there are currents and tendencies whose definitive synthesis has not been made. Even in the Torah, the harmonizing of the different lines of development, represented by pieces more juxtaposed than blended, give rise to discussion. The concept of individual retribution, and of Messianism is not the same in the sects we have just mentioned, no more than is the list of books considered as sacred. Finally, the recourse to Scripture cannot always be sufficient to resolve the controversies, since they crystallize divine revelation in its successive stages: whence there are apparent contradictions between equally inspired passages, but born at different periods and in different places, answering very different needs and resolving them in a more or less complete manner. The reason for this state of fact only appears in the light of the New Testament. In fact, Judaism is only a provisory and preparatory economy which tends towards a "fulfilment." Christ, in His person, His work and His teaching, "will fulfill the Scriptures," finally making explicit their meaning and their import, by reason of the divine plan which, from the very beginning, led toward it.

Thus, we will finish this rapid synthesis. The reader will not forget that in sketching it, we have incorporated into it more than one hypothetical element, when critical problems were raised that have not been definitively solved. Not that the value of the Bible as historical document would thereby be questioned. But today it is not sufficient to affirm this value as a whole without going into detail in order to determine the exact dates of the events, the dates of the inspired books and their places of origin. It is from this point of view that questions are still being asked. To make a choice in these debates, to propose probable points of view founded on serious arguments, was the only possible attitude in matters where research is not complete. It is then legitimate to hope that after these approximations there will come firmer certitudes and that our knowledge of the Old Testament will grow in accuracy even in its minute details. Discussions of this nature moreover leave intact the properly doctrinal value of the Sacred Books: whoever be their human authors and whatever be their dates, God speaks to us through them, and what is essential is to grasp His message. But if, furthermore, it is possible to reconstitute in a sure way the steps of divine pedagogy which led our Fathers in the faith (cf. Gal 3, 24) to Christ, then the relation of the Old Testament to Christ only becomes clearer, and faith finds in this an additional benefit. This is why the critical study of the Old Testament is worthwhile attempting: far from leading to skepticism, its only aim is to penetrate further into the knowledge of Revelation.

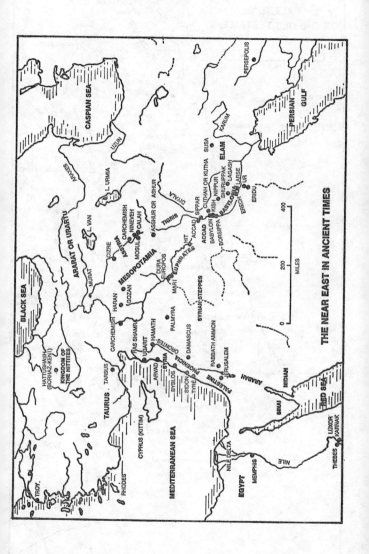

THE NEAR EAST IN ANCIENT TIMES

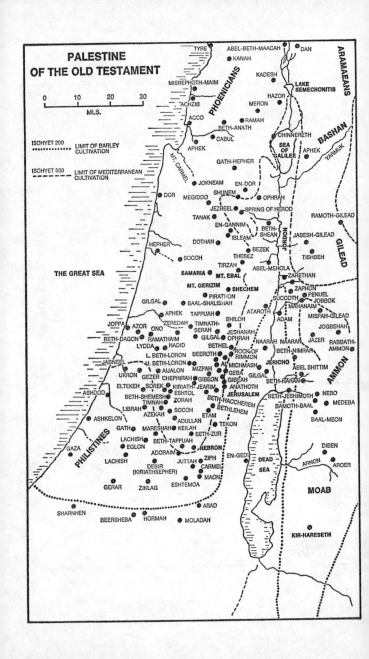

PALESTINE OF THE OLD TESTAMENT

INDEX OF AUTHORS

INDEX OF SUBJECTS

INDEX OF BIBLICAL REFERENCES